G000154073

"This book cuts through the noise that clutters the d tough, but the reading is easy."

—

"Highly readable, thoughtful, and very informative, tl excellent introduction to the topic. While the author's style is succinct, he manages to provide a comprehensive review of the key issues in an insightful, honest and entertaining manner."
— *André Croppenstedt, Food and Agriculture Organization of the United Nations (FAO)*

"In clear and sometimes witty ways, and drawing upon a depth of expertise, Willem van Eekelen assesses what works, what does not, and why. It's refreshing, it's engaging, it's that rare creature: a student textbook that is also a page turner."
— *Catherine Cameron, Director at Agulhas Applied Knowledge (a company specialised in strategic portfolio evaluations) and Visiting Fellow at the University of Surrey*

"Willem van Eekelen's impressive and original effort to reinvent the traditional student textbook is accessible, thoughtful, witty and stylish, and is guaranteed to bring alive the subject of rural development for students at all levels."
— *David Lewis, London School of Economics and Political Science*

"Willem van Eekelen's 'Rural Development in Practice' contributes a highly accessible, insightful and, in places, critical perspective on its topic. Its core arguments are skilfully illustrated by examples and personal experience. This book provides a unique entry point into international development for students and interested readers."
— *Armando Barrientos, Professor Emeritus of Poverty and Social Justice, Global Development Institute, University of Manchester*

"Willem van Eekelen rightly challenges some of the long-held hypotheses that have underpinned the narrative in international development in a courageous, thought-provoking and engaging way. This is a very useful book, not only for students, but for anyone seeking to improve their knowledge and understanding of rural development in an evolving global context."
— *Tina Fahm, Commissioner of the Independent Commission for Aid Impact (ICAI)*

"I am amazed by the way this rich compilation of information and analysis is woven into a compelling narrative. It is a 'must read' for anyone who wishes to understand the role of agriculture in global development, and its impact on countries' socio-economic and political dynamics. Watch out for the humour, too."
— *Girish Menon, Chief Executive of ActionAid UK*

"This is a highly relevant, well-written and well-researched textbook that is useful for students and anyone with an interest in rural development. It is a skilfully crafted synthesis of accessible and digestible information and evidence on the topical problems affecting rural development today."
— *Nyasha Tirivayi, United Nations University*

"An insightful, enjoyable and timely publication. With a practical style the book helps to understand the complexity of international development and the important role rural development plays in addressing the pressing challenges of our time. Agriculture and the ability to sustain life on the planet are presented with convincing evidence that a brighter future for all is possible."

— Oscar Garcia, Director of the Independent Office of Evaluation of the International Fund for Agricultural Development (IFAD)

"An intellectual and practical boost for the mind and soul. A no-nonsense and enlightening read with wit, great stories and practical examples. This book is a must-read for all people interested in development."

— Saleh Saeed, development practitioner and currently Chief Executive of the Disaster Emergency Committee (DEC)

"As an evaluator, Willem van Eekelen is professionally sceptical of whether projects have really made as much difference as the people who started them hope. So when he says the world has made huge progress in reducing extreme poverty in the last 50 years, believe it. If you want to know how: Willem describes both what worked and what got in the way, in plain language, for any reader."

— Laurie Lie, Chief Executive of CARE International UK

"This is an excellent publication, well-written, informative, and presented with an attractive freshness. The informality of the narrative does not spoil the academic value and the topics that the author highlights are very appropriate, topical, and should be essential reading for students hoping to work in the field of international development."

— Frank Rennie, Professor of Sustainable Rural Development at the University of the Highlands and Islands

"This is a must-read textbook. Stylishly innovative, it sucks the reader into a cutting edge exploration of the key issues that will shape the next phase of rural development in the Global South."

— Mesfin Mergia Mekonnen, Water for Food Institute, University of Nebraska

RURAL DEVELOPMENT IN PRACTICE

Rural Development in Practice focuses on the evolving nature of rural development in the Global South. It outlines how we got to where we are today, checks what we can learn from history, and explores the development drivers, facilitators, and obstacles most likely to shape the years ahead.

The book covers the management of fishing grounds, forests, grazing lands, water sources and soil, and looks at the effects of infrastructure, trade mechanisms, and new crop varieties on farming. The author discusses the opportunities and challenges of microfinance, social safety nets and migration, and assesses the way ICT and climate change are changing everything, rapidly. Real-life examples, exercises, role-plays, textboxes, anecdotes, and illustrative artwork are used to bring concepts and theories to life, and every chapter concludes with a section that explores how best to tackle the tough and complex dilemmas of our time.

Rural Development in Practice is essential reading for students at all levels and may be of benefit for programme and policy staff in rural-focused government departments, multilateral agencies, and non-government organisations.

Willem van Eekelen is an evaluator in the field of international development and teaches on that subject at the University of Birmingham, UK.

Rethinking Development

Rethinking Development offers accessible and thought-provoking overviews of contemporary topics in international development and aid. Providing original empirical and analytical insights, the books in this series push thinking in new directions by challenging current conceptualizations and developing new ones.

This is a dynamic and inspiring series for all those engaged with today's debates surrounding development issues, whether they be students, scholars, policy makers and practitioners internationally. These interdisciplinary books provide an invaluable resource for discussion in advanced undergraduate and postgraduate courses in development studies as well as in anthropology, economics, politics, geography, media studies and sociology.

For more information about this series, please visit: www.routledge.com

RURAL DEVELOPMENT IN PRACTICE

Evolving Challenges and Opportunities

Willem van Eekelen

Routledge
Taylor & Francis Group

LONDON AND NEW YORK

First published 2020
by Routledge
2 Park Square, Milton Park, Abingdon, Oxon OX14 4RN

and by Routledge
52 Vanderbilt Avenue, New York, NY 10017

Routledge is an imprint of the Taylor & Francis Group, an informa business

© 2020 Willem van Eekelen; illustrations, Micky Dirkzwager

British Library Cataloguing-in-Publication Data
A catalogue record for this book is available from the British Library

Library of Congress Cataloging-in-Publication Data
Names: Eekelen, Willem van, author.
Title: Rural development in practice: evolving challenges and opportunities /
    Willem van Eekelen.
Description: Abingdon, Oxon; New York, NY: Routledge, 2020. |
    Includes bibliographical references and index.
Identifiers: LCCN 2019058549 (print) | LCCN 2019058550 (ebook) |
    ISBN 9781138575356 (hardback) | ISBN 9781138575363 (paperback) |
    ISBN 9781351272001 (ebook)
Subjects: LCSH: Rural development—Developing countries. | Economic
    development—Developing countries. | Developing countries—
    Economic policy. | Developing countries—Rural conditions. |
    Developing countries—Economic conditions.
Classification: LCC HN981.C6 E365 2020 (print) | LCC HN981.C6
    (ebook) | DDC 307.1/412 091724—dc23
LC record available at https://lccn.loc.gov/2019058549
LC ebook record available at https://lccn.loc.gov/2019058550

ISBN: 978-1-138-57535-6 (hbk)
ISBN: 978-1-138-57536-3 (pbk)
ISBN: 978-1-351-27200-1 (ebk)

Typeset in Bembo
by Apex Covantage, LLC

Visit the eResources: www.routledge.com/9781138575363

CONTENTS

TABLES

BOXES

ACKNOWLEDGEMENTS

The biggest perk of conducting evaluations (which is what I do for a living) is that I get to listen to rural women, men, and children from all over the world. I am grateful to all who shared their thoughts and experiences with me. I am also grateful to the many development professionals I interviewed as part of my work. In no more than an hour, they shared insights gained in the course of years, and this often made for steep learning indeed.

I would like to thank Maha, my dear wife, for being my dear wife. We both work internationally, so we don't see each other a whole lot, but when we're together she's the best possible reason for taking a break. I'd like to thank Zena and Hans for helping me fine-tune some of the text and text editor Greg Morse, whose editing made this book far more readable than it would otherwise have been.

I would like to thank Mazvita Mutambirwa, a particularly talented ex-student of mine, for finding many and checking all of the facts and figures I've used throughout. Thanks also to Ajaz Khan, for getting me interested in microfinance and for commenting on the microfinance chapter; to Fiona Nunan for co-writing the chapters on the commons and climate change; and to Micky Dirkzwager for her lighthearted cartoons. Thanks to Helena, Matthew, Elizabeth, Aoife and Autumn, from Routledge and their associates, for being ever-encouraging and for turning this text into a book.

Thanks to my colleague and friend Robert Leurs. We spar and play table tennis, and together we teach a module entitled *Rural Poverty and Development* at the University of Birmingham's International Development Department. Routledge invited me to write this book on the basis of this module's lecture notes.

PREFACE

A while back, Routledge's Helena Hurd phoned me to discuss the need for new textbooks in the broad field of international development. I made a few suggestions but also said that today's students don't read textbooks because they live in an era of endlessly creative information overflows, and they find textbooks dull.

Helena challenged me to write a textbook that students would actually read, about the ways in which rural development is evolving – one of the gaps in Textbook Land.

I accepted and learned that writing an interesting textbook is really hard. In a lecture, you can re-engage sleepy students with a quick audiovisual intermezzo, an anecdote, or an exercise. But a textbook is one-dimensional: it's all just 'words on a page'.

I asked Micky Dirkzwager to add a few cartoons. I hope this helps a bit. I also added an exercise at the end of each chapter and used examples and anecdotes to illustrate key points. But still: this book isn't quite the light bedtime read I had intended it to be. I hope you will persist, find it useful, and consider some of the suggestions in each chapter's section titled *Why is all this relevant, and what does it mean for you?*.

INTRODUCTION

This book is about the evolving nature of rural development in low- and middle-income countries in Africa, Asia, and Latin America – 'the Global South'.

What the chapters are about

The first chapter outlines how we got to where we are today and what we could learn from history. What has caused the last half century's substantial increases in average life expectancy, income levels, and literacy rates, for example? The chapter identifies obstacles that make development very nearly impossible (such as war) and things that could either facilitate or impede development (such as a country's infrastructure). It then explores why some countries in Asia developed so much faster than most of the rest of the world over this period, and why some other countries seem stuck in poverty and fragility.

The other eight chapters cover the issues that are likely to matter most in the years to come.

Chapter 2 examines common agricultural practice, the results this has achieved, and the damage it has caused. It looks at soil and water management and the effects of rural infrastructure and new crop varieties on farming. It discusses what helps farming, pastoralist, and fishing communities to move towards practices that cause less damage and result in higher yields, and what such practice would look like.

Chapter 3 looks at fishing grounds, forests, grazing lands, and water sources that are neither government property nor in private hands. These 'common resources' aren't being managed well enough and, without change, they will deteriorate until they're gone forever. Why is the management of these commons such a problem, and how could it be improved?

Chapter 4 argues that trade is not working particularly well for poor rural people. Often, they pay more per unit of almost anything than everyone else. They are also less likely to have access to the things they need to produce sellable products, and the things they *can* buy are more likely to be of low quality. If they do manage to produce sellable products, they struggle to find a market for them and get paid little per unit of output. The chapter explores the reasons for all this and suggests what could be done to ensure that trade facilitates rural development without leaving behind the poorer segments of rural communities.

Chapter 5 is on microfinance. This includes loans, savings, insurance, leasing, and pensions. The global microfinance sector is large and has been growing non-stop ever since the 1970s, yet its impact has been modest, and sometimes it has caused harm. What could explain this growth path, and why is microfinance likely to have much more impact in the future than it has had in the past?

Chapter 6 is on 'information and communication technology' (ICT). Its opportunities are endless and its impact is enormous and very diverse. In what ways are ICT solutions changing agricultural practice, trading, microfinance, and almost everything else? What is that all-important 'digital divide', and what could be done to bridge it?

Chapter 7 is on migration. What inspires or forces people to migrate, and where do they go? What does their migration mean for the households and communities they leave behind, and in what ways do the effects depend on government policies?

Chapter 8 is on social assistance. In much of the Global South, large-scale social safety nets are a recent phenomenon, and they are changing the nature of rural poverty. The chapter discusses school meals and other forms of food distribution, public work programmes, in-kind support, fee waivers, and cash transfers, and comes to the conclusion that, in most cases, cash transfers are preferable to other types of social assistance.

Chapter 9, the book's final chapter, is about climate change. It explores how climate change is aggravating many of the problems and threats that rural communities are facing, and how it adds importance and urgency to many of the good practice principles discussed in previous chapters.

These are the issues I think will matter most in the years to come, but my judgement may be wrong. There are no chapters on health and education, for example, but new pandemics and changes in the way we learn may require the addition of such chapters to a second edition. In that edition, one or two of the current chapters might disappear. I think microfinance has a very bright future and social safety nets will continue to expand, but I might be mistaken, and if so, the next edition will not give much attention to either issue.

What the chapters look like

Many textbooks start each chapter with an overview of that chapter's content. This book doesn't – instead, all chapters start with a prologue that aims to tickle your interest in what's to come. Textbooks often end each chapter with a set of bullet points that repeat the main points made, but this book doesn't do that either. Instead, all chapters end with the same three sections:

- *Why is all this relevant, and what does it mean for you?* This section assumes that you are or will soon be in a position of some influence. It also assumes you've read the chapter – if you haven't, this section's suggestions won't make much sense.
- *Further reading.* These are lengthy sections, as they don't merely list relevant, high-quality publications but also explain what these books and papers are about, why you might want to read them and, sometimes, what their core conclusions are. Wherever possible, I suggest short papers and summaries of books that don't make things more difficult than necessary and don't use much jargon. Within this group, I prioritised open-source publications over ones that cost money. The reference of such open-source publications ends with 'online'. Papers that are only downloadable after successfully seeking the author's permission (a feature in ResearchGate, for example) or that appear to be online illegally are *not* marked as 'online'.
- *Exercise.* The exercises are best done in a group. They typically ask you to come to a conclusion, find a solution, or make a decision, but the learning objective is really to sharpen your understanding of the dilemmas that a range of stakeholders are facing and of their sometimes irreconcilable interests. After you've done an exercise, you could go to the eResource tap of www.routledge. com/9781138575363, for some reflections on the exercise.

A few technical notes

- *References.* Whenever the main text presents a quotation, fact, or figure, there will be an endnote that provides the reference to the publication it came from. These references are not normally listed in the further reading section, unless the source happened to be a particularly readable publication about sound research on a particularly important issue.
- *Acronyms and jargon.* This book does not have a list of acronyms because I barely used any, and the ones I did use (such as SDG, UN, and NGO) are so very common that they all appear as the first hit of a web search (at least in Google, where I tested this). The book doesn't use much jargon either. Where I did feel that a term was a little jargonistic, I <u>underlined</u> it, which means that it's defined in the endnote that follows it.
- *Corrections and additions.* If you spot an error, disagree with something I wrote, or find something unclear, please email me. My email addresses are willem.vaneekelen@gmail.com and, possibly more temporarily, w.v.eekelen@ bham.ac.uk. Please start the title with "Rural development in practice".

Now let us start.

1

THE DEVELOPMENT DRIVERS, FACILITATORS AND OBSTACLES OF THE LAST 50 YEARS

Don't be discouraged if you find this first chapter long and difficult. This is probably because it's very densely written, as it covers such vast ground. The other chapters are shorter and easier to digest!

Prologue: we're doing really well

If you study anything development-related, you're being taught to see problems everywhere. People are poor, ill, illiterate, abused or abusive, and they're destroying the natural environment. They are living through a civil war or have lost their loved ones in an earthquake. They face suppression and discrimination – perhaps because they are girls, elderly, migrants, or drug users, or because they have disabilities or belong to an ethnic minority. Corrupt officials, climate change, periodic flooding and cyclones, pollution, trade policies, and unnecessary bureaucracy all add to the misery.

You are educating yourself for the purpose of solving these and many other problems. After graduation, this focus on problems continues. You will find that some of them appear unsolvable and that this has turned some of your colleagues in the development sector into cynics. I recently bumped into a friend I once studied with. She was leaving the sector, she said, after coming to the conclusion that "everything always only gets worse".

This is not true.

Yes, the natural world is facing unprecedented challenges. But most people are doing well. The Sustainable Development Goals[1] point at issues that require further progress, but most of their predecessor goals – the Millennium Development Goals – have been achieved in large parts of the world. In the next few pages, we will see that the proportion of people living in extreme poverty has fallen, uninterruptedly, for decades. We will also see that life expectancy and literacy rates are higher and infant mortality is lower than ever before. To a lesser degree, <u>gender gaps</u>[2] are narrowing and, while inequality within many countries is increasing, the world in its entirety is slowly getting less unequal.

Rapid economic development in Asia in particular is shifting global power patterns. Jaguar, that British icon, is now the property of Tata, of India. When the euro faced a crisis, politicians suggested that perhaps China could help out, by buying billions of Europe's currency. *China!* Fifty years ago, this was one of the poorest countries in the world and a country that had only just overcome the world's largest-ever famine. And now Europe wants China's help to stabilise the euro!

So we're doing really well, but some parts of the world are developing faster than others. The average Indonesian village now has electricity, running water, a school, and basic health facilities, while in the 20th century it did not. However, life in the average village in Malawi has not improved all that much over the last 50 years.

In this chapter, we will look at overall development patterns in developing countries, and discuss the main drivers, facilitators and impediments of the last half-century. Some key patterns will emerge; they are relevant today and will remain relevant in the years ahead. In the rest of the book, we will zoom in on some of them, but we will also cover other issues that have become increasingly important in recent times, and that are likely to shape the future much more than they shaped the past. This book is about *rural* development, but we live in a highly interconnected world, and the issues we discuss, in this chapter and later, shape rural life but are not always exclusively rural issues.

What are we talking about?

The internet is full of interactive maps and charts that show development trends for countries, continents, and the world. These maps and charts are often more up to date than anything you could find in printed books, including this one – so go there, not here, if you're looking for the latest facts and figures. Try *gapminder.org*, for example. Select the countries and development indicators that interest you, and let the graphs move from the 1960s to the present. For most development indicators, you will see progress over time, but you'll also see how life expectancy drops during a country's years of war and famine, and it will be obvious just how much your prospects still depend on the continent in which you were born. Almost irrespective of the criteria you use, you will see that Europe and the Americas score better than Asia and Africa, but that many of the gaps are steadily narrowing.

Here are a few bottom-line facts. Read the bold-printed bits only if figures bore you.

- *People live **far longer** than ever before.* The global life expectancy from birth jumped from 53 years in 1960 to over 72 years today. Prospects are not so good in low-income countries, but they are catching up, with a life expectancy that jumped 24 years, from 39 back in 1960 to 63 now. This narrowed the difference with, say, the USA, where life expectancy increased by 'only' nine years in that same period (from 70 to 79).[3]

- *Far fewer infants pass away before the age of five than ever before.* In 1990, more than nine out of every hundred infants died before the age of five. Nowadays, all but eight African countries[4] perform better than that, and the global average under-five mortality rate has dropped from 9% to under 4%. This is still a massive problem – but the progress is obvious.[5] Under-five mortality is strongly associated with malnutrition: the World Health Organization estimates that "around 45% of deaths among children under five years of age are linked to undernutrition. These mostly occur in low- and middle-income countries".[6] This problem is slowly being tackled.
- *Children are better nourished than ever before,* though the figures are still distressing, and the long trend of progress seems to have come to an end in 2015.[7] In 2017, and among the under-fives only, some 150 million children were stunted[8] – which means that they have been chronically undernourished and may never grow to their full potential. This is grave and equates to 22% of the total number of children in that age group. But look at the progress: around the turn of the century, the figure was a third higher – almost 200 million children in this age group were stunted – nearly a third of the total. There is a relatively new and increasing problem, though: obesity has tripled since 1975,[9] and some 38 million under-fives were overweight in 2018.
- *Literacy rates are higher than ever before.* Today, some 86% of the over-15s are literate, compared to only 69% in 1976. The percentages are even better among young people.[10]
- *Many diseases affect fewer people now than they did in the past.* Smallpox no longer exists, and polio is close to being eradicated. Malaria has been on a slow but steady decline (down 20 million between 2010 and 2017, to 219 million people),[11] and it may not be much longer before there's a malaria vaccine.[12] Progress on AIDS has been moving faster. There is no decline in the number of people who are living with HIV yet, but this is part of the success: because medication is better and easier to access than before, HIV no longer necessarily leads to AIDS, which means that far fewer people living *with* HIV die *because of* HIV.
- *Extreme poverty is declining.* The percentage of people living in extreme poverty dropped from 36% in 1990 to 10% in 2015.[13]
- *There is a gradual reduction in global inequality.* Inequality within countries has been increasing throughout the past three decades, and there are only a few exceptions to this rule (a few countries in Latin America have become less unequal, for example). However, *globally*, the economic rise of China and India in particular have finally reversed, around 1990, a trend of ever-increasing inequality that started during the Industrial Revolution and lasted at least 170 years (before which there are no data).[14]
- *The 'gender gap' is narrowing, though the process is painfully slow.* The Global Gender Report features a *Global Gender Gap Index* that is a combination of (a) economic participation and opportunity; (b) educational attainment; (c) health

and survival; and (d) political empowerment. Every year since the report first appeared in 2006, the gap narrowed a bit. Progress is slow (the 2018 report says that, at this speed, we need another 108 years to reach equality) but it is clear and deliberate. Dozens of countries are in the process of, for example, strengthening their legislation to address violence against women and girls.[15]

Apart from the impact of climate change, which makes problems worse, threats graver, and prospects bleaker (see Chapter 9), there is progress everywhere, and it is so strong that it outpaces population growth. For example, there were far fewer extremely poor people in 2018 than there were in 1980, even though the total population was 70% higher.[16]

In almost all dimensions of development, some Asian countries have done *particularly* well over the last 50 years. If you exclude the main oil-producing countries on *gapminder.org*, you will see that Asian and African countries were in the same ballpark for most economic development criteria in the 1960s and early 1970s – and you will also see that, after that, most Asian countries took off and African countries did not. Some Asian countries that lagged behind initially have recently jumped on the 'fast train' as well. Much of the rural population in Bangladesh is still poor, for example, but far *less* poor than it was a few decades ago.

Sub-Saharan Africa does not really have comparable success stories. Yes, it is obviously impressive that life expectancy jumped by over 20 years between 1960 and 2017.[17] But sustained economic development? Not so much. In 2015, most of the extremely poor people in the world (56%) were in Sub-Saharan Africa and, if the current trend continues, it will be 90% by 2030.[18] Central and South America are different from either Asia or Africa. Their level of development in the 1960s was higher, but their progress has been less impressive than that of Asia – most countries in the Americas are still very unequal,[19] and political turmoil, suppression, violence, and poor policy choices have stunted economic growth and most other forms of development for much of the last 50 years.

So what explains the differences across countries and continents? There are obstacles, facilitators, and drivers, and we will cover the key ones in turn.

Obstacles that make development nearly impossible

The road out of poverty is filled with obstacles. Some of them just take a bit of effort. Little water? Use drip irrigation. Mountainous terrain? Drill tunnels. No navigable rivers? Dig a canal or build a railway. Other obstacles are more fundamental, and some of them are caused or reinforced by poverty itself – hence the term 'poverty trap'. This section covers seven obstacles that make development very nearly impossible.

1 of 7: conflict and war

A conflict does not necessarily halt a country's development if that conflict is limited to a certain region. Indonesia developed rapidly during its regional conflicts in Aceh, East Timor, and Papua, for example. But if a conflict engulfs a country, development becomes impossible for a few mutually reinforcing reasons.

- War and conflict destroy a country's economic infrastructure. This destruction is often deliberate, as warring parties aim to cause maximum damage. It is more attractive to blow up a bridge or an electricity plant than a field of grass. The result is immobility and a loss in economic production. If investments in infrastructure and other things vital for development continue at all, they are not informed by economic development objectives but by war strategy.
- Economic actors that do manage to continue operations are often the ones that don't develop but destroy. They are breweries that fuel violence as they stay open by paying militia off with alcohol[20] and companies and criminal networks that produce and trade weapons and illicit drugs. Some 95% of hard drugs are produced in countries in conflict. Growing poppy is a lifeline for local farmers (even if the crop they grow destroys lives elsewhere), but it also causes conflicts to drag on: "a study of 128 conflict-affected countries found that conflicts financed at least partially by illicit trafficking (primarily in drugs and diamonds) lasted six times longer, on average, than conflicts without these factors".[21]
- War and conflict affect a government's ability to provide public services (electricity, education, health care, and suchlike). They also lead to casualties and injuries, mass displacement, disease, malnutrition (up to the point of starvation), and a host of other things that count as 'development in reverse'.[22]

Once a country is embroiled in violent conflict, it is often difficult to get out of it. Peace agreements are hard to come to and easy to break. Look at the country ranking of the *Human Development Index*, and you will see that many of the countries at the bottom have been in long and often recurrent conflicts. Yemen, South Sudan, and the Democratic Republic of Congo, to give just three obvious examples, will be at the bottom of the global development league for years to come, and their next peace agreements may not hold. When the conflict in these countries eventually ends, things will not just return to normal. Education will take years to re-establish itself, for instance, and the effects of the disruption of people's schooling will last for decades. Still, the end of conflict opens the door for development processes to resume, and these countries will soon see high economic growth figures, if only because they come from such a very low base.

2 of 7: the resource curse

There is a strong correlation between poverty and conflict, and it is even stronger in countries with resources like gold, diamonds, and oil in the ground. These 'underground resources' (often referred to as 'natural resources', but not in this book as I reserved that term for water, forests and air and such) attract people who are poor and have no other prospects, and who form or join rebel groups that promise a way out of poverty by gaining or keeping control over these resources.

As is the case with illegal drugs, underground resources have the tendency not just to start and exacerbate conflicts but to *prolong* them too. This is because groups that gain control over such resources will often use the revenue to finance further conflict to defend and expand their territorial control. Central governments that control resource-rich regions may be similarly violent as they defend their territory. They may commit crimes against humanity themselves, or they may tolerate such crimes being committed by militias that protect the interests of unscrupulous extractive companies (which, just to be clear, is a sub-set within the extractive industry – this is *not* a sweeping, sector-wide accusation). The ties between such companies and national governments, or decision-makers within these governments, are often strong.

3 of 7: absence of incentives to produce

In the 20th century, a number of communist and socialist countries used farming models where people were expected to work hard for some sort of greater good, rather than for their own profit. It never worked.[23] Around 1960, it contributed to the three-year 'Great Chinese Famine' that killed tens of millions of people.

The simple truth is that, like almost everybody else, farmers work harder if they get rewarded for that work. In 1978, the farmers in a Chinese village proved this when they secretly moved from a collective farming to a family-based farming model. This was a risky and illegal move, and the farmers faced possible execution if the authorities found out. (They had agreed that, if this happened, the survivors would take care of the orphaned children.) They came to this courageous decision after the famine of the 1960s had killed more than half the people in the village.

When the Chinese government heard of the experiment, they did not arrest and execute the farmers. Instead, they assessed the results of their experiment and found them convincing. The government took swift action and moved the country from collective farming to family-based farming over the next five years.[24] Vietnam followed a similar track, in the second half of the 1980s. There, too, it led to an agricultural production boom. Agricultural production in Cuba will rapidly increase as well, if ever Cuba gets rid of the requirement for farmers to sell a large part of their harvest to the government (90% in the case of tobacco), at government-set prices.[25]

4 of 7: stifling rules and regulations

It is important to regulate business, but it is bad to stifle it. It is hard to find the right regulatory balance, but a good rule of thumb is that obstacles need to pose as little hindrance as possible, while effectively serving one or more of three good aims:

1   Generating money for the government. A government that is unable to generate money is unable to invest in health, education, infrastructure, and a range of other things that a government should provide. Obviously, taxation and other forms of money generation should not squeeze companies to the point where making a profit is no longer interesting.
2   Preventing harmful consequences of business activity – such as poisoning a river or failing to prevent workers getting injured in the course of their work.
3   Preventing unfair competition. An example of unfair competition is 'dumping', where a company sells products below the cost price to drive competitors

out of business – after which the company increases the sales price again and has a bigger market to sell to.

In reality, business regulation is often overbearing *and* fails to serve the purposes it is meant to serve. The private sector can manage a fair bit of unnecessary bureaucracy (and corruption, see Box 1.1), but there is a limit beyond which you kill the entrepreneurial spirit – and it is nearly impossible to develop a country without entrepreneurialism. India provides the world's best illustration of the impact senseless bureaucracy can have. The country used to have an awful business climate between its independence in 1947 and the early 1980s. It then slashed its bureaucracy and turned from "the biggest beggar in the world" to "an object of envy among developing countries".[26] Its current business climate is not at all great (the country scores 77 out of 190 countries on the *Ease of Doing Business Index*, and it's been as bad as 142 in recent times),[27] but it is not nearly as stifling as it once was, and there are plenty of businesses managing to thrive there.

BOX 1.1 CORRUPTION

Corruption can be a facilitator if there are unreasonable rules that you can bribe your way out of. In such cases, corruption 'greases the wheels of growth'.[28] Corruption can also be an obstacle that adds to the costs and hassle of doing business – and it can be far more serious if large sums of money meant to do something useful just disappear out of the country, or if corrupt officials look the other way when companies dump toxic waste.

There is strong correlation between corruption and poverty. Take a look at the Transparency International's Corruption Perception Index, and you will see that the richest countries are never very corrupt and that the poorest countries are almost invariably very corrupt. While the correlation is strong, the causal link (as in what causes what) is not entirely obvious. It seems certain that, in the longer term at least, corruption slows development and increases inequality. However, it may also be true that economic development causes corruption to gradually decline and that high inequality stimulates corruption as much as it is reinforced by it.

---

5 of 7: overreaching leadership

Nigeria and Indonesia have a lot in common. They are both multi-ethnic former colonies with oil in the ground, a history of internal conflict, and comparable levels of poverty until the 1970s. Since then, development patterns could not have been further apart. As Nigeria was squandering its hundreds of billions of dollars in oil money *and* building up a heavy debt burden, Indonesia moved forwards. The results are obvious: today, Indonesia significantly outperforms Nigeria in pretty much everything. Take extreme poverty: in 1984–85, the proportion of extremely poor people was higher in Indonesia than in Nigeria (71% versus 53% of the population).

A few decades later, the proportion of extremely poor people in Nigeria is still the same, while in Indonesia, it has declined to less than 6%.[29]

Nigeria could have benefited from a few learning visits to Indonesia. Instead, Nigeria looked at Western countries and wanted to 'modernise' in the way *they* had done. This did not work out well. Nigeria overreached, trying to build sophisticated industries without having sorted out the basics of reliable electricity, infrastructure, an appropriate skills base, a business-friendly environment, and markets for its products. Ghana did the same. Other African countries saw massive money wasting endeavours as well – sometimes not even to grow the economy but merely to glorify the leaders (see Box 1.2, or check YouTube for a taste of the 1976 coronation of Bokassa, the 'emperor' of the Central African Republic). Whether for the purpose of personal glorification or because of their attempts to 'modernise', countries taxed agriculture to finance some of the costs and got loans for the rest. The taxation kept Africa's agricultural sector poor and underdeveloped, and the result of the loans was that countries ended up with the same levels of poverty, broken dreams, and an unserviceable debt burden.

BOX 1.2 MOBUTU'S BIRTH VILLAGE

If, in the early 1990s, you travelled overland from Uganda to the Central African Republic, using the northern 'highway' of Zaire (now called the Democratic Republic of Congo), it would take you a few weeks on an uneven red gravel road. Sometimes you needed to fill potholes to be able to proceed, and the road was so deserted that you could stop the car on the road to have lunch.

Then, one day, this red gravel road would turn flat and smooth, then broaden, and then gravel would turn into asphalt. Streetlights would appear, and flowerpots would separate the two directions of travel. You would see a giant satellite receiver and signs for an airport. A bit later, the streetlights would disappear, and so would the other features, until it was an uneven gravel road again. You had just passed the birth village of the late Mobutu Sésé Seko, Africa's foremost kleptocrat and squanderer, the man who milked Zaire from 1965 until 1997.

FIGURE 1.1 The road to our people

6 of 7: crippling debt burdens

It makes sense to borrow money if you use this money for something that generates more than the value of the loan plus its interest payments. For example, a country could usefully borrow money to build the infrastructure needed for a coastal holiday zone, if this then inspires private investors to build hotels and if tourists then come. Such a loan could result in the government receiving tourist and income tax, which it could use to pay off the loan and accrued interest. The net result of the loan would be jobs for its citizens and an ongoing flow of extra money into the government's coffers.

A loan might also make a bit of sense if it covers a lean period, if there's reason to believe better times are just around the corner. But it makes no sense at all to borrow money to finance things for the here and now, without reasonable expectation that you are going to be able to repay your loans without major sacrifices later. Yet, in many poor countries, this is what happened, especially in the 1970s and early 1980s, and the effects are lasting even today. It got countries into a debt spiral, where delays in repayments incurred additional fines and interest charges, which made it even harder to service the debts, which then led to further fines, and so forth. Debt waivers have been important for the development of many of the poorer parts of the world. Without it, it would have been virtually impossible for heavily indebted countries to develop.

7 of 7: bad neighbours

Bad neighbours bring you down. If conflict is raging next door, it will threaten your own stability, as conflict often spills across borders. It will affect your trade and tourism industry. It will force you to increase your military spending, which could in turn spark a regional arms race. It will deter foreign investors and may burden you with a large refugee population, which could cause friction and pose a financial burden.

Your neighbours' conflicts aren't the only problems they may present you with. If you are surrounded by countries with unnecessary bureaucracy and corruption, you won't look bad if you, too, are bureaucratic and corrupt. Your neighbours' practice in relation to health, education, and social safety nets is similarly contagious: you will probably invest in these sectors if all your neighbours are outperforming you, but you may not prioritise them if the regional standards are low.

Being landlocked is not necessarily a problem; it doesn't bother Switzerland or Luxembourg. But your prospects are grim if you are landlocked and surrounded by chaos.

Things that could either facilitate or impede development

The obstacles we just discussed make it very nearly impossible to develop at all. This means that it is crucially important for a country to

- Maintain or build peace and stability, within the country and in the wider region. This is particularly challenging if the country is financially poor, but rich in resources.
- Create and maintain a reasonably business-friendly environment that incentivises productivity.
- Avoid making massive investments in high-risk endeavours and then facing crippling debt burdens if these investments fail to generate a good return.

Sticking to these principles does not guarantee development, but it certainly increases the odds.

This section presents a few other things that help explain why some countries developed so much faster than others. They could be facilitators or impediments, depending on the country and context. In some cases, progress is simultaneously a form of development in itself *and*, in a chicken-and-egg sort of way, stimulates other forms of development. Good education, for example, is a form of development. It also reduces poverty levels, which enhances education, which reduces poverty levels, and so on.

We'll cover seven issues. Seven is not a magic number, and the similarity with the previous section is coincidental.

1 of 7: the ease of transport of people and things

There is air, water and land transport, and in all cases it is not about distance but about the costs and time required to go from A to B. In short,

- In 2018, 24 of the 30 cheapest airlines were in Asia and the Middle East. Europe and most of the Americas came next, followed by the rest of the world. Flights within Africa are generally expensive, though a few budget airlines now exist.[30]
- The turnaround time for a container ship is less than a half a day in most of Europe, the Americas, and Southeast Asia. It is a little longer in the Middle East and South Asia, and it takes multiple days in most African ports.[31]

The differences are more pronounced in transport by road and rail. Check out the *World Logistics Performance Index*, and you will see that countries in Sub-Saharan Africa (with the exception of South Africa) score far worse than almost all other countries on almost all sub-indicators. In most of Sub-Saharan Africa, infrastructure quality, safety, maintenance of roads and vehicles, policing and law enforcement, and aid dependency (traditionally on European and North American infrastructural support but increasingly on China's loans and workers) are all really bad. Moreover, the best roads are the ones meant for the export of underground resources, rather than local transport or the export of agricultural products (which would benefit far more people, as agriculture is more labour intensive than mining).[32] In addition, inefficiency, bureaucracy and corruption mean that borders take more time in African countries than in the rest of the world – which is a problem for the continent's many landlocked countries in particular. Perhaps the biggest trade impediment, though, is uncertainty: you never know when your container is going to arrive, and this adds to the trading costs and reduces the export potential of perishable goods.

Together, high costs and uncertainty, in combination with high levels of corruption, lead to 'adverse selection': the few investors willing to do business in your country may be the type of investors you don't actually want (see Box 1.3).

BOX 1.3   THE ADVERSE SELECTION PRINCIPLE

When Save the Children contracted me for a brief assignment in Juba, South Sudan, I had to travel to Kenya to apply for my visa and then visit the South Sudanese embassy every day for a week until my name appeared on the 'approved-for-visa' list. A ticket for the next-day flight was really costly (though far less expensive than my first-ever trip to Juba, for which the UN had to charter a private plane from Khartoum), and the flight got cancelled. I was booked onto another flight but did not get on the plane because there was a security incident in Juba the night before my flight, and Save the Children cancelled the visit altogether. Ten days wasted, no work done. A few years before, my dear wife, Maha, had caused me distress by flying out of Juba with an airline that had been blacklisted by the UN because of its track record of crashes.

If you work in the humanitarian sector, this sometimes happens, and it affects your nerves but not your income. If you are a businessperson, though, such safety risks are not inevitable, and such time wastage cuts into your profits – and there is not much obvious profit to make in Juba to begin with.

Such difficulties create an 'adverse selection principle', and large parts of Africa are suffering from it. The thing is: bona fide businesses like safety, stability, predictability, and speed. Singapore offers all of this, and Juba offers none of it – so bona fide businesses gravitate towards Singapore, not South Sudan or, say, Liberia. The investors who *are* willing to face tedious bureaucracy and corruption, unreliable flights and security incidents, are often the type of investors you don't want. They probably don't come to Juba to grow maize or produce shoes – they come to make a lot of money quickly, by exploiting the country's natural riches, and may not mind violating some rules and rights in the process.

---

2 of 7: the money you have and the way you use it

Earlier, we discussed the 'resource curse'. But of course oil, ore, and diamonds do not *have* to cause conflict, and their extraction does not *have* to be mismanaged (see Box 1.4). Dubai very successfully used oil money to diversify its economy. To a lesser extent, this is true for Chile, Malaysia, and Botswana as well. Foreign financial support is potentially useful too, and American budget support in particular helped a number of countries kick-start a positive development spiral. Marshall Aid helped Western Europe recover after the Second World War, to give just one example.

3 of 7: the nature and extent of your trade barriers

Many people have strong opinions about the merits of global free trade. On the one extreme, and until President Trump of the United States changed the country's trade policy, there was the 'Washington consensus'. According to this consensus among the big players in Washington (which are the World Bank, IMF, and the US government),

- Free trade is good.
- Exerting pressure on countries that are restricting imports is a worthwhile thing to do.

Its theoretical frame is called 'neo-classical economics'. On the other side, there are (or really there mostly *were*) theories – such as dependency theory and world-systems theory – which argued that

- Trade benefits high-income countries but harms low-income countries.
- Global trade is increasing inequalities, making rich people richer but poor people poorer.

Such theories concluded that poor countries should protect their industries to give them time to develop, and only open the borders once they have successfully done so (this is called the 'infant industry argument').

Research on countries that have successfully developed their economies concluded that the truth is in the middle. A rigorous border closure has never helped any country, but countries that have temporarily protected and supported the development of specific, not-yet-competitive economic sectors have sometimes done so with great success – as the economic success stories of South Korea, Taiwan, Japan, China, and India all illustrate.

Consequently, the discourse amongst economists is no longer as polarised as it was between the 1960s and the 1990s, and today's fairly wide consensus is that

- Free trade is good, once you have reached a certain level of development.
- Some forms of strategic protectionism may be needed to get to that level or to compensate for subsidised agricultural products from other countries (see Chapter 4, on trade, for more on this).

- Temporary protection really needs to be *temporary*, and needs to be closely monitored to avoid fighting battles that cannot be won. In the field of ICT, for example, protection won't help you, as the global development of ICT products and services moves *so* fast and is *so* complex that you'll never catch up from behind a protective wall.

As many countries have now reached the level of development needed to compete successfully on global markets, import tariffs have been reduced around the world (though, as you would expect, less so in low-income countries). The result of these tariff reductions has been that trade has increased. At least for the countries that provide a reasonably healthy business climate, this growth has been good for national production and employment.

The expansion in global trade has reduced inequality across countries. This is because labour-intensive industries that produce shippable goods tend to move to

---

BOX 1.4 THE DUTCH DISEASE

Underground resources may cause and prolong conflict. A less dramatic problem with such resources is that they sometimes cause 'the Dutch disease'.[33] The phenomenon is named after a problem that the Netherlands faced when it discovered huge natural gas reserves. It has two components. First, a high-value underground resource causes capital and talent to flow there, at the expense of other sectors. After all, why would you focus your investment on growing potatoes if you can make vastly more money pumping oil, and why would you work anywhere else if the salaries are highest in the petroleum sector? Second, the value of a country's currency is roughly reflective of that country's economic production, and the value of oil can be *so* high that the currency becomes expensive (as in, you used to pay a dollar for a dinar, but now you need two dollars to buy that dinar). An expensive currency is a problem because it makes all your domestic production cost more in dollar terms. For example, if your currency doubles in value, a worker who used to cost the equivalent of 10 US dollars now costs 20 dollars per hour – without having had a salary raise in dinars and without producing anything extra. Such high costs in dollar terms make your exports too expensive and make imports cheaper and therefore hard to compete with.

Particularly unwise governments face additional problems. They expand their cadre of civil servants when the oil price is high and then fail to pay their salaries when a lower oil price reduces government income. This then increases corruption because civil servants who do not receive their salaries will need another way to gain an income. Such governments also use their oil wealth to convince banks to lend them extra money – until they are hopelessly indebted. Or they are proud of their expensive currency and keep the formal exchange rate artificially high when the currency's value goes down with the declining oil price (which then creates a black market for that currency).

FIGURE 1.2   The mixed blessings of oil

countries that have good infrastructure and relatively low salary costs, and over time this will cause these salaries to increase. This is what happened in India and China, for example. Trade critics argue that international trade has increased inequality *within* countries. This did indeed happen in India and China and in a range of other countries. However, this rising inequality is generally caused by the rise of a very wealthy elite and some high-income professions, not because the poorest segments of society got poorer in absolute terms.

Though economists broadly agree that free trade is worth striving for, the trend towards lower trade barriers is a fragile one, and at the time of writing – 2019 – it seems to be reversing. Support for trade wars is understandable because there *are* losers in international trade. Open borders mean that some companies are established and flourish but also that other companies do not survive, as they cannot compete with the world's most efficient producers. Globally, this dynamic leads to a continuous productivity upgrade, but this is hard to appreciate if you work for a company that just went bankrupt or moved to a country where salaries are lower.

4 of 7: the percentage of the people in your country that are doing useful work

The workforce ratio is the number of people who are working or looking for work, as a proportion of the overall number of people in a country. For a healthy and growing economy, this ratio needs to be high. Moreover, the unemployment rate within the work force needs to be low, and the work they do needs to be useful.

The smaller the proportion of economically active people, the harder it is for them to cover their own living costs *and* the living costs of the people who are not participating in economic life – and *then* still have enough money left to invest in the future. There are four critical elements:

1   *The levels of unemployment and underemployment* (see Box 1.5). If everybody wants to work but there are no productive jobs, development prospects are bleak.

2   *The proportion of children in the population.* Take a look at population statistics, and you will see that by far the highest birth rates are in Africa.[34] High birth rates are a problem, as they mean there are many children and relatively few people who earn the money needed for their upbringing.

3   *The proportion of women in the labour force.* You don't see many women in the streets of northern Pakistan. This poses an economic problem, as human capital is a key component of wealth creation, and economies that underutilise women (and virtually all economies do but to very different extents) do not develop as fast as they could.[35]

4   *The proportion of elderly people in the population.* This is going to be China's next big economic and workforce problem. Already, the work force ratio in

---

BOX 1.5   UNDEREMPLOYMENT

Last June, I had lunch with an old African friend who now works for her country's Bureau of Statistics. At the end of our lunch, I walked her back to her department, and she invited me in for coffee. We walked through a number of empty offices until we reached a 'common room' where, I was told, people were supposed to be if they were not working. At the moment, there was no work, and the room was crowded. I asked when the work would start again. In September, she said.

The people in her department are 'underemployed': they have a formal job, but for much of the time, they do not actually *do* anything. For a country to develop, it is not enough for people to have a job: they need to actually be *doing* something, and their work needs to be useful.

China is low, because life expectancy has increased while the labour force has not. This problem is going to get much bigger once the parents of the one-child generation retire.[36]

5 of 7: your people's level of education

Literate women are more likely to have their own income than illiterate women, and their income goes up with their educational attainment. This is not just because office jobs require education: literate women can read the instructions for the use of fertiliser and pesticides, and use smart phones to gain access to information; both could be income boosters.

The benefits of literacy are intergenerational. Literate women marry later than illiterate women and have fewer children. These children are healthier (partly because their mothers can read their medication information wrappers) and are more likely to go to school. After that, they are more likely to find employment than the children of illiterate women, and they get higher levels of income.

The effects of education, on women and men, are manifold and significant. They are also often exaggerated (see Box 1.6), and they are very different across countries and continents. In the 1990s, the link between education and income was far stronger in Latin America and Sub-Saharan Africa than in the Middle East, for example.[37] Even where the effects are strong, they are often not powerful enough to withstand the effects of serious adversity. Take a look at literacy rates (through the UNICEF website or *ourworldindata.org/literacy*), and you will see that many African countries have higher literacy rates than some of the Asian countries, while they are lagging behind in most other forms of development.

**BOX 1.6   TAKE SWEEPING WEBSITE STATEMENTS
              WITH A PINCH OF SALT**

UN, NGO, and government websites often make sweeping statements about the benefits of whatever they do. In the case of education, "every additional year of schooling for girls and boys increases GDP by 0.37 per cent!"

Take such slogans with a pinch of salt. First, many such statements do not refer back to credible research or generalise the finding in a single country into a global statement. For example, the statement above is from Canada's "feminist international assistance policy",[38] with a footnote that refers to the website of the Global Partnership for Education. That website in turn refers to a UNESCO report, and that's where the trail runs dry: the UNESCO report makes the same statement, without substantiation or reference – so we just don't know what that 0.37% is based on.

> Second, organisations regularly change these statements to befit their requirements. For example, that same "feminist international assistance policy" of Canada says that
>
> > "In developing countries, girls who have completed seven years of schooling will, on average, marry *four* years later."[39]
>
> ActionAid did not think this was sufficiently impressive, so they added a year and wrote that
>
> > "Girls who have completed seven years of education will marry on average *five* years later than uneducated girls."[40]
>
> Third, correlation and causality are not the same. Yes, there is strong correlation between education and income – but this does not necessarily mean that the educational achievements *cause* higher income. An alternative causal link

is one where a household's higher income increases its investments in education – and in reality it is generally a bit of both.

6 of 7: your people's health and nutritional status

Good health and nourishment create a positive spiral that benefits individuals and the country in which they live. Poor health and undernourishment does the opposite: "productivity losses to individuals are estimated at more than 10 percent of lifetime earnings [and] gross domestic product . . . lost to malnutrition runs as high as 2 to 3 percent".[41]

In the short term, the economic effects of poor health are bigger if the health problem disproportionately affects key parts of the labour force. AIDS is a good example. Southern African truck drivers who had unprotected sex in the course of their journeys often contracted HIV. They spread the virus and then became ill and died, leaving behind their wives and others in poor and deteriorating health *and* leaving a key gap in the labour market.

In the much longer term, health and nutrition have inter-generational effects. Healthy, well-nourished children are likely to grow into physically and cognitively well-developed adults, able to generate an income that benefits themselves and their own children's development. The opposite creates a negative spiral: if the physical and cognitive growth of today's children is compromised, they are more likely to remain poor, and *their* children are more likely to suffer the same fate.

7 of 7: culture and climate? Probably not

An argument commonly used to explain global differences in the speed of development is that some cultures are hard-working and some are, in effect, lazy. Proponents of this argument point at religion and say that religious communities tend to be fatalistic and focused on the spiritual rather than the materialistic side of life – and are therefore not inclined to improve their plight.[42] People advocating for this explanation also point at climate: countries in the tropics are poor because it is hot and tough there, and it is hard to grow crops, and therefore people from tropical cultures do not really try to improve their lives.

There are two problems with these arguments. First, they smack of racism and anti-religiosity, and it seems to me that wealth tends to reduce religiosity, rather than religiosity reinforcing poverty. Second, the arguments seem to shift from one culture to the next, depending on who is behind on the development trajectory. When China, India, and other Asian countries were lagging behind, people often quoted Max Weber, who believed that entrepreneurial capitalism was incompatible with Confucianism, Taoism, Hinduism, and Buddhism. Books and papers often quoted him until these countries' economies took off. When this happened, Weber's arguments did not disappear but moved to Africa, and now people argue that *Africans* are lazy, instead of Indians and Chinese. If Ethiopia is going to be the next economic miracle (which I think is likely, albeit from a very low base), the argument will not fade out but will just move again, southwards or westwards, and so forth.

Why have many Asian countries been outpacing the rest of the world?

Did you spend a bit of time on *gapminder.org*? If so, you'll have seen the rapid and almost uninterrupted socio-economic development processes of Thailand, South Korea, Malaysia, Indonesia, then China, and more recently India and Vietnam, with early signs that other Asian countries are following. Different countries started their rapid development at different times – but once they started, there was no stopping them and even disasters such as the Asian financial crisis of 1997 only dampened progress for a few years. Income, life expectancy, health, nutritional status: everything rapidly improved. How did they do it?

First, they ended or dramatically reduced wars and internal conflict, as happened in Vietnam, South Korea, Cambodia, and Indonesia.

Second, they avoided major pitfalls. By and large, the successful Asian countries managed to avoid the resource curse (which has been much more of an African and Latin American problem), and instead, they used the money generated by their underground resources – and by American financial aid – more or less wisely. Asian countries were also less likely to accumulate unserviceable debt burdens.[43]

Third, they terminated some awful policies. As mentioned earlier, China and Vietnam got rid of agricultural models in which there was no link between performance and income, and this led to a rapid increase in agricultural production. In India, the government used to be the Grand Master of making anything other than small-scale business impossible through corruption and obstacles-without-a-purpose. In the 1980s, an Indian researcher tried to establish a company, just to see how many steps it required (close to a hundred, if I remember correctly) and how much time it would take (close to a year, and the process was concluded only after paying a few bribes to avoid a total standstill).[44] The Indian economy only took off when its government removed, hesitantly in the 1980s and more forcefully in the early 1990s, thousands of unnecessary rules that had stifled business for so long.

AND THEN, FINALLY, ON PAGE 22...

FIGURE 1.3 This book's readers, mid–way chapter 1.

Fourth and last, they recognised that most people were *rural* people and that development efforts therefore had to start in *rural* regions. Asian leaders saw a large rural population, lots of land, and an inclination to engage in small-scale farming – and they built on this by making small-scale farming more rewarding.[45] To do this, many Asian countries invested far more heavily in rural development than African or Latin American countries have ever done. These Asian countries typically

- Increased the amount of cultivated land (destroying many forests in the process).
- Constructed and improved many, *many* thousands of kilometres of rural roads.
- Encouraged irrigation-based agriculture which, in many places, helped to double or even triple production. To achieve this, they invested in irrigation networks, often using labour-intensive digging methods so that the construction itself generated an income for local people (see Chapter 8 for more on these 'public work programmes').
- Promoted, through subsidies and awareness campaigns, the use of high-yielding varieties of rice, rubber trees and cotton plants, pulses, cereals, soybean, rapeseed, maize, and a range of other key crops. They also often subsidised inputs, such as fertiliser and pesticides (we'll discuss the pros and cons of such subsidies in Chapter 2).
- Offered minimum prices for rice and other crops.
- Invested in other parts of rural life, such as schools, health-care centres, and electrification.

...THE AUTHOR REALISED THAT THIS BOOK IS ABOUT **RURAL** DEVELOPMENT.

FIGURE 1.3   Continued

The focus on rural development was costly and required strong and sustained commitment of political leaders, but it paid off (see Table 1.1 for three examples). The farmers' increased income created a higher demand for education and health services, which, as we discussed, then tends to create a positive spiral in which progress in income, health, and education all reinforce each other. These higher incomes also led to a demand for a more diverse range of consumer products and services, and this sparked a diversification of rural economies.

This diversification meant that people's economic activities were no longer confined to farming. Though farming was much more profitable than it had been before, millions of people moved to an ever-expanding range of occupations that catered for a booming demand for, say, fixing motorbikes, organising weddings, and local eateries. Some of the demand came from new arrivals: tourists. Once particularly pretty parts of the rural world had reasonable road access, electricity, and running water, they sometimes managed to turn into rural and nature-based tourism destinations. This was a tiny niche in the 1970s but has grown year on year. This niche has received a major new push with the arrival of Airbnb and other platforms that allow individual households to market their spare capacity on the global marketplace.

In essence, the rapid rural development in Asian countries was first a matter of removing obstacles, then promoting and supporting good farming approaches, and then letting the market work its magic. Countries often did not quite know what their next steps ought to be, and much was therefore a matter of trial and error. Once it was clear what worked, success was quickly replicated, with lots of room for contextual adaptation and for dealing with unforeseen developments – something China's President Deng Xiaoping described, in 1978, as "crossing the river by feeling for stones".[46]

TABLE 1.1 Examples of Asian countries' strong focus on rural development

Malaysia	Indonesia	Vietnam
• Started in the 1960s. • Poverty fell from 45% in the early 1970s to 0.2% in 2015.	• Started in the 1970s. • Poverty fell from 92% in 1984 to 27% in 2017.	• Started in the 1980s. • Poverty fell from 80% in 1992 to 8% in 2016.
Malaysia subsidised a rejuvenation of its rubber plantations and settled landless and marginal farmers onto new farmland. Agricultural land almost tripled, between 1961 and today, *and* production per acre of land increased because of better irrigation and better seeds and other inputs. Other key development drivers were free trade zones that created a boom in labour-intensive manufacturing, and free health and education.	Rural economies grew and diversified because of a strong and multifaceted rural push that included subsidised seeds and fertilisers, guaranteed minimum prices, new and improved irrigation systems, rural roads, schools, health centres, and electricity networks. A big focus on rice turned Indonesia from the world's largest importer to a net exporter of rice.	More and better irrigation, land reform that focused on poor farmers and that allowed for better use of agricultural land, and a subsequent liberalisation of trade caused a rapid increase in the production of, primarily, rice and (later) coffee. Initially, the increased agricultural production was mostly for internal consumption. This changed, and export crops got a major push when America lifted its trade embargo in 1994, and when Vietnam joined ASEAN a year later.

Details and sources: Poverty figures in this table are from *data.worldbank.org/indicator*, indicator of 'Poverty headcount ratio at $3.20 a day (2011 PPP) (percentage of population)', accessed on 29 September 2019. The only exception is Malaysia's early 1970s figure, as the World Bank database does not go back that far – so that figure is from Asian Development Bank (2006) "Pathways out of rural poverty and the effectiveness of poverty targeting" *ADB evaluation study*, online. The figures showing that Malaysia's agricultural land almost tripled – from 30,847 to 86,270 square kilometres between 1961 and 2016 – are from *data.worldbank.org/indicator*, indicator of 'agricultural land (sq. km)', accessed on 29 September 2019.

Looking at each step individually, and with the benefit of hindsight, action was often clumsy, frequently corrupt, and included expensive measures that we now know to be largely ineffective (such as these fertiliser subsidies, which we'll come back to in the next chapter). But looking at all efforts combined, that single-minded focus on improving life in the countryside worked strikingly well. And because this rapid development occurred in several countries in the region, in the same few decades, it created regional momentum – illustrating that a 'neighbourhood effect' can be positive as well.

Several of these governments have continued their rural investments until today (though not at the level of the 1980s and 1990s),[47] and agricultural production continues to grow. In parallel, these countries' manufacturing industries grew and evolved (see Box 1.7). This process of growth and increasing sophistication was

BOX 1.7 ON FLYING GEESE

On a flight from Kunming in China to Dhaka in Bangladesh, a talkative Chinese man in the seat next to mine talked about the five textile factories he owned. He'd made a lot of money, he said, but it was now getting increasingly difficult to generate a profit in his native China. This was a labour-intensive industry, and salaries in his factory had been pushed up by Chinese development, from a monthly $50 when he had started in the 1980s to $200 now. He was therefore in the process of moving these factories to Bangladesh, where the labour costs were still significantly lower.

This is an example of the 'flying geese theory' in practice. The theory is named after the flying formation of geese. Towards the two tail ends of the V are the countries that produce the simplest products on the basis of basic technology and low salaries. As they develop, they move to increasingly sophisticated products, paying higher salaries. This pushes up the overall salaries in these countries, which means that they are no longer able to produce the more basic items at competitive costs – so, as these countries move up the V, the production of these basic commodities moves to poorer countries, where the salaries are still very low.

The flying geese theory was developed in the 1930s by Akamatsu, a Japanese economist, and is still relevant today. As Bangladesh develops and its labour costs increase, the textile industry is likely to move again – and early signs suggest that the next move will be to Ethiopia.

sparked by governments improving their business environments (regulation and infrastructure, mostly), which attracted foreign investors who proceeded to produce an ever-increasing proportion of their products in Malaysia (first) and China (then). Investments then spilled over to other Asian countries, and some Asian countries turned into large investors themselves.

Why is all this relevant, and what does it mean for you?

Climate change is deeply concerning, as it creates and aggravates a wide range of problems and risks. The conflicts in today's world cause great and non-reversible harm as well and, for many conflict-affected countries, a peace treaty will merely be a fragile starting point. If you see an opportunity to help solve the climate puzzle or to help move along the process towards a lasting peace somewhere, then that's the best thing you could possibly do.

In all other fields: don't be pessimistic. Recognise that things are going well, and that we now understand, much better than we did in the 20th century, how development processes are affected by a range of drivers, facilitators, and obstacles.

Keep the basics in mind. Education and health care are fundamental building blocks, and so are a high labour force ratio and non-discriminatory labour force access. If your country scores poorly on the 'ease of doing business' ranking, or if it has overregulated or ignored its agricultural sector, or if there are non-sensible trade barriers you could remove, then these are some low-hanging fruits to focus on. If you do so,

- Do not blindly follow the advice of development banks. The most successful countries of the past 50 years found their own way, which was often distinctly different from what the World Bank and IMF thought would be best.
- Do not get discouraged by your neighbours' poor performance, but do take inspiration from regional examples of good practice. Together with your neighbours, you could create a positive 'neighbourhood effect', instead of bringing each other down with a negative one.
- Consider the grave effects of corruption but be careful when trying to reduce it, as powerful interests will cause a hostile response. Depending on context and location, work in this field may cost you your life.

If your country has just found oil or ore or diamonds, look at South Sudan, Nigeria, Venezuela, and the Democratic Republic of Congo to understand the risks of what you've found. For lessons on how underground resources can be a *good* thing, look at Chile, Botswana, Malaysia, or any of the other countries that managed their resources relatively wisely. Use your oil money to strengthen other parts of your country's economy, and focus your diversification efforts on sectors and regions where the largest number of people will benefit from the investments.

If you have a financial role in government, remember the importance of borrowing with care. It is never wise to invest in megalomaniac projects or to take risks that your citizens will bear the burden of if they materialise. If you contribute to making budget decisions in a rich country's government, debt cancellations have proven worthwhile investments. (More suggestions on ways to spend money follow in later chapters.)

If you are an African policymaker, understand that there is more to learn from comparable Asian countries, and East Asian countries in particular, than from Europe or the USA. If you invest in infrastructure, wonder if many cheap rural roads might have more impact than a few big and shiny ones, and consider constructing them using labour-intensive methods, if unemployment is high or the months prior to the harvest are lean. Realise that transport is not just about smooth tarmac but also about roadblocks and the speed of border crossings. If you do need smooth tarmac, plan not only for its construction but also for its maintenance. If China offers its construction support, check the finance conditions, and see if you might be able to change the practice of flying in a thousand Chinese construction workers and use and strengthen local capacity instead. Also keep in mind that China's focus is generally on resource-rich regions and that its infrastructure support may not reach poor rural communities.

Lastly, if you are a policymaker from one of the Asian countries that have developed at such remarkable speed, kudos to you, but don't be complacent and remember that many millions of people have not yet benefited from Asia's rapid development (see Box 1.8).

BOX 1.8 HOMELESSNESS IN INDIA

A few years ago, and for the first time since 1992, I returned to Mumbai and was struck by its metamorphosis. There is so much more ostentatious wealth, and there are so many more well-to-do people than I saw in the early 1990s!

After a week, I took a 4:00 a.m. taxi back to the airport and was struck again, this time by the thousands of homeless people sleeping on pieces of cardboard at the side of the road. They are among the many millions of people, in urban and rural environments alike, who have not yet benefited from India's rapid economic growth, and who are not yet reached by any type of social assistance.

Further reading

In this first chapter, we covered a *lot* of ground, so I limited the suggestions to only one or two papers per topic. If you want to know more, use Google Scholar, as its search engine is far more advanced than whatever library search engine you might have access to. Google Scholar offers the option to limit your search to the last few years, which makes sense if you are interested in recent developments or if your field of interest is rapidly evolving (such as in the case of ICT as a facilitator of rural development). Then, once you have found abstracts that look interesting, use your online university library to get access to the full paper, if you can, as Google Scholar often won't give you full access unless you pay for it.

The meaning of 'poverty'

Poverty is not an easy concept, and in this chapter I am assuming you know about the ways 'poverty' can be defined and analysed. If this is not the case, you may want to read Ehrenpreis, D., editor (December 2006) "What is poverty? Concepts and measures", *Poverty in focus*, International Poverty Centre, online.

Pages 10 and 11 of that publication give very brief summaries of four key interpretations of poverty: the so-called (1) monetary, (2) capability, (3) social exclusion, and (4) participatory approaches. For a bit more depth on each of these approaches, read section 3 of Laderchi, C.R., Saith R. and Stewart, F. (September 2003) "Does it matter that we do not agree on the definition of poverty? A comparison of four approaches", *Oxford Development Studies*, volume 31, number 3, pages 243–274, online.

Up-to-date statistics

As mentioned at the start of this chapter, the internet is full of interactive maps and charts that show development trends for countries, continents, and the world. These maps and charts are typically more updated than anything you could find in printed books. Two particularly powerful and user-friendly databases are accessible through *data.worldbank.org* and *gapminder.org*.

The complex relations between conflict and development

If you are looking for a quantification of the extent to which conflict affects development, then read this difficult but insightful paper: Gates, S. et al. (2016) "Development consequences of armed conflict", in Pérouse de Montclos, M.A., Minor, E. and Sinha, S., editors, *Violence, statistics and the politics of accounting for the dead; demographic transformation and socio-economic development*, volume 4, Springer. If your library does not stock this publication, then read an earlier version that virtually all academic libraries have and that is nearly the same: Gates, S. et al. (2012) "Development consequences of armed conflict", *World Development*, volume 40, issue 9, pages 1713–1722.

If you're looking for an exploration of *reasons* for the link between conflict and development, rather than just a confirmation *of* that link, read MacGinty, R. and Williams, A. (2016, 2nd edition) *Conflict and development*, Routledge. Make sure to get that second edition.

The resource curse

For a long and sobering read, get Bebbington, A., editor (2012) *Social conflict, economic development and extractive industry; evidence from South America*, Routledge. Or, if you are more interested in African examples, read some of Chapters 3 to 10 in Omeje, K., editor (2017) *Extractive economies and conflicts in the Global South; multiregional perspectives on rentier politics*, Routledge.

But not all is bad – after all, there have also been countries that managed to avoid that curse – such as the previously mentioned trio of Botswana, Chile, and Malaysia. A quick web search will present you with case studies of each of these countries, and several of them are available free of charge without a library subscription. For a comparison of the attributes and behaviour of successful and unsuccessful resource-rich countries, see Torvik, R. (2009) "Why do some resource-abundant countries succeed while others do not?" *Oxford Review of Economic Policy*, volume 25, number 2, pages 241–256, online.

Producers' disincentives and stifling rules and regulations

This chapter mentioned that agricultural production in China and Vietnam rapidly increased when their governments allowed farmers to make money, and that the economy of India took off when the government slashed bureaucracy. The following papers describe these transitions well:

- **China:** China's transformation from collective farms to family farms improved the lives of hundreds of millions of farmers. For a nine-minute presentation on the topic, go to *coursera.org*, and look for a free course titled

"China's economic transformation part 1: economic reform and growth in China course" – and then select "1.4 Decollectivisation of agriculture". Formally, the new system was based on "yin di zhi yi" ("work on the basis of local conditions"), and the process is often portrayed as one where local communities were at liberty to choose the farming model that worked best for them. In reality, governmental directives may have been just as forceful as they had been before – but the choice for family farming was simply a much better one than the previous choice for collective farms. Jonathan Unger interviewed farmers at the time (in 1983) and describes this dramatic transformation process in Chapter 5 of Unger, J. (2002) *The transformation of rural China*, Routledge.

- **Vietnam:** For the agricultural transformation of the second half of the 1980s, see Wolz, A. and Duong, P.B. (2010) "The transformation of agricultural producer cooperatives: the case of Vietnam", *Journal of Rural Cooperation*, volume 38, number 2, pages 117–133, online. For the country's subsequent development pathway, see Vandemoortele, M. and Bird, K. (2011) *Viet Nam's progress on economic growth and poverty reduction: impressive improvements*, ODI, online.
- **India:** Aiyar, S.S.A. (October 2016) "Twenty-five years of Indian economic reform; a story of private-sector success, government failure, and institutional weakness", *Policy Analysis*, number 803, online. This paper covers both the stifling bureaucracy until the 1980s, the rapid growth that occurred when this bureaucracy was slashed, and the many business obstacles that still exist. Swaminathan Aiyar's style is journalistic (in fact, he *is* a journalist). If his style is too casual or emotive for you, read Panagariya, A. (2004) "India in the 1980s and 1990s: a triumph of reforms" *IMF Working Paper number 04/43*, online.

Corruption

Search for the word *corruption*, in combination with the name of a UN organisation, a development bank, or a relevant NGO such as Transparency International, and you will find papers that explain why and how corruption should be fought and that say things like this:

- "The World Bank Group considers corruption a major challenge to its twin goals of ending extreme poverty by 2030 and boosting shared prosperity for the poorest 40% of people in developing countries" (World Bank [October 2018] "Combating corruption", *Brief*, online).
- "The costs of corruption for economic, political and social development are becoming increasingly evident" (OECD [2014]. "The rationale for fighting corruption", *CleanGovBiz*, online).

Often, papers of international organisations look like academic publications – such as this one, which found that "high and rising corruption increases income inequality and poverty by reducing economic growth": Gupta, S., Davoodi, H. and

Alonso-Terme, R. (1998) "Does corruption affect income inequality and poverty?" *IMF working paper*, number 76, online. But beware: these are not independent publications, and their findings tend to be aligned with the prevailing paradigms of these organisations.

There is less consensus among independent researchers. To give just two examples,

- For the finding that a "strong negative correlation between corruption and growth in genuine wealth per capita is surprisingly robust", see Aidt, T.S. (2009) "Corruption, institutions, and economic development", *Oxford Review of Economic Policy*, volume 25, number 2, pages 271–291 (with the quote taken from page 272).
- For the finding that "corruption is . . . a stimulus for [foreign direct investment]," which "lends empirical support to existence of the 'helping hand' type of corruption with regard to foreign investment", see Egger, P., and Winner, H. (2005), "Evidence on corruption as an incentive for foreign direct investment", *European Journal of Political Economy*, Volume 21, pages 932–52 (with the quotes on pages 932 and 949 respectively).

All in all, it is clear that there is a strong inverse relation between corruption and development, and corruption is nearly certainly bad for development in many cases – but there are also conditions in which corruption 'greases the wheels of growth' and the causal link may not be as straightforward as all these UN, World Bank, and IMF publications suggest.

Debt burdens

A paper that summarises previous research on the link between official debt relief and development, and then adds to it, is Cheng, G., Díaz-Cassou, J. and Erce, A. (2018) "Official debt restructuring and development" *World Development*, volume 111, pages 181–195. Their research suggests that "the strategy of fostering development through nominal debt relief paid off" and that this strategy helped to "accelerate per capita GDP growth, reduce poverty and improve income distribution. This improved performance also resulted in a decline in infant mortality" (page 192).

The 'neighbourhood effect'

For an account of the effects of civil war in a neighbouring country, read the first part of Chapter 2 of Collier, P. et al. (2003), *Breaking the conflict trap. Civil war and development policy*, World Bank and Oxford University Press, online. There's also a study on the effects of war on agriculture in particular, on war-torn countries and their neighbours, but it's only for econometricians who like a challenge: Lukongo, O.E. and Rezek, J.P. (2018) "Investigating spatial dependence and spatial spillovers in African agricultural Total Factor Productivity growth", *The American Economist*, volume 63, issue 1, pages 41–58, online.

In this chapter, I went beyond war and argued that a country's corruption and bad policies and practices also negatively affect its neighbours' growth prospects. And some research concluded that, even *after* considering the effects of bad neighbours on a country's trade and tourism and suchlike, economic growth is *still* adversely impacted by, well, *just being in Latin America or Africa*!

This conclusion led to the introduction of the 'Latin American dummy' and the 'African dummy'. These are dummy variables that are added to regression analyses that seek to identify what causes economic development. These dummies "imply that the growth rate for Latin American and Sub-Saharan African countries were 1.47 and 1.28 percentage points below the level that would be predicted by the countries' other characteristics". [This quote is from Sala-i-Martin, X., Doppelhofer, G. and Miller, R.I. (2004) "Determinants of long-term growth: a Bayesian averaging of classical estimates (BACE) approach", *American Economic Review*, volume 94, number 4, pages 813–835.] Other researchers have used other methods to come to comparable conclusions. Yet other papers have discredited such research, to some extent, by showing that "the presence of the African dummy . . . results from misspecification", such as Burger, R. and Du Plessis, S. (2006) "Examining the robustness of competing explanations of slow growth in African countries", *CREDIT research paper*, number 06/02, online (with the quote on page 2).

The ease of transport of people and things

For the state of transport across the world, see *outlook.gihub.org/region*. It covers airports, seaports, railways, and roads. The *World Logistics Performance Index* also provides an instant comparison, and you will see that, not counting South Africa, Sub-Saharan Africa is behind in everything transport-related. For insights and analysis rather than facts and figures, see Gwilliam, K. (2011) Africa's transport infrastructure: mainstreaming maintenance and management, online; or Chris, N. and Ferrantino, M.J. (2011) "Land transport for export: the effects of cost, time and uncertainty in Sub-Saharan Africa", *World Development*, volume 39, number 10, pages 1749–1759. For insight into the increasing role of China in global (and specifically African) infrastructure, see Edinger, H. and Labuschagne, J.P. (March 2019) "If you want to prosper, consider building roads; China's role in African infrastructure and capital projects", *Deloitte Insights*, online.

Fairly free trade

Academics do not consider *Wikipedia* to be a credible reference, but as introductory texts for schools of thought *Wikipedia* works well, as its descriptions are generally succinct, readable, and well-referenced. Also, *Wikipedia*'s many cross-references allow you to jump from one school to the next.

For quick insights in the discourse on the benefits (mostly) and drawbacks (some) of free trade, check out the *Wikipedia* link for the "Washington Consensus," which argues that trade is good, or take a look at the website of the World Trade Organisation (*wto.org*), which has, as it's raison d'être, "to ensure that trade flows as smoothly, predictably and freely as possible." By means of counterweight, check out the *Wikipedia* pages of "Dependency Theory" or "World-Systems Theory." Both are outdated as academic schools of thought, but their call for protectionism lives on in policy discussions. To understand why so many people still call for trade barriers even though economists by and large agree that such barriers are counter-productive in the long run, read Klein, M. (2018) "When economists agree, but (many) others do not: duelling narratives on international trade", *The Fletcher Forum of World Affairs*, volume 42, number 1, pages 5–19.

Population growth, the work force ratio, and development

- For issues related to population growth: the annual UNFPA "State of the world population" reports are a good place to start. This is the UNFPA's one-sentence summary of its 2018 report: "The power to choose the number, timing and spacing of children can bolster economic and social development."
- About the underutilised women in the labour force: see Wodon, Q. and Brière, B. de la (2018) "Unrealized potential: the high cost of gender inequality in earnings", *The cost of gender inequality notes series*, World Bank, online. Or take a look at the UN Women website, which has a good set of infographics.

Education

There is a *lot* of research on the links between education and other dimensions of development, so do a web search for your country and field of interest, and you'll find plenty. For example,

- Education ←→ child mortality and fertility: Shapiro, D. and Tenikue, M. (2017) Women's education, infant and child mortality, and fertility decline in urban and rural sub-Saharan Africa, *Demographic Research*, volume 37, issue 21, pages 669–708, online.
- Education ←→ income in Pakistan: Awan, H., Awan, S. M. and Waqas, M., (2011) Impact of education on poverty reduction, *International Journal of Academic Research*, volume 3, number 1, pages 659–664, online.
- Education ←→ economic development and child marriage: World Bank (2017) *Economic impact of child marriage: educational attainment brief*, online.

Health and nutrition

For an analysis of links between health, nutrition, and economic development in general, see World Health Organization (2004) *Investing in health for economic development*, online. In essence, it finds what you'd expect: "cross-country macro-economic studies suggest that health positively affects growth" (page 16).

For research on the economic effects of the particularly ferocious malaria, see Gallup, L.J. and Sachs, D.J. (2001) "The economic burden of malaria", in Berman, J.G., Egan, A. and Keusch, G.T., *The intolerable burden of malaria: a new look at the numbers*, Supplement to Volume 64, issue 1 of the *America Journal of Tropical Medicine and Hygiene*, online. A key finding (presented in the last paragraph of the "Poverty and malaria" section) is that the

> growth of income per capita 1965–1990 for countries with severe malaria has been 0.4% per year, whereas average growth for other countries has been 2.3%, [more than] 5 times higher. . . . More than a third of the countries with severe malaria (11 out of 29) had negative growth between 1965–1990.

For the role of Southern African truck drivers in the spread of HIV, read Ramjee, G. and Gouws, E. (2002) "Prevalence of HIV among truck drivers visiting sex workers in KwaZulu-Natal", *Sexually Transmitted Diseases*, volume 29, number 1, pages 44–49. In the main text, I specified Southern Africa, but the problem is more widespread than that. For example, for comparable research in India, read Singh, Y.N. and Malaviya, A.N. (1994) "Long distance truck drivers in India: HIV infection and their possible role in disseminating HIV to rural areas", *International Journal of STD and AIDS*, volume 5, issue 2, pages 137–138. Other mobile groups spread HIV as well. See, for example, Silver, M. (June 2019) *The dark secret of Lake Malawi: trading sex for fish*, NPR, online.

Culture and climate

For a good example of the use of the arguments presented (and, I hope, discredited) in this chapter, see the eight-minute and often-watched YouTube clip titled "Why some countries are poor and others rich". For the father of the theory that a country's culture and religion determine its development prospects, see the *Wikipedia* page of Max Weber, which is a great deal more readable than Weber's original texts on Confucianism, Taoism, Hinduism, and Buddhism. For an example of a paper that does not dispute the line of thought itself but shifts Weber's argument away from a particular group that recently disproved the theory, see Chung, C.H. Shepard, J.M. and Dollinger, M.J. (1989) "Max Weber revisited: some lessons from East Asian capitalistic development", *Asia Pacific Journal of Management*, volume 6, number 2, pages 307–321.

Why Asian countries have outpaced much of the rest of the world

A while ago (2006–11), David Henley led on a research initiative titled "tracking development", which researched the reasons for the vast differences in the speed of development in Sub-Saharan Africa and Southeast Asia. It led to a fascinating series of publications, which are increasingly hard to find and do not always seem to be available online. Examples include the following:

- Donge, J.K. van, Henley, D and Lewis, P. (2010) *Tracking Development in Southeast Asia and Sub-Saharan Africa: the primacy of policy*, African Studies Centre, Leiden.
- Henley, D. (2010) *Three principles of successful development strategy: outreach, urgency, expediency*, KITLV Leiden, online.
- Henley, D. (2015) *Asia-Africa development divergence: a question of intent*, Zen Books, London.

Henley's inaugural lecture of October 2012 is the best of the lot, but it no longer seems to be online.

A more recent and equally good publication is Vos, R. (2018) "Agriculture and rural transformations in Asian development: past trends and future challenges", *WIDER Working Paper 2018/87*, online.

The flying geese theory

For the original flying geese theory of economic development, search for papers written by Akamatsu (starting in the 1930s!) and, later, Ozama. For a good example of quite a number of papers that use the flying geese paradigm to assess the current and likely future transfer of manufacturing capacity from Asia to Africa, see Brautigam, D., Xiaoyang, T. and Xia, Y. (2018) "What kind of Chinese 'geese' are flying to Africa? Evidence from Chinese manufacturing firms", *Journal of African Economies*, volume 27, Issue 1 (supplement), pages i29–i51, online.

Exercise on prioritisation: getting Fragilistan back on its feet

The situation

Thankfully, the civil war has ended. But the economic infrastructure has been destroyed, much of the population has been displaced, and the people with the biggest brains have either died or left. The government budget for the coming year is one billion *quasi* (Qs). This could be expanded by 50 percent, if the government of Fragilistan is willing to accept the debt burden.

The background

Fragilistan is a country prone to floods and cyclones, and is situated in a region typified by war and environmental degradation. Many people believe that the root cause of the civil war was a recent string of natural disasters.

It is also a country with large and beautiful primeval forests and beaches. Before the war, it was the primary tourism destination of the entire continent (Fragista).

Recently (and this is something else that may have caused the civil war), very large oil reserves have been discovered. Several major companies have already indicated their interest in these reserves.

The task

Together with your colleagues, you are responsible for allocating the next year's budget. Around the table, there are

1   The Minister of Defence. She also acts as the Interim Prime Minister, and she will listen, contribute to the discussion, and ultimately decide on the budgetary priorities.
2   The Minister of Agriculture.
3   The Minister of Infrastructure.
4   The Minister of Oil and Industry.
5   The Minister of Disaster Risk Reduction.
6   The Minister of Other Things.

If you are with fewer than six people, please combine a few of the roles.

Make a table in which you distribute the budget across health, education, defence, disaster preparedness, pensions, infrastructure, tourism, the petroleum sector, and everything else that the government may want to spend money on. Decide if you take that loan to increase your budget. And, importantly, explain the rationale behind your choices.

Note for the Minister of Agriculture

As the population of Fragilistan is largely rural, you are convinced that Fragilistan's first and foremost priority should be agriculture. Develop and present your own reasons for this.

Note for the Minister of Infrastructure

You are convinced that Fragilistan's first and foremost priority should be infrastructure. Develop and present your own reasons for this. Perhaps it is something like this:

You are not sure if the Fragilistani economy will be based on oil, industry, tourism, or agriculture — but you do know that, whichever sector will be the motor of the country's economy, infrastructure will be vital for this sector's success. In addition, there is a morale-building dimension to infrastructure: the internal wounds of war will not heal as long as the country's veins — its roads — are so visibly scarred.

Note for the Minister of Defence

You are convinced that Fragilistan's first and foremost priority should be defence. Develop and present your own reasons for this. Perhaps it is something like this:

- Without a strong military presence, the civil war will start again.
- Without a strong military presence, the neighbouring countries, which have a history of war and invasion, may invade Fragilistan.
- The various armed factions that fought in the civil war of the past decade need to have a role in the post-war society. The only role they are familiar with and trained for is a military one.

Note for the Minister of Oil and Industry

You are convinced that Fragilistan's first and foremost priority should be oil exploration and exploitation. Develop and present your own reasons for this. Perhaps it is something like this:

An annual budget of 1–1½ billion Qs is much too small to run Fragilistan. The petroleum industry is rich. They will pay good money for drilling rights. You then have more money to invest in the rest of the economy.

Note for the Minister of Disaster Risk Reduction

You are convinced that Fragilistan's first and foremost priority should be the prevention of any further natural disasters. They caused this war and aggravated its effects. You want money for dikes, sturdy shelters, and a lot of awareness raising.

Note for the Minister of Other Things

You are the Interim Minister for

- *The Ministry of Banking and Finance.* You do not want to overspend, as sound monetary policies and financial management are key to a healthy economy.
- *The Ministry of Tourism.* Fragilistan has great tourism resources, and tourism is a very labour-intensive industry. Developing tourism means employing the nation.
- *The Ministry of Social Safety Nets.* The economy is in shambles, and unemployment is high. Without a safety net, these unemployed people will grow hungry. A hungry population may go to war again.
- *The Ministry of Health.* Health is important, both for the well-being of individuals and for the national economy. After a war, the Fragilistani health situation is dire – the consequence of a combination of malnutrition and uncontrolled epidemics.
- *The Ministry of Education.* The children are the future. Do not let them go through the same misery that the current generation has gone through. Make

sure they are educated. Do not let them suffer the consequences of the current generation's inability to maintain the peace.

If you haven't agreed on a sensible budget after trying for 20 minutes

Forget about your respective roles, and reconvene as 'a group of experts'. This should make it a lot easier to come to a sensible budget.

Notes

1   The Sustainable Development Goals (SDGs) are 17 goals that the UN General Assembly of 2015 confirmed as the 'Global Goals' that need to be achieved by 2030. They are of the type of "End poverty in all its forms everywhere" (SDG 1) and "End hunger, achieve food security and improved nutrition, and promote sustainable agriculture" (SDG 2).
2   The 'gender gap' is the gap between women and men in a range of dimensions, including educational attainment, health and nutritional status, political participation, and earnings. The World Economic Forum introduced a *Global Gender Gap Index*, back in 2006. This index includes some (but far from all) ways in which there are gaps between women and men, and in the way in which members of these two groups are treated.
3   These figures come from *data.worldbank.org/indicator*, indicator 'life expectancy at birth, total (years)', accessed on 26 September 2019. You will see the global figures at the top and the figures for countries and specific groups of countries when you scroll down. Tip: play with the data. For example, the first graph you see when you use this link gives you the option (in the left top corner) to turn the graph into a map of the world, which in turn shows you the life expectancy for each country, for different years.
4   Benin, Chad, Central African Republic, Mali, Nigeria, Sierra Leone, Somalia, and South Sudan. Sub-Saharan Africa is the region with the highest under-five mortality rate in the world overall – almost eight out of every 100 infants do not survive the first five years. See UNICEF, WHO, World Bank and United Nations (2018) *Levels and Trends in Child Mortality Report*, available through childmortality.org/reports.
5   From *data.worldbank.org/indicator*, select indicator 'mortality rate, under-5 (per 1,000 live births)', accessed on 22 September 2019.
6   See World Health Organization 2018 Malnutrition fact sheet, available through *who.int/news-room/fact-sheets*, accessed on 26 September 2019.
7   For a report on that reversal, see FAO, together with IFAD, UNICEF, WFP, and WHO (2019), *The state of food security and nutrition in the world 2019. Safeguarding against economic slowdowns and downturns*, online.
8   This and all unreferenced figures in this paragraph are from page 12 of the executive summary of the *Global Nutrition Report* (2018) *2018 Global nutrition report*, accessible through *globalnutritionreport.org*. The same page also notes that, in 2018, 7.5% of the children in this age group were 'wasted'. For the latest data, historical comparisons, and telling graphs, see *data.unicef.org/topic/nutrition*. Note that wasting is not the same as stunting:

- A *stunted* person has been chronically undernourished and, consequently, has not reached his or her full physical and cognitive potential. Importantly: undernourishment is not just a matter of nutritional *intake* but also of the *absorption* of nutrients. Diarrhoea and worms reduce absorption and are therefore an important cause of stunted growth.
- In most cases, *wasting* is a severe process of weight loss – which often means acute starvation or a very serious disease.

9 See the World Health Organization (2018) *Obesity and overweight fact sheet*, available through who.int/news-room/fact-sheets, accessed on 26 September 2019.

10 See *data.worldbank.org*, indicator 'literacy rate, adult total', and *data.unicef.org/topic/education/literacy*, both accessed on 20 September 2019.

11 World Health Organization (2018) *World malaria report 2018*, online.

12 It's best to do a web search for the latest on that vaccine because, at the time of writing this chapter, Africa's first large, three-country malaria vaccine experiment has only just started. See Schuerman, L. (9 July 2019) "RTSS malaria vaccine could provide major health benefits", *The Lancet*, online. See Box 2.1 of Chapter 2 for another field of research that may lead to malaria eradication.

13 Isn't that amazing? Why is this never in the news? See World Bank (2018) *Poverty and shared prosperity 2018: piecing together the poverty puzzle*, online, page 19.

14 World Bank (2016) *Poverty and shared prosperity 2016: taking on inequality*, online, figures 4.3 and 4.5, the text around these figures, and the conclusions on pages 87–88. The 2018 version of this annual report – World Bank (2018) *Poverty and shared prosperity 2018: piecing together the poverty puzzle*, online – stepped away from the traditional measure of inequality (the 'Gini coefficient') and uses a range of inequality indicators instead. This is sound but hard to summarise in a sentence. One key conclusion of that 2018 report was that the poorest half of the world's population is slowly increasing its share of the global income (see figure 2.1.7).

15 World Economic Forum (2018) *The global gender gap report 2018*, online, page 15 for the 108 years and the slowly upward-sloping *Global Gender Gap Index*, and page 19 for more about that legislation to address violence against women and girls.

16 See *data.worldbank.org*; select 'world' for indicators 'Population, total' and 'Poverty headcount ratio at $1.90 a day (2011 PPP)' and multiply these two indicators. Accessed on 26 September 2019. PPP means 'purchasing power parity', and a PPP of $1.90 in 2011 terms is the lowest of the World Bank monetary poverty indicators. It reflects 'extreme poverty' (see the button 'details').

17 From 40.4 in 1960 to 60.9 in 2017. See *data.worldbank.org/indicator*, indicator 'Life expectancy at birth total (years)', for Sub-Saharan Africa.

18 World Bank (September 2018) *Decline of global extreme poverty continues but has slowed: world bank*, online. See also the World Bank clip titled "New ways of looking at poverty", on YouTube.

19 Though less so now than in 1990. In 2014, 16 of the 25 most unequal countries in the world were in Central and South America (and the remaining nine were all in Africa). See *gapminder.org* (search for 'Gini' and then for 'ranking') – and you could then move the big dot on the X-axis to see how countries have become more or less unequal over time.

20 If this interests you, search for this saying from the Democratic Republic of Congo: "You can bomb a hospital, but not Bralima."

21 World Bank and United Nations (2017) *Pathways for peace: inclusive approaches to preventing violent conflict*, page 11, online.

22 A term discussed in Collier, P. et al. (2003) *Breaking the conflict trap. Civil war and development policy*, World Bank and Oxford University Press, online.

23 The Israeli kibbutz might be an exception to this rule – but kibbutzim do not really count, as people do not *have* to join a kibbutz in the same way North Korean agricultural workers *have* to join a farmers' collective.

24 This was the first change that increased farmers' income. It was followed by a change from low government-set prices for agricultural products to higher and eventually market-driven prices, which caused subsequent income increases.

25 Jones, K. (June 2019) "Cuba, the centrally planned cigar, and its rivals", *The World Economy*, pages 1–24, online (the fact is mentioned on page 5).

26 Aiyar, S.S.A. (October 2016) "Twenty-five years of Indian economic reform; a story of private-sector success, government failure, and institutional weakness", *Policy Analysis*, issue 803, page 2. This is not to say that there was no progress in India, before the 1980s:

in the 1970s, the Green Revolution had already significantly reduced extreme poverty and malnutrition (see Chapter 2).

27 World Bank (2019) *Doing business 2019: training for reform*, online, Table 1.1 on page 5; for India's worst scoring in recent times (142 out of 189), see World Bank (2015) *Doing business 2015: going beyond efficiency*, online, Table 1.1 on page 4.

28 A term coined and a case first made in Leff, N.H. (1964) "Economic development through bureaucratic corruption", *American Behavioral Scientist*, volume 8, issue 3, pages 8–14.

29 See *data.worldbank.org/indicator* and then select Nigeria, Indonesia, and the indicator 'Poverty gap at $1.90 a day (2011 PPP) (percentage of population)'. The most recent data are 2009 for Nigeria and 2017 for Indonesia. Accessed on 29 September 2019. For a personal comparison made by a Nigerian journalist, see Cunliffe-Jones, P. (28 September 2010) "How Indonesia overtook Nigeria", *Focus on Africa Magazine*, BBC News, online. It is an entertaining read, but take it with a pinch of salt please, as it's a very partial analysis.

30 'Cheapest' is in terms of costs per mile of transportation. See Rome2rio (April 2018) *2018 global flight price ranking: what's the world's cheapest airline?* online.

31 See page 14 of Ducruet, C., Itoh, H., and Merk, O. (2014) *Time efficiency at world container ports*, discussion paper 8, International Transport Forum, online. Also note the *huge* increase in the number of vessels docking at Chinese ports, between 1996 and 2011.

32 Moreover, the best roads are sometimes 'white elephants': beautiful, flashy highways that were built with foreign assistance and that the country is unable to maintain. They will soon be full of potholes.

33 The Dutch disease is a phenomenon that is not limited to underground resources. In Chapter 7, on migration, we explore how remittances (the money that migrants send home) can cause the Dutch disease as well.

34 The United Nations Population Fund has a set of interactive world maps that show the population, population growth, and fertility rate per woman and suchlike indicators, and changes therein over time. See *unfpa.org/data/world-population-dashboard*.

35 For statistics on issues such as the percentage of women in the labour force, see the indicator on "labor force, female" in the World Bank database (note that the World Bank followed the American spelling). You will find that the percentage of women in the labour force is *far* lower in the Middle East and North Africa (20% in 2018 and on a very slow growth path) and in South Asia (26%, *down* from 30% in 1990) than in the rest of the world, where the percentage is typically between 40 and 70% (Data accessed on 20 September 2019).

36 The website of the United Nations Population Division has a section for 'graphs', where you can select a country and look at the past, present, and predicted future 'population pyramids', which show the proportions of people in that country or region within each ten-year age bracket (see *population.un.org/wpp/graphs/demographicprofiles*). For China, this 'pyramid' does not look like a pyramid at all – it is more like a pagoda.

37 See Psacharopoulos, G. and Patrinos, H.A. (2004) "Returns to investment in education: a further update", *Education Economics*, volume 12, issue 2, pages 111–134, online (the relevant pages are 112–113).

38 Global Affairs Canada (2017) *Canada's feminist international assistance policy*, online, page 26.

39 Global Affairs Canada (2017) *Canada's feminist international assistance policy*, online, page 26, emphasis added.

40 See *actionaid.org.uk*, searching '*Women's economic empowerment*', selecting the subheading '*Girls' education*' in the tabs on the left-hand side of the webpage, accessed on 27 September 2019; emphasis added.

41 World Bank (2006) *Repositioning nutrition as central to development: a strategy for large-scale action*, page 2, online.

42 Proponents of this argument make an exception for the USA, which is both successful and religious, and say that this is because American Protestants work hard, as they believe that their economic success says something about their prospects in the afterlife.

43 By means of illustration: during the height of the debt crisis, in the first half of the 1980s, there was only one Asian country (the Philippines) among the 38 countries that were forced to engage in 'multilateral debt renegotiations' (which are a most unequal affair that countries don't undertake until they have run out of options, in which a heavily indebted country negotiates, all by itself, with a block of creditor countries). For this list of 38 countries, see footnote 1 on page 397 of Sachs, J. (1986) "Managing the LDC debt crisis", *Brookings Papers on Economic Activity*, volume 1986, issue 2, pages 397–440, online.

44 I am working from memory, as I could not find the paper that discussed this business registration fiasco. If you find it and are the first one to send it to me at willem. vaneekelen@gmail.com, I will send you $100. I will also do this if you send me proof of another memory I could not trace back to a paper, about an Olympics-style sports stadium, built in India in the 1980s, in which athletes broke all running records on the inaugural day because, as it later turned out, corrupt contractors had cut costs by slightly and proportionately reducing the size of the stadium, which had reduced the length of its running tracks.

45 Note the striking difference with some African leaders, who saw what they did not have (modern, industrialised economies) and aimed for an economic metamorphosis that never happened and that indebted their countries.

46 Quoted in Gebriel, S.J. (2008) "Economic liberalization in post-Mao China: crossing the river by feeling for stones", *China Essay Series*, essay issue 7, online. An alternative translation is "feeling our way across the river", quoted in Ravallion, M. (2009) "Are there lessons for Africa from China's success against poverty", *World Development*, volume 37, issue 2, page 308.

47 For current and historical data on this, see IFPRI (2019) *Statistics on public expenditures for economic development (SPEED): 2019 global food policy report table 2*, International Food Policy Research Institute, online. Of the historically big spenders, China and Vietnam in particular are still maintaining their levels of agricultural investments.

2

AGRICULTURAL PRODUCTION PRACTICE

Take the figures presented in this chapter with a pinch of salt. Researchers use a range of definitions and methods to measure the same things and come to significantly different guestimates. Data sets for a few small plots of land are liberally presented as country-level averages, and there's a whole lot of fearmongering.

It wasn't declining water levels that killed my broccoli this summer.

I just failed to follow good growing practice.

Prologue

Some Western schools have 'partner schools' in Africa, and entire classes travel to meet their peers. They tend to bring nonsensical presents – my friend's daughter brought the hockey sticks that the school cook now stirs the soup with.[1] The Western kids feel good because they help build new classrooms and other things (which could all have generated a bit of local employment at a fraction of the cost). They return home with stories about the welcoming and grateful nature of their peers and about their happiness in the midst of poverty. It's well-intentioned, but it's not very useful.

A while ago, I bumped into something far less common: Ugandan kids, from a rural school, visiting their partner school in the Netherlands. They were having lunch in a park and kindly agreed to an impromptu 'focus group discussion' (or FGD – something most development practitioners do a lot). I asked them about the key differences between the Netherlands and their home country.

Most of the responses were unmemorable, but two kids mentioned the fields and the greenhouses they had seen from their bus. What had amazed them was the sheer density of the crops. Fields of maize in Uganda and the Netherlands were, they said, *very* different things.

They were right: a hectare in the Netherlands generates more than four times as much cereal as a hectare in Uganda and almost six times the Sub-Saharan average.[2]

This is all the more striking because Dutch *inputs* are far less than four and six times as high. The Dutch are 'precision farmers': they take pride in producing as much value as possible with as little of the various inputs – water, pesticides, fertiliser – as they can.

As a result, this tiny country is the world's second largest exporter of agricultural produce. (The largest is the USA, which exports only a little bit more and is over 230 times as large.)[3] To get to this position, the Dutch have overcome significant challenges. They don't have much land, so they reclaimed land from the sea (a quarter of the country is below sea level).[4] Farmers owned oddly shaped bits of land, and this is inefficient, so the country went through a process of 'land consolidation', where land was redistributed until the country's farms were all pretty much perfectly rectangular. There is not much sunshine in the Netherlands, so farmers built greenhouses. They took promising crops from around the world and tweaked both crops and their own local soil conditions to create the perfect match. Over the past few decades, the Dutch have been applying their skills in many other countries. The Ugandan kids could have seen some of them on their way to the Netherlands, as there are Dutch farmers in Uganda, conveniently close to the main airport, exporting roses to the world.

The Netherlands is a Grand Master of maximising yields.[5] High yields are not *always* a good thing and may occasionally drive farms into bankruptcy (see Chapter 4, on trade). In general, however, getting more of something useful out of a hectare of land, without harming that land, is a good thing to aspire to. This chapter looks at ways, for farmers and their governments, to achieve good agricultural yields, and to do so efficiently and sustainably.

What are we talking about?

With ever-more people and more disposable income per person, the demand for food is higher than ever before, and it's still on the rise. But so is global food production. In 2014, it was 350% of what it had been in 1961 (see Table 2.1; more recent

TABLE 2.1 The situation in 2014 (compared to a 1961 baseline of 1)

	Food volume	Population size	Food per person
East and Southeast Asia and the Pacific	6.0	2.2	2.7
Latin America and the Caribbean	4.6	2.7	1.7
South Asia	4.0	3.0	1.3
North America	2.3	1.8	1.3
European Union	1.4	1.2	1.2
North Africa and the Middle East	5.2	4.2	1.2
Sub-Saharan Africa	3.8	4.2	0.9
World	**3.5**	**2.4**	**1.5**

Sources: data.worldbank.org, indicators for *Food Production Index* and total population, 1961 and 2014 data (which were the most recent for food production), combined with the FAO deflated *Food Price Index*, from the September 2019 data file for food prices index, available from the *FAO Food Index* webpage, both accessed on 2 October 2019.

figures are not available at the time of writing). In this same period, the proportion of the world's <u>agricultural lands</u> only increased by a few percent.[6]

Globally, this growth in food production far exceeds the global population growth of the last few decades. Regionally, the picture is different. In East Asia, the percentage increase in per capita food production has been highest. This achievement is the result of the region's relatively modest population growth, compared with the rest of the developing world, in combination with heavy investment in rural development and lots of research, trial and error, and learning about what works and what doesn't. On the other end of the spectrum, and in that same half century, the per capita food production in Sub-Saharan Africa *declined*; shortly after the turn of the century, the region became a net importer of agricultural products.[7] There is a striking paradox: Sub-Saharan Africa is the only region in the world where more people are working in agriculture than in all other sectors combined, yet it does not produce enough food to feed its population.[8]

All other regions are in between these two extremes (see Table 2.1). The picture does not change if you consider *all* crops, instead of food crops only (in other words, if you also include crops for biofuel and crops such as flowers or tea and coffee, and other consumables that are not considered 'food' because they lack nutritional value).[9]

The problem, at present, is not the size of the world's food production as a whole, but the lagging production in some countries. Often these are countries with high population growth rates, which add to the problem. Another complication is that many also have relatively little water and cultivated land per person *and* have agricultural practices that further reduce the quality and quantity of these two key resources every year. Moreover, many countries in this group do not protect their agricultural lands against competing usage (this is called 'functional zoning'). Cairo's wealthier residents have their holiday homes in villa parks along the River Nile, for example, built on chunks of the country's narrow fertile strip that used to be farmland. The risks are grave: if imports stop, for whatever reason, famine will hit Egypt very quickly. Lastly, countries that face all these problems are often also very unequal and have large gender gaps. Millions of poor people in these countries face a life-and-death 'food justice problem': they face chronic malnutrition and food insecurity, not because there is no food but because they're unable to access it.

None of this is inevitable. There is a lot to learn from success stories, and there are plenty of them – especially in Southeast Asia. There's also plenty to learn from mistakes, made around the world, that have contributed to desertification, resistant pests, declining water levels, and soil degradation.

So what are the issues, and what have we learned?

Issue 1 of 4: in poor regions in particular, yields could improve significantly but, also in poor regions in particular, soil quality is deteriorating

The world's agricultural production has been growing for decades and is at an all-time high. But yields vary vastly across countries and regions.

Part of this is related to natural soil conditions. In the Middle East and North Africa, most countries have to import most of their food because there's a lot of desert and too little fertile land to feed the region's population. This region is the world's most extreme illustration of a recent global study's "ultimate . . . conclusion . . . that the food production volume . . . depends most on natural conditions".[10] After the Middle East and North Africa, soil conditions are the worst in Sub-Saharan Africa, and then there's the rest of the world.[11]

Soil quality clearly matters, but it is possible to improve it – even in the desert![12] – and to tailor farming crops and methods to the soil you have. If you optimise farming, the gains could be enormous. Table 2.2 shows the percentage of the potential yield that is currently realised in the various regions.

So global agricultural production is at its highest point in history, *and* the scope for further growth is significant. In many places, though, the picture is very different. There are large stretches of land where the soil's production potential has deteriorated (it's called <u>soil degradation</u>),[13] in part because modern farming practice has had harmful effects. A 2017 report summarised the extent of recent soil degradation as follows:

> Worldwide, on more than 9 million km^2 of land, there is a persistent, significant decline in net primary production (excluding the effects of climate change), showing decades-long negative effects of human activities and land management practices. . . . The most dramatic developments are taking place in Sub-Saharan Africa, where over 15% of the land area is affected. In most other regions, the figure lies between 5% and 10%. . . . More than half of the 9 million km^2 affected, worldwide, is cropland and pasture, an area of 4.7 million km^2, corresponding to about 12% of all agricultural land on the planet.[14]

TABLE 2.2 Actual yield as a percentage of potential yield

Region	Percentage
East and Southeast Asia	83
European Union	74
North America	69
Latin America and the Caribbean	47
South Asia	45
Sub-Saharan Africa	27
North Africa and the Middle East	No data
World	**55**

Source: Tabulated from tables 41 and 49 of the statistical annex of Fischer, G. and Shah, M. (2010) *Farmland investments and food security*, International Institute for Applied Systems Analysis, online. These estimates are based on 2005 data for a sample of countries in each of these regions. This sample did not include any eastern European EU members or any countries in the Pacific. Keep in mind that simulations in this field use imperfect and incomplete data and use rigorous assumptions that won't always hold true. An example of such assumptions is that the figures in this table assume that there is a direct correlation between the suitability of the land for agriculture and the quality of management of and inputs to the land (as in, the better the land, the better it will be utilised). Of course that's not always true.

The problems of soil degradation are not new. Five thousand years ago, overgrazing and intensive agriculture probably started the formation of the Sahara desert on land that had been, until then, green and fertile. Three thousand years ago, farmers in China caused very long-term problems of <u>soil erosion</u> by cutting down forests to create new farmland.[15] And in the 17th century, the complex society on Easter Island disappeared because the combination of forest burning and intensive agriculture in the centuries before had caused such topsoil erosion that harvests failed and people starved until the entire civilisation collapsed.[16] However, the problems are more common today than they were back then, because there are so many more people on the planet, who exert far more pressure on the land. And there are far fewer stretches of new land that can still be developed – at least not without serious loss of biodiversity.

Scenario modelling suggests that soil degradation will continue and accelerate and that Africa will end up suffering most.[17] Within countries and regions, *poor* people's farmland is particularly prone to degradation: the quality of their lands' soil is often not great to begin with, and poor farmers have the least knowledge, access to tools and techniques, government support, and incentives to prevent or reverse the degradation of the land they farm.

So how could farmers optimise their yields without causing harm to the land they farm and the wider ecosystems in which they operate, and how might they even reverse harm previously done? How could this happen equitably – without increasing the gap between poorer farmers and wealthier ones? To a large extent, the answer is that farmers need to feel certain of their long-term control over the land they are farming, and they need to be able and eager to use the right inputs, at the right time and in an appropriate manner. Getting this to happen is difficult. It needs research, as well as investment in farmers' ability and incentives to follow good practice, along with a supportive and safe environment in which markets work, property is safe, and effective support services are available. Let us first look at a few key inputs and then at the requirements for that supportive and safe environment.

Issue 2 of 4: changes in the DNA of crops and livestock can make a massive difference

Crops and livestock evolve. In terms of nutritional value and yield, the maize that was grown in the Americas some 8,000 years ago was far inferior to what farmers grow now. The ancestors of Holstein-Friesian cows produced only a fraction of the milk they produce today. Bananas are easier to peel than they used to be, and they no longer have seeds. Potatoes used to be poisonous.

The gradual improvements in these and many other crops and animals were generally the consequence of deliberate breeding. Farmers used two methods:

- *Selective breeding.* Take the seeds of your biggest fruits to grow consistently bigger fruits in the future. Selective breeding started over 30,000 years ago,

SELECTIVE BREEDING

FIGURE 2.1 Improved wolves

when people domesticated wolves and gradually turned them into dogs, which then evolved into today's Chihuahuas and labradoodles. Between 8,000 and 10,000 years ago, people started improving wheat in the Middle East and maize in Central and South America. Then farmers around the world gradually improved the other crops we eat today.

- *Cross-breeding.* If you use a Holstein-Friesian bull to inseminate a zebu cow, chances are that their hybrid calves retain some of the zebu's resistance to heat and some of the Holstein-Friesian ability to produce lots of milk.

In the last 70 years, this process of crop and livestock improvement has accelerated. Farmers and researchers made plants and animals more resistant to disease. They created crops that are unaffected when a farmer sprays herbicides to kill weeds. New crop varieties produce higher yields per harvest *and* more nutrients per kilogram of produce. Some new varieties give more harvests per year (up to three, in the case of rice), as they grow quickly and do not require a specific season's temperatures or specific daylight hours. Some crops look more appealing than they used to – we now have 'golden kiwis' and suchlike. It is in part a matter of trial and error. A new crop that looks better or that produces bigger fruits may initially have inferior taste or nutritional value. This, then, is a matter of breeding taste or nutrients back into the crop or of starting again.

This acceleration was caused by the involvement of scientists with big budgets, scientific rigour, and a few new crop development methods (see Box 2.1). In only a few decades of selective breeding, World Fish created a type of tilapia – it's a fish – that grows more meat per kilogram of feed than tilapia had done before, and is more resistant to changes in water temperature. In even less time, researchers developed wheat varieties that produced larger seeds and had sturdier stalks to carry their weight. Most importantly by far, researchers developed 'miracle rice', also known as 'IR8', in 1966. It started in the Philippines but was quickly adopted in India and elsewhere. This IR8 and its even better descendent varieties allowed harvests to jump from a typical 2 tons to 4 (easy), 6 (common), 8 (sometimes), and 10 (exceptional) tons of rice per hectare.

BOX 2.1 GENETIC ENGINEERING

In parallel with selective breeding and cross-breeding, scientists use two more recent sets of techniques:

- *Mutagenesis.* Expose an organism to chemicals or radiation that causes genetic mutations, and check if the mutations might have been beneficial. If they have been, you have created a new and better version of that organism, which is then called a 'mutant variety'. In China, mutagenesis created rice variety 'Zhefu 802', which is the genetic parent of rice types that can cope with low temperatures, grow quickly and in abundance, don't need very much care, and are relatively resistant to rice blast (a disease that ruins harvests). Mutagenesis has also improved types of sesame, barley, cotton and lots of other crops – as of 2019 a UN database has registered over 3,300 mutant varieties.[18]

- **Genetic engineering.** Find a gene that causes a problem or that limits growth, and neutralise it. Or take a gene from one organism and implant it into another one in order to make that second organism bigger, better, or more resilient to drought or disease. The first commercially produced genetically engineered food crop hit the shelves in 1994. It was the *Flavr Savr*, a sturdy tomato with a longer-than-normal shelf life. Genetic engineering also brought us coffee beans without caffeine, tobacco without nicotine, and apples that don't get that brownish colour when you slice them. The world's most widely grown engineered crop is maize, which has been made increasingly resistant to pests, herbicides and, more recently, drought.

These recent techniques arouse strong emotions. Some religious groups resist them because it is not up to us to tamper with God's creations. Some resist them because these new crop varieties favour wealthier farmers over poorer ones (see main text). Others have objections that are related to consumer safety and to the risk of genetically engineered species spreading into nature.

Whatever your opinion and your country's policies, genetic engineering is unstoppable. You could possibly keep genetically engineered crops out of your country, but you can't keep them out of the global marketplace, and in some cases, the quality difference is so significant that genetically engineered varieties will simply push yesterday's varieties out of the market. Moreover, the challenge to feed the world is enormous, and it's going to get worse – and genetic engineering will help meet this challenge. It will also help solve other problems. If we manage to eradicate malaria in the course of the next few decades, for example, it may well be because of re-engineered fungi that contain venom that kills mosquitoes.[19]

Farmers didn't get their miracle harvests by merely sowing such new types of seeds. These new 'high yielding crop varieties' were demanding. To grow well, they needed reliable irrigation[20] and the systematic use of fertilisers and pesticides. A number of governments in Asia and the Americas recognised this, and they dug canals, built roads to facilitate the trade of inputs and harvests, and did lots of other things to create the conditions needed for farmers to adopt and get the most out of these new crop varieties. Where the necessary conditions were met, the results amounted to a 'Green Revolution'.

The impact, on individual farmers and on large parts of the Global South, was dramatic. Indeed, this 'Green Revolution' explains most of the rapid expansion of the agricultural production in Asia and Latin America between the late 1960s and today.[21] Satellite pictures show that regions get greener, for a larger part of the year, when they widely adopt new seeds. New seeds turned some Asian countries from net importers to net exporters of rice. They helped avoid a massive famine in India and reduced malnutrition elsewhere. Because of the Green Revolution, people – women more than men – started to live longer and have fewer children. As the latter effect was bigger, the Green Revolution slowed total population growth. In fact, "the developing world would have contained more than one billion more people in 2000 if the Green Revolution had not happened".[22] These high-yielding crop varieties also had a major effect on the wider economy: a group of researchers compared data from 84 countries in the Global South, and found that "a 10 percentage points increase in HYV adoption increases GDP per capita by about 15 percent". (HYV means high-yielding crop varieties, and GDP stands for gross domestic product, which reflects the total value of economic activity in a country.) They concluded that "investments in the development of HYV crops have been by far the most successful form of foreign aid to developing countries in the past half century".[23] In some countries (most notably in India, Brazil, and China), the effects of nationally financed research have been similarly dramatic.

In part, the Green Revolution's accelerating effects on economic growth were caused by the positive spirals that Chapter 1 has already touched on. The initial increases in production led to higher earnings among farmers, who were therefore able to eat better and be in stronger health. This enabled them to work harder, which had positive effects on production, and so forth. The increased agricultural production reduced some of the local food prices, which benefited non-farming households. In some regions, it increased the price fetched for export crops, as the increased crop volume made these regions more attractive to international buyers. As a consequence of the higher income levels, rural economies diversified, and this generated non-agricultural employment. The higher rural incomes and diversified income opportunities enabled millions of households to help some of their members move out of the countryside and into cities and industrial zones. This is what provided China with the workers needed to kick-start its industrialisation process. Some of the factory workers sent money to their home villages, and some of that money was invested in better farming practice. (Admittedly, another effect of these remittances[24] was that it led people to neglect their farms, as farming seemed very cumbersome for the little money it generated – see Chapter 7, on migration.)

But not all was good. The thirst of the new seeds required an expansion of irrigation that lowered groundwater levels and caused soil salinisation.[25] The economic diversification that followed added to the overuse of water reserves as cities, industry, and tourism consumed ever-increasing amounts, and groundwater usage proved to be really hard to regulate. Excessive use of pesticides built resistance among pests.

The unwise use of fertilisers and pesticides, and the move towards monoculture, affected soil fertility. Together, these side-effects negated some of the results of the Green Revolution. Moreover, the Green Revolution benefited the world at large but did little for, and sometimes harmed, regions that were unable to arrange suitable growing conditions for the new varieties. Even within regions in which all the necessary inputs were widely available, the Green Revolution sometimes harmed the poorest people. The poorest farmers could not afford to swap to the new seed varieties, and landless workers sometimes lost their jobs because of the mechanisation that accompanied the Green Revolution on larger farms.

These drawbacks were avoidable. They can be – and sometimes have been – addressed by continuing to invest in further crop development, by supporting regions to create suitable growing conditions, and by fine-tuning agricultural practice. One key component of good agricultural practice is the sustainable use of water. This is not yet common, so water scarcity is on the rise, and parts of the world are running out of time.

Issue 3 of 4: truly sustainable water management is hard to achieve but crucial (and not yet common)

All crops need water – just enough, preferably, and at just the right time. If crops don't get enough water when they need it, they won't produce the best possible harvests or – at worst – will die. Crops with *too much* water around them are similarly problematic. An olive tree, for example, can withstand drought quite well, but for it to thrive, its soil needs to drain well and the groundwater level can't be too high.

The water used for agricultural purposes does not necessarily have to come from irrigation. In fact, most of it doesn't. In the Netherlands, only some 11% of the agricultural land is irrigated.[26] Dutch farmers can often do without irrigation, as it rains a *lot*, and the focus tends to be on drainage[27] instead. In other regions, where rains are less regular and plentiful, irrigation is far more important. Recent experience in a number of Asian countries illustrates this well. In these countries, there was a huge expansion of irrigated land in the latter part of the 20th century, in part to cater for the thirst of new high-yielding crop varieties. This expansion explains a good part of the region's agricultural productivity boom: fields with good irrigation systems produce better yields per harvest and sometimes allow for more harvests per year.

These massive yield gains in Asia reduced poverty and malnutrition and had many other benefits, but all this progress came at a cost. Water reserves have dwindled, stagnant parts of irrigation networks have been breeding grounds for flies and mosquitoes, and some of the irrigated lands have suffered from salinisation, as even freshwater leaves bits of salt behind and, over time, these tiny salt deposits build up.

Five things are likely to happen in the coming decades.

Prediction 1 of 5: the percentage of agricultural land under irrigation will continue to increase

This is part of national development plans in countries across the dry parts of the world. So far, Africa in particular has been lagging behind. Estimates differ widely, but the African Union says that

> for Africa the percentage of arable land that is irrigated is 7 percent (barely 3.7 percent in Sub-Saharan Africa) while the corresponding percentages for South America, East and South-East Asia and South Asia are 10 percent, 29 percent and 41 percent respectively.[28]

Moreover, African irrigation systems have often delivered far less than they could. Systems were often short-lived, as they required maintenance skills that were not available, and poor design and practice caused damage to ecosystems and soil conditions.

It doesn't have to be this way. Africa has plenty of unused freshwater reserves. Profitably and sustainably using these reserves for irrigation is a matter of careful system design, construction and usage, and adequate maintenance (all of which requires a lot of capacity building). The continent will probably make major investments in irrigation over the next few decades. China is likely to expand its already long-standing support in this field but with more attention to small farms and system maintenance, and with better use of appropriate technology.[29]

Prediction 2 of 5: water management will become more efficient and less harmful

Farmers would need far less water if water always predictably reached the plant roots of the best possible plant varieties at the right time in the right quantity. On average, for example, the world uses over 200 litres of water to grow a kilo of tomatoes (and water-poor China uses considerably more than that), but in the Netherlands, they can do it with less than ten.[30]

I don't think the Dutch hyper-efficiency will be replicable in large parts of the world anytime soon, but much of today's irrigated and rain-fed agriculture could certainly be improved. In the coming years, there's likely to be a global move towards more efficient forms of irrigation (such as drip irrigation),[31] better rainwater harvesting, and more – and safer – re-use of sewage and industrial water. These efficiency gains will save water and are likely to reduce the harm that irrigation sometimes causes, as mosquitoes can't breed in water that flows through pipes, and salinisation is less of a problem if crops only receive the volume of water they actually need. In this context, countries should be mindful that water subsidies disincentivise efficient water use. After all, why would you be careful with something that costs almost nothing?

FIGURE 2.2 Drip irrigation

Prediction 3 of 5: there will be a gradual movement toward crops that require relatively little water

Agriculture consumes far more water than any other economic sector, but not every crop is equally demanding. If you have 30,000 litres of irrigation water, you could produce a ton (1,000 kilograms) of potatoes or just 4 kilograms of pistachios. You need 80 litres for a kilogram of barley or maize, 340 for wheat or rice, 500 for olives, and 900 for cashews. Rainwater requirements are generally several times higher, and ideally, you also have additional water to flush out the pollutants that the farming process put into the soil.[32] Producing a kilogram of meat (including fish farm meat) requires more water than a kilogram of most consumer crops, if you include the water required to produce the necessary fodder.

Because of climate change and the overexploitation of water reserves, there are already lots of local water shortages, and some of the water is getting saltier. This will get worse and more widespread. This will result in shifts in crop choices, towards crops that require less water, as well as crops that thrive on water with higher salt content. In the long run, water shortages will change consumer behaviour as well, as water-intensive crops will become increasingly pricey. In China, for example, I expect the booming meat consumption of the last few decades to continue only if 'clean meat' (or 'cultured meat' – the burger that is produced in a laboratory) becomes commercially viable.[33] If not, Chinese meat consumption is likely to start its decline before 2050, even in conditions of further economic growth. If you allow me an even bolder claim: 50 years from now, people in China will be growing and consuming more potatoes than rice, as potatoes require far less water to grow.[34] If the trade war that started under President Trump of the USA continues and spreads, then these changes in crop choice and consumption will happen even sooner. This is because the dangers and costs of trade barriers will cause countries to intensify efforts to achieve food self-sufficiency, and limited water reserves mean that this just won't be possible without a major shift in production choices and eating habits.

Prediction 4 of 5: ongoing research will develop ever-more water-efficient crops and livestock, and farming practice will follow

As funding for crop and livestock development has provided high returns on investment, it will continue to be available. It comes from the international donor community but also from national governments and, increasingly, commercial companies.[35] This research will lead to new breakthroughs, and several of the next major gains are likely to be related to water. We are already seeing the beginning of this, with more drought-tolerant rain-fed crop varieties and varieties that can deal with erratic water supply or with water that has high salt contents.

Farmers will not automatically adopt these new crop varieties, but that's largely a matter of genuine engagement between farmers and researchers, and of combining the wide availability of appropriate and affordable seed varieties with intelligently designed training, information, and incentives (see 'issue 4 of 4', on page 55).

Prediction 5 of 5: serious water shortages will lead to more cross-border cooperation and not to widespread cross-border conflict

The River Nile flows through 11 countries before it reaches the Mediterranean. The populations of each of these countries are higher than they've ever been, and they're continuing to rise. Collectively, they would like to use more of the river's water than actually exists.

Technicians could temporarily reduce the pressure by increasing the efficiency of water usage, and they could increase supply by reducing en route water wastage. For example, and in addition to the possibilities outlined earlier, they could replace leaking pipes and safely recycle used water. Or, far more important, they could find ways to reduce water evaporation, which is a massive problem when water reserves have a large surface area, as is the case with shallow rivers and reservoirs like Lake Nasser in Egypt. But whatever they manage to achieve, it will cushion and postpone rather than solve the problem of water distribution across the countries of the Nile basin.

In addition to these technical measures, these countries therefore need to negotiate the distribution of user rights. So far, the region's efforts to come to an agreement have not been successful. Egypt in particular is very worried about its water supply and most prominently about a massive dam that is under construction in Ethiopia. Egypt objects to this construction and, in 2013, the late Egyptian president threatened that "all options are open" if Ethiopia's dam were to reduce Egypt's access to Nile water. Around that same time, a group of Egyptian politicians discussed sabotaging the dam's construction, without knowing they were on live television.[36] Such sabre-rattling is part of a bigger trend towards the protection of resources through the threat of military might ('I want it, and if you try to take it, I will kill you').[37]

It doesn't have to be like this. In fact, "cooperation, not conflict, is the most common response to transboundary water management issues. [Between 1948 and 1999] there have been more than 200 international water agreements and only 37 cases of reported violence between states over water".[38] Such agreements are not just paper formalities: history shows that they pave the road for long-lasting cooperation.

The next few decades will see an increase of the number of local conflicts over dwindling water resources,[39] but I'm less worried about occasional cross-border threats and tough talk as the world's track record of dealing with such transboundary problems is, overall, good. Increasingly serious water shortages are likely to lead to increasingly committed cross-border cooperation. If this pattern holds, then the war between the city-states Lagash and Umma in Mesopotamia, 4,500 years ago, will remain the world's only-ever all-out water war.[40]

Issue 4 of 4: achieving sustainable yield gains requires farm support to be useful and used

Imagine this:

> You're a farmer, farming the plot of land on which you were born. You went to school nearby and, as a child, combined your school days with part-time work in the field. In the course of your childhood years, your parents taught you all there is to know about farming on this particular type of soil and with this particular type of weather. They, in turn, had learned it from *their* parents, and so forth. Based on generations of experience with the lands around this village, you and your fellow villagers know the conditions better than anybody and know exactly what is needed to get the best and safest possible harvest.

Sounds plausible?

No, it doesn't! For a number of reasons:

- Local knowledge is important, but importing good ideas from elsewhere is powerful too. Without this, all coffee beans would still come from Ethiopia.
- Climate change has changed the weather. Rains are no longer predictable and, on average, it is warmer than it used to be. Cyclones, hurricanes, and typhoons (these are all the same type of storm, occurring in different parts of the world) have increased in intensity. Your land might be getting saltier, especially if you're close to the coast.
- If you stick to your parents' seeds, you won't be able to compete with farmers who have moved on to new varieties.
- Agricultural pests and diseases have evolved, in part because they gradually built resistance to pesticides and antibiotics and in part because of changes in our climate. New diseases are affecting the health of your livestock, and some of the diseases of the past are no longer a problem.[41] The types and costs of available pesticides have changed as well, so following your parents' practice is no longer possible – and if it were, it wouldn't work.
- It's the same with fertilisers: lengthy, intensive usage of chemical fertilisers alters the chemistry of the soil, which means that a simple continuation of past practice won't necessarily have the same effects.
- New rural roads mean that there are better opportunities to trade, so it may well make sense to grow more cash crops and fewer subsistence crops (which are crops that you grow to consume within the household).
- You might have had the opportunity to link up with a region's irrigation network, which will have had profound implications for the way you farm.

So yes, there is value in the transfer of knowledge from one generation to the next. But yesterday's practice is often no longer relevant today, and sticking to it may well be to your detriment. Farm life is changing, and for farmers to get the most out of their land, they need up-to-date knowledge and real-time, tailor-made advice.

There are many ways to gain this knowledge and get that advice. You can get information from better-informed peers, radio shows, leaflets, and instructional apps. Tailored advice is available from cooperatives (if you're a member), agricultural extension centres,[42] and the vet. You can see and sometimes try out good practice at model farms and at the local agricultural research centre. Whatever the channel used, if farmer support is sound and leads to behavioural change, it is likely to push up production, reduce harm inflicted on soil and the wider environment, or both.

Almost 3,000 years ago, centrally managed technical advice led Chinese farmers to adopt crop rotation and to drain their fields.[43] In the 1970s and 1980s, the most commonly used type of farmer support had a similar top-down, centralised approach. It was called the 'Training and Visit System': in a massive effort to upgrade farming practice, *everybody* was encouraged to grow new and better rice varieties / replace old rubber trees with new and better ones / follow a particular pattern of fertilisation and using pesticides. Later, the support became more situation-specific and based on the idea that farmers could learn by experimenting and then decide what worked best on *their* particular farms. That's the basic idea behind 'Farmer Field Schools' that started in the late 1980s: 'let's try this out and see what happens, and then we talk about it and learn from it, and then you draw your own conclusions'.

Whatever the model used, these and many other types of farmer-focused information and advice have not always led to changes in farming practice. 'Integrated farming' (see Box 2.2), for example, is often a good idea – but the uptake has so far been disappointing.

BOX 2.2 INTEGRATED FARMING

Integrated farming is a system of farming that combines crops with livestock and/or edible water creatures. Combinations must be of mutual benefit. Fish benefit from rice plants, as these plants provide shade, keep the paddy water cool, attract insects (food for fish), and filter harmful chemicals out of the water. Rice benefits from fish as well, as fish eat weeds and bump against rice stems to throw off tasty insects. Their excrement is fertile, and their bumping rids rice leaves of water droplets that could otherwise feed a fungus that causes rice blast (that harvest-destroying disease I mentioned in the previous box – it's a big deal).

In integrated farming, you avoid the use of polluting inputs to the extent possible and put lots of farming by-products and 'waste' to good use. Instead of importing soya bean meal, you feed your livestock no- or low-value parts of your farm-grown crops. Your rice paddy hosts fish, crabs, shrimp, or ducks.

You harvest rain for irrigation, sunlight for electricity, and your livestock's manure – and possibly your own faeces as well (yes, indeed) – to maintain your land's fertility. Where possible, you keep pests at acceptable levels without using harmful pesticides – by, for example, deploying insects that eat pests or use them as hosts for their eggs, which kills them in the process. As you do all this, you continuously monitor the results, learn, and adapt the way you farm. Integrated farming looks a little like old-fashioned farming (in parts of China farmers have combined fish and aquatic plants for thousands of years), but with 21st-century seeds, management practices, and technical solutions.

Integrated farming is meant to keep costs low and generate a reasonable level of income for small-scale farmers. It is also meant to spread risks: a mono-crop farmer is left without an income if the harvest fails, but a farmer with multiple sources of income won't be hit quite as hard. The produce is organic, or close to organic, and the practice in its entirety is meant to be sustainable: no harmful inputs, little waste, soil that maintains its fertility, and water use that doesn't exceed replenishable levels. Where needed, integrated farming could even *restore* and *increase* the quality of the land and water resources, instead of gradually reducing it.

All in all, integrated farming has its attractions and plenty of promoters – but in many parts of the world, it's still far from common practice among smallholders.

Where support does not improve farming practice, there seem to be one or more of three persistent problems: the advice is bad, the support does not reach the target farmers, or it reaches them, but they choose not to follow it.

Problem 1 of 3: advice is not necessarily valuable

Some of the advice that farmers are exposed to is genuinely meant to improve agricultural practice. In other cases, the 'advice' is really just meant to boost sales. "This fertiliser works much better than organic manure. Why don't you try it for free, for a month?" Farmers don't always recognise the difference between technical advice and a sales pitch.

Another problem is that the information and advice may be provided by people who are insufficiently rewarded and motivated, or lack adequate and up-to-date expertise. And even if there is an overwhelming consensus of what good practice looks like, the advice given may later be discredited. In the 1970s, it was common to advise farmers to adopt a one-size-fits-all mono-cropping model with intensive use of pesticides and fertilisers. Nowadays, few people would still argue that this was wise. A last issue worth mentioning is that there are *many* non-governmental organisations, in Africa in particular, that use donor money to push some sort of niche agenda. This village needs bicycles! Start a crab farm! Grow this weird unknown vegetable and sell it to that fancy hotel's organic fusion restaurant! Some of these ideas may be good, but collectively these organisations contribute to the fragility and fragmentation of farming efforts. These organisations come and go, and their Great New Ideas tend to come and go with them.

Problem 2 of 3: advice doesn't always reach farmers

As an evaluator, I have visited quite a number of agricultural extension centres and model farms. Some of them were bustling. Others seemed to generate no farmer interest at all. There were no visitors and the 'experts' were mostly just sitting around. In some cases, the dysfunctionality was instantly obvious: dilapidated premises, backyards that had turned into 'equipment graveyards' (where lots of broken-down tools are left to rust – see Box 2.3) and piles of dusty leaflets in languages that local people do not understand. In other cases, these facilities seemed to be active but had morphed into places where 'research' and 'demonstration' were merely labels used to get subsidies to grow crops and breed livestock, which were then sold on the local markets. This was formally 'to cover some of the operational costs', but in reality these revenues disappeared or were under-reported, and I suspect they formed a significant salary supplement for the people working there.

BOX 2.3   CHECK THE BACKYARD BEFORE DONATING EQUIPMENT

In countries with weak institutions, 'equipment graveyards' are a common feature of places such as agricultural extension centres and cooperatives, hospitals and health clinics, fire brigades and schools. Equipment gets discarded because it is inappropriate (you can't use an X-ray machine in a clinic without electricity) or because donated equipment is of uncommon brands and therefore unmaintainable, as the knowhow is missing and spare parts are unavailable. Or, as the hockey stick example in the prologue illustrates, things get discarded because people just don't know what to do with the 'presents' they receive.

In such cases, I generally saw little or no evidence of outreach work either. Typical excuses were that "we would like to visit farmers, but we have no cars or motorbikes / we have no money for petrol / our motorbikes broke down / it is the rainy season, and the roads are inaccessible". Providing means of transport and petrol did not necessarily solve the issue. A while ago, I evaluated an organisation that had given 'model farmers' bicycles to visit and inspire other farmers, but I could find no evidence of them actually doing so. In another evaluation, an organisation had donated two motorcycles to a veterinary outreach office. One had lasted a few months and then broke down beyond repair. The other one was used by the office manager for joy rides with his girlfriend, during workdays, claiming mileage. (This is not a manner of speech: they passed by my lodge on their way to the beach, fully packed to spend the day, and asked if I fancied joining them.)

The farmers formally targeted by these facilities don't benefit from their existence but do sometimes face the unfair competition from their subsidised produce in the local markets.

Problem 3 of 3: farmers are not always able and eager to follow advice

Investing in a pension would be of benefit to almost everybody, but lots of people don't do it, even where pensions are easy to arrange and have reasonable and transparent terms and conditions. This is because this investment costs money that not everybody can afford to spend, and requires an interest in the long term that not everybody has.

It's the same for farmers who choose not to follow sound advice.

Some advice is cumbersome and therefore unattractive. Organic manure has many advantages, but it is also a time-consuming, smelly, heavy hassle. Other advice is costly. High-yielding seed varieties, greenhouses, and permanent crops may all generate good income and present low crop failure risk, for example, but they also require high upfront investments. Even if credit is available, farmers are often too risk-averse to make these investments. This is understandable, as the burden of failure may include skipping meals and selling family assets — and that is a heavy burden to carry (see Chapter 5, on microfinance).

Unused advice related to the long-term productivity of land is particularly common. There are two reasons for this.

First, life for poor people in particular is often too harsh, and the immediate problems are too pressing, to have the peace of mind to think much beyond the present (see Box 2.4). School drop-out, failure to take HIV medication with the necessary regularity, and fatty diets in high-income countries all cause problems in the long run and are all most common among poor communities — not because they don't care, but because they don't have the peace of mind (or 'mental bandwidth') needed to do what they generally know is of importance for their future. It's the same with smart agricultural investments: 'I'll do it next year' . . . but the following year, there will be other urgent distractions.[44]

Second, farmers are unlikely to invest in long-term conservation if they are not confident about their continued control over the land they farm. They do not necessarily need to *own* the land to feel protected: in China, where all agricultural land is state property, user lease agreements last for decades, and that's fine too.[45] But some sort of formal entitlement needs to be in place, and farmers need to feel certain that this entitlement is enforceable.

This is often not the case: "a mere 30% of the global population has legally registered rights to their land and homes".[46] This is a problem because people who can't prove they are entitled to use the land they farm may be vulnerable to losing it. In some countries, women are at particular risk. This is the case where land is

---

BOX 2.4 FOR SOME PEOPLE, WORRYING ABOUT THE FUTURE IS AN UNAFFORDABLE LUXURY

A 15-year-old orphan with four younger siblings worked as a sex worker to make ends meet. In an interview, she told me that she regularly agreed to unprotected sex, though she knew about the risks. AIDS and the prospect of pregnancy did not bother her much, she said, as both felt irrelevant. All that really mattered was that she earned enough money to feed her siblings and herself. This is what extreme hardship does to you: it leads to a fixation on meeting today's needs, irrespective of the longer-term implications.

---

traditionally owned, by formal registration or community consensus, by 'the man of the house'. If a woman loses her husband, she may lose her household's land as well.[47]

Small-scale farmers could lose their land to wealthier local farmers. These wealthier farmers may buy land after failed harvests (so when times are rough for poorer farmers and land prices are therefore low) or gain control over land through intimidation, threats, violence, bribes, contacts in high places, or legal procedures (see Box 2.5).

BOX 2.5 VICTORY FOR LANDLESS FARMERS IN BANGLADESH

Even if official government policy is to prioritise poor people's access to land, they may face an uphill struggle. Bangladesh has a policy that says that landless farmers may use unused government-owned land, but when rich farmers took such land instead and landless farmers protested, the leader of the protests was jailed, and both his legs were broken.

The story ends well: the imprisonment and torture did not deter this man or his movement. They continued their protest and eventually got what they fought for.

Source: I came across this man and his organisation in the course of some evaluative work I conducted a few years ago. I don't name them here because of safety concerns.

Farmers can also lose their land to companies. Long-term and large-scale lease agreements between foreign companies and governments (the formal owners of land in absence of evidence to the contrary) spiked in the 2000s – particularly after the food crisis of 2008. This phenomenon is sometimes called 'land grabbing'.

The term is a little unfair because not *all* such agreements are bad news for the people living on such land. Sometimes, leasing agreements include commitments to invest in infrastructure and to create employment, and some companies take such commitments seriously. However, three problems are common. First, these lease agreements are rarely the result of transparent tender processes, and the fees rarely reflect the economic potential of the land. Second, the agreements frequently include land that people – farmers and pastoralists – believe is theirs. The agreements are typically signed without genuine consultations with these people, and they are taken by surprise when they lose their traditional user rights and homes. Third, such agreements often include a 'stabilisation clause' that stipulates that the government cannot change the rules of the lease agreement later. This means that it's hard to take corrective action if the lease turns into an environmental, social, or economic disaster.

Until far more land ownership (or 'land tenure') is formalised, the typical poor household's access to farmland remains uncertain. Because of that uncertainty, it would be odd for such households to invest much in the long-term health of their land. After all: why would you invest time and money in conservation efforts that you may not benefit from? Why go through the hassle of flattening fields and installing drip irrigation to reduce water wastage; using no-till seed drills to avoid soil damage; planting unsellable cover crops in seasons when land would otherwise be empty; or maintaining rows of trees at a field's edge to break the wind - if you may end up doing it all for somebody who kicks you off your land, possibly even *because* you ensured its continued fertility?

These problems can be overcome

In most cases, and for now, wealthier farmers are better positioned to progress than poorer farmers. They have better access to information, advice, and financial products and services. They can afford to invest in their own expertise and are therefore better able to distinguish good advice from advertising. They more commonly have legal title over the land they farm and are therefore more inclined to focus on the long-term fertility of that land. And on average, the wealthier farmers' land is flatter and less erosion-prone to begin with.

The implication is that land degradation (which is soil degradation plus issues such as water shortage and the disappearance of surrounding vegetation) is more common among poor than among wealthier farmers. But it's not all bad news for poor farmers. There are lots of initiatives under way to formalise land ownership for them too, and ICT developments are equalising people's access to useful information and advice. Chapter 6 covers the issue of ICT, so here I'll just give a single example: extension centres.

Extension centres don't have a great name, and in many countries they don't have an impressive track record. However, ICT and better insights into the nature of learning processes are providing new opportunities. Today's best-functioning extension centres are partly virtual, and therefore some of their information and advice is instantly accessible in areas where farmers are online. They are also part of bigger knowledge systems, in which information flows through a range of channels to and from farmers and stakeholders like research centres, cooperatives, traders, and relevant government agencies. They don't limit themselves to giving blanket advice on what you and all other farmers should do. Instead, their advice is grounded in established good practice but tailored to the particular needs of a farm or group of farms, and they facilitate <u>experiential learning</u>.[48] They also use apps to collect local data from farmers, which helps them to identify and respond early to emerging problems and new opportunities. This regular two-way communication creates a positive spiral of perceived usefulness and trust. This is crucial, as the main challenge of centres that do not have a track record of success is to persuade farmers that they are worth engaging with.

All in all, for poor farmers to receive and use relevant information and good advice more consistently, parallel tracks of progress are required. Seed varieties and other inputs need to suit the small farm's soil and other conditions and should lead to profitable harvests – even for farmers with modest expertise and management skills. Information and advice needs to be relevant to the farmer's particular circumstances. The channels through which the communication takes place need to be easy to access, and increasingly this requires ICT hardware (a farmer needs to have coverage to a mobile network), software (the extension centre needs to have a handy app), and relevant, timely interaction (the app needs to be live, and advice needs to be available in real time). Basic literacy and numeracy helps too. Ideally, microfinance products enable the farmer to seize opportunities, and certainty of land access is needed for the farmer to *want* to follow up. Reasonable infrastructure is needed to ensure that the inputs required are available and the harvest can be sold.

The poorer and more remote the region, and the more dispersed its farmers, the longer it will take to create the environment in which a farmer can action advice. Creating such an environment requires governments that consider these regions worthy of their money and attention. Chances of this happening are better in countries with decentralised government structures, as poor and remotely located farmers are pretty much invisible to decision-makers in capital cities.

Why is all this relevant, and what does it mean for you?

The evidence is overwhelming, and the trends are clear. Without decisive actions that protect our water and soil, we are heading towards an unmitigated global disaster – though, at least initially, poorer countries and regions are likely to suffer far more than wealthier ones. Our food production will continue to increase for a while, then plateau, then fall – probably well before the world population reaches its peak. Increasing numbers of people will live with freshwater scarcity. There will be water-related violence, migration-induced conflict, and hunger. The poorest communities within poor and fragile countries will suffer most. Within these communities, people's identity will determine the level of suffering they face:

an illiterate disabled orphan girl from an ethnic and religious minority may well face life-threatening challenges.

Another looming disaster is related to employment in Africa in particular. Unemployment is already high, and the population continues to grow (though the growth path is slowing down). There are large slums, there are many conflicts that are aggravated by lack of prospects, and there is lots of migration pressure already. These issues are likely to worsen, but just as rapid rural development prevented communist uprisings in Thailand and Malaysia in the 1970s, it could prevent instability and mass migration in Africa in the 2020s and beyond. Such rapid rural development needs to be pro-poor, as was by and large the case in Asia. So far, few governments in Africa show clear signs that they are up to the challenge.

So what does this mean for you? It means that you could usefully focus your work on three big things.

First, make or encourage appropriate, sizeable, and sustained investments in rural development

In Chapter 1, we saw that Asia's large and sustained investments in rural development distinguished the continent from Latin America and, even more, from Africa. These investments underpinned the impressive growth of Asia's economies. Their focus was on small-scale farming, and this helped reduce rural poverty with high speed and at large scale. In many African countries, the importance of public rural investments is now recognised as well,[49] and this recognition is a good first step – but not all spending is equal, and agricultural spending choices, in most African countries and in low-income countries around the world, are often unwise.

At the start of the Green Revolution, input subsidies helped to persuade farmers to take the risk of growing new crop varieties, and the impact has been phenomenal. Then subsidies outlived their usefulness. Nowadays, subsidies on fertilisers, seeds, water, electricity, petrol, and pesticides are often worse than 'just' a waste of money: they create dependencies and lead to inefficient and damaging uses of scarce resources. They disincentivise innovation, as there's no reason to think creatively about water or energy efficiency if water and electricity cost practically nothing. Moreover, subsidies tend to favour wealthier people[50] and are often so non-transparent that much of the money seems to evaporate.

One particular type of subsidies may gain usefulness at some point in the near future. These are subsidies that encourage sustainable land use, land restoration, or transitions to water-efficient crops. Progress in this field requires strong land registration and systems that offer little scope for corruption (e-government comes to mind – see Chapter 6, on ICT). It also requires the use of low-cost satellite imagery to monitor farms' conservation efforts. In countries that have these conditions in place, conservation-related subsidies may turn out to be money well spent – and we return to them in Chapter 9 on climate change.

Until that time comes, economists broadly agree that it is generally much better to spend public funds on agricultural infrastructure, such as electrification, feeder roads, markets and efficient forms of irrigation. However, politicians are reluctant to follow the economists' advice because subsidies influence election results in ways that infrastructure does not.[51] This is because subsidies are instant, while it takes a long time for infrastructure to be constructed, and farmers often need to spend time and money to connect their farm to that infrastructure (e.g., to get the farm ready for irrigated agriculture, after the government digs the larger canal). Maintaining existing infrastructure is even less of a vote-winner: dikes need costly maintenance, but it's hard to see the difference between a well-maintained and a leaky dike – until it's tested by high waters. Within the field of infrastructure, there is a bias towards a few highly visible large-scale initiatives over many small-scale networks – even if the smaller networks make more sense from the point of view of rural development.

And the best spending, on average, may well be on pro-poor research and development (R&D), conducted in close consultation with people from the target group. Of course, not all investments in this field are useful, and bad research may even have negative effects, but imagine the effects of fully utilised research that improves yields, pest resistance, and the shelf life of drought-resistant crops that are grown on remote rain-fed plots with poor soil conditions! It would dramatically improve millions of lives.[52]

Sadly, the current reality is that subsidies absorb a lot of low-income countries' agricultural spending, and research gets nearly nothing. It's hard to change this because of the 'status quo bias': taking away almost any subsidy will deeply upset people who have grown accustomed to that subsidy. I hope the next generation of policy-makers will have the courage to break through that bias and withstand the short-term outrage of subsidy recipients. It might be helpful to work closely with farmer groups that have a genuine interest in the long-term health of the agricultural sector. Such groups could help raise awareness about the long-term benefits and drawbacks of different types of agricultural spending, thereby reducing resistance to a gradual refocus from subsidies to types of spending with better returns. If you follow this path, make sure your spending does not end up favouring wealthier farmers over poorer ones. Keep in mind that poor farmers are invisible to policy-makers unless these policy-makers go out of their way to reach them, as poor farmers tend to live in remote and poorly connected parts of the country and do not have a loud voice or political clout.

Second, help farmers focus on the long run

Just as important as a government's spending on rural development is the way in which it facilitates or complicates farming with a long-term horizon. Formalising land ownership should be a priority, as it gives people confidence about their continued access to the land they farm, and this may have positive effects on land conservation. If you are able to change legislation or cultural practice that excludes women from land ownership, your work would have positive effects on women's peace of mind and agricultural practice. If neither is a problem in your country, it might be worth looking at unnecessary complexities of formal land transfer and land rental arrangements that often make it all but impossible for poor people to formally buy, sell, or rent land. It would also be useful to look at possibilities for 'functional zoning' and specifically at possibilities to earmark fertile lands for agriculture. In countries without that type of spatial planning, anybody who is wealthy enough can choose to do anything with the land he or she is able to buy. Without limits on such choices, you may end up with holiday parks, golf courses and new cities, but no food.

Third, contribute to regional collaboration

Sustainable water management in particular often requires long-term cross-border agreements on the distribution of limited water resources. In the long run, Egypt's attitude of 'we want it all, and if you build a dam, we may bomb it' is bound to backfire: you need agreements that share the pain and that work for all parties.

Neighbours also present opportunities. If you work for the government of a country in which it is really hard to register new seeds, for example, your country's farmers do not benefit from sturdier and better-yielding varieties to the extent that they could. They would benefit from a system whereby approval for the use of a new seed variety is given regionally, rather than by each individual country.

If farmers are indeed enabled and persuaded to improve their yields without damaging their land, the ongoing deforestation to meet the need for ever-more farmland might slow down. For this to happen, the world needs a good response to climate change as well. That's the topic of the final chapter.

Further reading

To appreciate the extent of the Green Revolution's impact

Start with Gollin, D., Hansen, C.W., and Wingender, A. (2018) "Two blades of grass: The impact of the Green Revolution", *NBER Working Paper 24744*, National Bureau of Economic Research. This is a riveting read. The abstract is available online, and underneath it, you will find a box in which to type your email address. If it's a university address, you'll receive a link to the full paper, free of charge. Or take a look at Fuglie, K. (2015) "Accounting for growth in global agriculture", *Bio-based and Applied Economics*, volume 4, issue 3, pages 201–234, online.

There's a lot of praise for East Asian countries in particular, in the two chapters you've just read and in Gollin's publication, but of course there are large differences among these countries. For an overview of the differences, see Le, T.L. et al. (2019) "Evaluation of <u>total factor productivity</u>[53] and environmental efficiency of agriculture in nine East Asian countries", *Agricultural Economics–Czech*, volume 65, pages 249–258, online. This paper starts with a few useful references to publications that make cross-country comparisons of agricultural efficiency in other regions.

About the state and likely future of the world's natural resources

For more on the state of the world's land and water resources, read FAO (2011) *The state of the world's land and water resources for food and agriculture (SOLAW); managing systems at risk*, FAO and Earthscan, online. A few years earlier, FAO also published 'state of the world' books on forests, food, and aquaculture. Or if you want to know more about soil and food security and where the world is heading, you could read a few of the chapters in Lal, R. and Stewart, B.A. (2012) *World soil resources and food security*, CRC Press.

For a meaningful look into an uncertain future, large-scale research endeavours use scenarios. *If* the population plateaus and then declines, *and* inequality is reduced, *and* we modify our consumption patterns, *and* we are increasingly skilful in the way we use our lands, *then* the future is likely to look so-and-so. Some such publications add recommendations: *if* this particular scenario materialises, *then* our recommendations for the world's decision-makers would be this-and-that. Three recent publications that explore scenarios related to land and water are

- IPCC (2019) *Climate change and land; An IPCC Special Report on climate change, desertification, land degradation, sustainable land management, food security, and greenhouse gas fluxes in terrestrial ecosystems*, Intergovernmental Panel on Climate Change. It has a 40-page summary (online) in which, unusually and helpfully, each paragraph refers to relevant sections in the main report.
- Van der Esch, S. et al. (2017) *Exploring future changes in land use and land condition and the impacts on food, water, climate change and biodiversity*, PBL Netherlands Environmental Assessment Agency, online.
- UNCCD (2017) *Global Land Outlook; first edition*, United Nations Convention to Combat Desertification, online.

The IPCC and Van der Esch publications in particular are clinical, in a good way. The authors did not write these papers to promote some sort of doom-and-gloom worldview. Instead, they conducted research, ran simulations, and reported on the (sometimes chilling) findings in a sober, factual manner.

About the depth of the challenges for poor communities in particular

For descriptions and applications of conceptual frameworks that help in understanding the complex interplay between poverty and the environment in which poor communities live, see Nunan, F. (2015) *Understanding Poverty and the Environment: Analytical frameworks and approaches*, Routledge.

For the way poverty-inflicted problems reduce people's 'mental bandwidth' and how this tunnels their focus onto immediate problems rather than long-term opportunities, see Mullainathan, S. and Shafir, E. (2014) *Scarcity; the true cost of not having enough*, Penguin (original 2013, Times Books).

About wise, less wise, and counterproductive government investments

Obviously, it is not good enough for governments to just 'invest in rural regions': you also need to know what is worth investing in!

For insights on this, a good place to start is the not-yet-dated World Bank (2007) *World development report 2008: agriculture for development*, online. Start on page 114, and follow the references to other sections. Or, for trends in, drawbacks of, and opportunities for African governments' rural investments in particular (which is where most work needs to be done), see the 40-page 'overview' of this massive book: Goyal, A. and Nash, J. (2017) *Reaping richer returns: public spending priorities for African agriculture productivity growth*, World Bank, online.

About input subsidies

For a nuanced assessment that distinguishes between subsidies in 'successful Asian green revolutions', 'post-Green Revolution situations in Asia', and 'current pre-Green Revolution Sub-Saharan Africa situations', see Dorward, A. and Morrison, J. (2015) "Heroes, villains and victims: agricultural subsidies and their impact on food security and poverty reduction", Chapter 9 of Robinson, G.M. and Carson, D.A. *Handbook on the globalisation of agriculture*, Edward Elgar Publishing. The chapter also covers subsidies in high-income countries.

For an overview of the pros and considerable cons of today's input subsidies in Africa in particular, see Jayne, T.S. and Rashid, S. (2013) "Input subsidy programs in Sub-Saharan Africa: a synthesis of recent findings", *Agricultural Economics*, volume 44, issue 6. You'll find a slightly more positive set of conclusions in a meta-analysis that is based on 31 studies from Africa and Asia (of which 15 are about Malawi!): Hemming, D.J. et al. (2018) "Agricultural input subsidies for improving productivity, farm income, consumer welfare and wider growth in low- and lower-middle-income countries: a systematic review", *A Campbell Systematic Review*, issue 4 of 2018, online. Or, for a focus on post-2005 'second generation, market-smart targeted subsidies', see Holden, S.T. (October 2019) "Economics of farm input subsidies in Africa", *Annual Review of Resource Economics*, volume 11 (apologies if the reference is not exactly right – I've only seen the unpublished draft version of this paper).

If you only have a little time and are looking for a set of bottom-line conclusions in this field, read the two-page concluding section of Gautam, M. (2015) "Agricultural subsidies: resurging interest in a perennial debate", *Indian Journal of Agricultural Economics*, volume 70, issue 1, pages 83–105, online. The rest of this paper is worth reading as well.

About research and development – R&D – in relation to agricultural inputs and practice

R&D conducted in the 1950s and 1960s started the Green Revolution, and R&D is still vitally important today. But the research *models* have evolved from the top-down knowledge transfer model ('here is a great new seed – now go and grow better rice!') to models where researchers and farmers interact and influence each other. For an overview of the impact of various models of agricultural research, see Faure, G. et al. (2018) "How different agricultural research models contribute to impact: evidence from 13 case studies from developing countries", *Agricultural Systems*, volume 165, pages 128–136.

The 13 case studies that Faure's paper is based on were all about internationally funded research (funded by the French CIRAD, to be specific), but it's not just international research that matters. For an assessment of the reasons for the striking successes of a government research institute from Brazil, read Correa, P. and Schmidt, C. (2014). "Public research organizations and agricultural development in Brazil: How did Embrapa get it right?" *Economic Premise*, number 145, online. One bit of learning: Embrapa never funded 'curiosity-driven research' and instead focused all its funding on concrete problems faced by Brazilian farmers. This led to crop varieties that were developed to thrive in local weather, on local soil.

Perhaps more important than the source of funding is the location of the research, as much of the agricultural R&D focuses on location-specific growing conditions. Research in India improved agriculture, first and foremost, in India – and so forth. Shifts in the geographic distribution of the world's agricultural R&D helps to predict where agricultural productivity will and will not continue to grow. For an overview of the shifts in R&D, from rich to middle-income countries and from public to private sector funding, see Parday, P.G. et al. (2016) "Agricultural R&D is on the move", *Nature*, volume 537, issue 7620, pages 301–303, online. One key conclusion: people in low-income countries get the short straw, as very little research is conducted in this group of countries.

Other issues

About agriculture in the Netherlands

If the prologue sparked an interest in Dutch agriculture, a good start is Viviano, F. (September 2017) *This tiny country feeds the world; the Netherlands has become an agricultural giant by showing what the future of farming could look like*, National Geographic, online. Or you could watch a short video, embedded in a brief column on the issue: Skillikorn, N. (2018) *How the Netherlands has innovated agriculture to become the world's #2 exporter of food*, online. Not everybody agrees with such glowing assessments. For a more critical review of Dutch agriculture, see Schröder, J. et al. (12 March 2018) "Dutch agriculture is not a beacon of good farming practice to the world", *DutchNews.nl*, online.

About ways to change DNA

For a brief history of breeding and more modern forms of genetic modification, see Rangel, G. (2015) "From corgis to corn: a brief look at the long history of

GMO technology", *BLOG*, online. This brief paper is part of the August 2015 Harvard University BLOG special issue on "Genetically modified organisms and our food".

About integrated farming systems

A good place to start is Walia, S.S. et al. (2019) "Integrated farming system: enhancing income source for marginal and small farmers", in Peshin, R. and Dhawan, A., editors, *Natural Resource Management: Ecological Perspectives*, Springer, pages 63–94. Or if you are interested in the rice-fish combination covered in Box 2.2, and how this relates to the Green Revolution's focus on rice as a mono-culture crop, see Lansing, J.S. and Kremer, J.N. (2011) "Rice, fish and the planet", *PNAS*, volume 108, issue 50, pages 19841–19842 (yes, really, those are the page numbers), online. There are also lots of manual-type publications on the ins and outs of integrated farming systems.

About land grabbing

For a dramatic read on Africa, take a look at Haller, T. et al. (2019) "Large-scale land acquisition as commons grabbing: a comparative analysis of six African countries", in Lozny, L. and McGovern, T., *Global perspectives on long term community resource management*, Studies in Human Ecology and Adaptation, volume 11, Springer. Or for a journalist-style account of land grabbing in Southeast Asia, with case studies of Cambodia, Indonesia, and the Philippines, read Borras, S.M. Jr. and Franco, J.C. (2011) *Political dynamics of land-grabbing in Southeast Asia; understanding Europe's role*, Transnational Institute, online.

For a good read with a more neutral tone, read Cotula, L. et al. (2009) *Land grab or development opportunity? Agricultural investment and international land deals in Africa*, FAO, IIED and IFAD, online. There are more recent publications on the issue, but this one is still current – and very clear and easy to read. The case studies are all from Africa, but the recommendations make sense in other contexts as well, and you should consider them carefully if you work in this field.

Formalising land ownership would reduce the scope for land grabbing. In endnote 46 I referred to a brief and interesting blog about this: Tuck, L. and Zakout, W. (25 March 2019) "7 reasons for land and property rights to be at the top of the global agenda", *World Bank Blogs*, online.

About farm size

One of the arguments sometimes used in favour of large acquisitions is that it increases farming efficiency. If this argument appeals to you, read Rada, N.E. and Fuglie, K.O. (April 2019) "New perspectives on farm size and productivity", *Food Policy*, volume 84, pages 147–152. The paper starts with references to a number of publications that argue that small farms are hindering agricultural growth and competitiveness. It then summarises findings from the other papers in this special issue of *Food Policy* (all interesting reads by themselves) and comes to a different conclusion. A quotation from the abstract suggests that it will take decades for this efficiency argument to gain minimum plausibility:

> Certain farm sizes face relative productivity advantages, such as small farms in Africa. But with economic and market growth, that smallholder advantage will likely attenuate, moving toward constant and eventually increasing returns to size. Yet, importantly, small farms may be quite dynamic, and need not be a drag on agricultural growth until perhaps well into the development process.

Exercise

You work as an 'expert advisor' in a local agricultural extension centre. Five years ago, you participated in a training course on the results of 'biofortification'. It was about crop varieties that have been modified to contain micronutrients such as vitamin A, zinc, and iron.

You had been fascinated by 'golden rice' in particular: a variety of rice packed with vitamin A. Farmers in a neighbouring country had been growing golden rice for several years, with quite some success. Golden rice seeds were available in your country as well.

You had wanted the farmers in your catchment area to move from the rice varieties they had traditionally been growing to this golden rice.

Question 1: what kinds of activity have you probably undertaken to make this happen?

Now, five years later, you acknowledge that your efforts have been unsuccessful. Most farmers ignored your advice. The ones that did follow it moved back to the traditional rice varieties one or two years later.

Question 2: what could have gone wrong?

Notes

1 I write this with her permission.
2 From *data.worldbank.org*, indicator on 'cereal yield', accessed on 4 October 2019. Select the Netherlands, Uganda, and Sub-Saharan Africa and then compare the yields. I used 2017 data.
3 According to *knoema.com*'s article titled *The world's leading exports of agricultural products* (online), the value of exported agricultural and food products from the United States was valued to be US$102.1 billion in 2017. In the same year, the Netherlands exported agricultural and food products valued to be US$86.9 billion. Knoema is one of several free websites that presents data from various credible sources. Figures used for this indicator are taken from the UNCTAD's online database, a public – but not particularly user-friendly – domain. The 'over 230' is from Google's answer to 'surface USA' and 'surface Netherlands'.
4 It's 26%, at the moment. This might disappoint you, as many sources incorrectly report that it's more than half, on the basis of a statement in a 2007 background note of the

IPCC. This note was corrected in 2010 – see Ireland, L. (2010) *U.N. climate panel admits Dutch sea level flaw*, Reuters, online.

5 In this book, yield refers to the weight of a crop per unit of land, such as the number of kilograms of rice per hectare planted. In other contexts, yield could also refer to the financial return of an investment, or to the production per unit, such as the volume of milk per cow.

6 In *data.worldbank.org*, the indicator 'Agricultural land (% of land area)' suggests that the global percentage of agricultural land increased from 36% in 1961 to 37% in 2016 – but note the 1991–92 cliff, which suggests a change in definition or an improvement in measurement technique in 1992. The term *agricultural land* includes three broad categories: crops that are 'permanent' (with olive trees probably being the world's most extreme example), pastures that are 'permanent' (which means they have been in use as pasture land for five years or longer) and 'arable land'. Arable land includes land that is used for short-term crops, land that is temporarily fallow (which means it is not being used for a while to restore fertility or because it does not make commercial sense to do so), as well as temporary meadows that are being used for mowing or pasture.

7 FAO (2018) *The state of agricultural commodity markets*, figure 1.6 on page 9, and pages 20–22, online.

8 The International Labour Organization (ILO) estimated that, in 2018, 51% of the African labour force worked in agriculture, including forestry and fishing. It was higher for Sub-Saharan Africa (55%) and higher still for the low-income countries in Sub-Saharan Africa (66%). The percentage is lower for all other continents and regions but comparably high in the sub-group of *low-income* countries in Asia (57%, versus 32% for Asia in its entirety). See ILOSTAT's *Employment by sector–ILO modelled estimates* (these estimates are from the November 2018 dataset, accessed on 3 October 2019). Because much agricultural work is informal and unrecorded, these figures are subject to many assumptions and involve a lot of guessing. Also note the vast differences in the participation of women and men in agriculture, across countries!

9 Again, figures are available from *data.worldbank.org*. Look for the indicator *Crop Production Index* and the more limited indicator *Food Production Index*.

10 The second part of this 'ultimate conclusion' is that this is not a big problem for oil-rich countries as "economic conditions . . . have the greatest impact on food consumption and security levels." Baer-Nawrocka, A. and Sadowski, A. (2019) "Food security and food self-sufficiency around the world: a typology of countries", *PLoS One*, volume 14, issue 3, online.

11 For a region-by-region division of agricultural land into 'prime', 'good', 'marginal' and 'not suitable' land, defined in terms of the capacity to reach certain levels of yield for a basket of crops, see tables 4–8 of Fischer, G. et al. (2010) "Scarcity and abundance of land resources: competing uses and the shrinking land resource base", *SOLAW Background Thematic Report TR02*, FAO, online.

12 In fact, desert agriculture is among the older forms of agriculture: some 5,500 years ago the Sumerians irrigated and grew crops in desert lands that are, nowadays, part of Iraq. See Trager, J. (1995) *The food chronology*, Henry Holt, New York, section on 3,500 BC.

13 Soil degradation is a decline in the soil's potential to produce useful things. Much of it is caused by soil erosion, salinisation, pollution, and nutrient mining (which is any agricultural practice that takes more nutrients out of the soil than it puts back into it).

14 Van der Esch, S. et al. (2017) *Exploring future changes in land use and land condition and the impacts on food, water, climate change and biodiversity*, PBL Netherlands Environmental Assessment Agency, pages 12–13, online. The two other regions that Van der Esch predicts to face particularly tough challenges are South Asia and the Middle East and Northern Africa (page 15). It's even worse if you include the effects of climate change: "About a quarter of the Earth's ice-free land area is subject to human-induced degradation." IPCC (2019) *Climate change and land; summary for policymakers*, Intergovernmental Panel on Climate Change, paragraph A1.5, online.

15 Trager, J. (1995) *The food chronology*, Henry Holt, New York, sections on 3,000 BC and 1,000 BC respectively.

16 Chamberlain, T.C. (2007) "Islands in time", Chapter 9 in Montgomery, D.R., editor, *Dirt: the erosion of civilization*, University of California Press, Berkeley.

17 Van der Esch, S. et al. (2017) *Exploring future changes in land use and land condition and the impacts on food, water, climate change and biodiversity; scenarios for the UNCCD Global Land Outlook*, PBL Netherlands Environmental Assessment Agency, online.

18 See *mvd.iaea.org*, which is the 'mutant variety database' of the Food and Agriculture Organization (FAO) and the International Atomic Energy Agency (IAEA).

19 See Vogel, G. (31 May 2019) "Fungus with a venom gene could be new mosquito killer", *Science*, volume 364, issue 6443, page 817. On pages 894–897, there is a more technical and longer report on the same issue.

20 Irrigation is the managed supply of water to land. Diverting water from the river to farmland, spraying water over farmland, and deliberately flooding a field – it all counts.

21 The Green Revolution is generally seen as a phenomenon of the 1960s and 1970s, but agricultural productivity gains in large parts of the Global South actually accelerated *after* that. See Fuglie, K. (2015) "Accounting for growth in global agriculture", *Bio-based and Applied Economics*, volume 4, issue 3, pages 201–234 (with the point I'm making here aptly summarized in conclusion 3 on page 224).

22 Gollin, D., Hansen, C.W. and Wingender, A. (2018) "Two blades of grass: the impact of the green revolution", *NBER Working Paper 24744*, National Bureau of Economic Research; quotation from the abstract.

23 Gollin, D., Hansen, C.W. and Wingender, A. (2018) "Two blades of grass: the impact of the green revolution", *NBER Working Paper 24744*, National Bureau of Economic Research, quotations from the abstract and page 33 respectively.

24 Remittances are sums of money that migrants send to people – and generally to close relatives – in their country of origin.

25 Salinisation is the build-up of the salt contents in soil.

26 From *data.worldbank.org*, select the indicator 'agricultural irrigated land (% of total agricultural land)' and select the Netherlands, 2016 figure, accessed on 6 October 2019. Estimates from other sources are different and generally lower.

27 Drainage systems are meant to remove excess water. In the most extreme case, this is to avoid waterlogging, which is the situation where the soil is saturated with water (which is bad).

28 AU and NEPAD (2003) *Comprehensive Africa Agriculture Development Programme; New Partnership for Africa's Development*, page 2, online. Other guestimates are proposed by Goyal, A. and Nash, J. (2017) *Reaping richer returns: public spending priorities for African agriculture productivity growth*, World Bank, page 23: "the irrigated area as a share of total cultivated area is estimated at 6 percent for Africa, compared with 37 percent for Asia and 14 percent for Latin America".

29 Chinese irrigation support to African countries started in the 1960s but wasn't initially successful, in part because they were not integrated in national plans and dependent on ongoing Chinese supervision.

30 Viviano, F. (September 2017) *This tiny country feeds the world; the Netherlands has become an agricultural giant by showing what the future of farming could look like*, National Geographic, online, in the infographic titled "doing more with less".

31 Drip irrigation is irrigation that minimises water loss by slowly releasing water directly to the roots of plants, using pipes or (in the past) pots with small holes. According to Postel, S. (June 2012) *Drip irrigation expanding worldwide*, National Geographic, online, drip irrigation is rapidly expanding ("over the past twenty years … at least 6.4-fold, from 1.6 million hectares to more than 10.3 million") yet, still, "less than 4 percent of the world's irrigated land is equipped with micro-irrigation systems" (of which drip irrigation is only part). As so often, other sources present different figures, but all agree that drip irrigation it still massively underutilised.

32 The figures I mentioned are rough approximations, as much depends on the irrigation technique, weather, and soil conditions. For an overview of the 'water footprint' of different crops, see Mekonnen, M.M. and Hoekstra, A.Y. (2010) "The green, blue and grey water footprint of crops and derived crop products; volume 1, main report", *Research Report Series*, issue 47, online. The figures stated in this paragraph are approximations calculated from the figures in table 3, on pages 16–20, and I thank Mesfin Mekonnen for kindly reviewing these calculations. Blue water is irrigation water: the rainwater that reaches crops through streams and groundwater. Green water is rainwater that is stored in the root zone and not flowing to the groundwater or streams. Grey water is the water required to flush the soil, post-harvest.

33 The time for this hasn't quite come yet, but we've come a long way from when the first 'clean' burger was fried and eaten in the presence of the media, in 2013. That burger had taken two years and $300,000 to produce (and was judged to be "a bit dry"). For a historic overview and an indication of progress, see Ireland, T. (23 May 2019) "The artificial meat factory – the science of your synthetic supper", *Science Focus*, online.

34 If you think this prediction is preposterous, please persuade me to remove this claim from this book's next edition (willem.vaneekelen@gmail.com), but keep in mind that China is already the largest producer *and* the largest consumer of potatoes in the world.

35 For an overview of shifts, see Parday, P.G. et al. (2016) "Agricultural R&D is on the move", *Nature*, volume 537, issue 7620, pages 301–303.

36 The quotation and the bit about politicians being televised are both reported in Pflanz, M. (12 June 2013) "Egypt: 'all options are open' in Nile dam row with Ethiopia", *The Telegraph*, online. If this issue interests you, you might want to read Yihdego, Z. (2013) "The Blue Nile dam controversy in the eyes of international law", *GWF Discussion Paper 1326*, online.

37 For more on that trend and its legal ramifications (but not for the 'quotation', which is not in fact a real quotation and merely added for the purpose of clarification), see Krieger, H. and Püschmann, J. (May 2019) "Securing of resources as a valid reason for using force? A pre-emptive defence of the prohibition on the use of force", *KFG Working Paper*, issue 31, online.

38 This is a UN statement of 2009, quoted in Brochmann, M. (2012) "Signing river treaties – does it improve river cooperation?" *International Interactions*, volume 38, issue 2, pages 141–163, with the quotation taken from pages 141–142.

39 This trend is already obvious. For a rather intimidating overview of conflicts that have had a water dimension, see *worldwater.org/conflict*, then select 'Chronological list', accessed on 6 October 2019.

40 This is the second conflict from the top, in that website mentioned in the previous endnote.

41 Cattle plague (or 'rinderpest') is the most notable example, and the only animal disease that has truly been eradicated, after killing nearly all cattle during outbreaks that spanned at least 5,000 years. In the worst outbreaks, food production plummeted, because there was no dung to fertilise the fields and no cattle to plough them. This caused mass starvation: in the Great Ethiopian Famine of 1888–1892, "speculative estimates of the human death toll in affected parts of East Africa reach as high as one-half to two-thirds of the population." Morens, D. et al. (2011) "Global rinderpest eradication: lessons learned and why humans should celebrate too", *The Journal of Infectious Diseases*, volume 204, issue 4, pages 502–505 (and the quotation is from 502); or read Roeder, P. (2011) "Rinderpest: the end of cattle plague", *Preventive Veterinary Medicine*, volume 201, pages 98–106.

42 Extension centres (or extension services) are places and virtual facilities that exist to provide information, advice, and sometimes other services related to good and sometimes innovative farming practice.

43 Trager, J. (1995) *The food chronology*, Henry Holt, New York, section on 800 BC.

44 For a convincing book on the way poverty limits people's peace of mind (or 'bandwidth', as they call it), read Mullainathan, S. and Shafir, E. (2014) *Scarcity; the true cost of not having enough*, Penguin (original 2013, Times Books). The examples I gave here are discussed in Chapter 7, on 'Poverty'.

45 Though leasing land is not as good as owning it, as you can't use leased land as collateral for a loan – see Chapter 5, on microfinance.

46 Tuck, L. and Zakout, W. (25 March 2019) "7 reasons for land and property rights to be at the top of the global agenda", *World Bank Blogs*, online.

47 For some statistics on the imbalance between the percentages of men and women owning land, see the online 'land' sheet of the World Bank series on 'understanding poverty'. For insights in the imbalance of land property rights and practice, and the international community's work to remove this imbalance, see *stand4herland.org*.

48 Experiential learning is doing things and then reflecting on what you've been doing and learning from these reflections. The Farmer Field Schools, mentioned before, are a good example of experiential learning in practice.

49 This recognition is formalised in the 'Maputo and Malabo targets' of allocating at least 10% of national government budgets to agriculture. In 2016, the Sub-Saharan countries that met this target were Benin, Malawi, Mali, Niger, Rwanda, and Senegal, and the Central African Republic and Ethiopia are getting close to it. For current and historical data on this, see IFPRI (2019) *Statistics on public expenditures for economic development (SPEED): 2019 global food policy report table 2*, International Food Policy Research Institute, online.

50 For example, the World Bank looked at ten developing countries and found that well over half (56%) of water supply and sanitation subsidies were spent on the wealthiest 20% of the people. Only 6% went to the poorest 20%. See Andres, L.A. et al. (August 2019) "Doing more with less: smarter subsidies for water supply and sanitation", *Water Global Practice*, World Bank, pages 32–34, online. (This is only a rough proxy of what we're talking about, as these figures are mostly about piped water, but the distribution of other subsidies tends to be similarly biased.)

51 A good example is the overwhelming re-election victory of Malawi's president Bingu wa Mutharika, in 2009, following a few bumper harvests that were widely seen to be caused by input subsidies. (After that election, things went downhill.)

52 Rates of return for agriculture-related government funding are really hard to estimate, and they are inevitably subject to heroic assumptions. A few Africa-specific efforts are reported on in Goyal, A. and Nash, J. (2017) *Reaping richer returns: public spending priorities for African agriculture productivity growth*, World Bank, online. On page 99, the report concludes that "Regarding spending on different agricultural functions, the estimated returns are 22–55 percent for research, 8–49 percent for extension, and 11–22 percent for irrigation." Elsewhere, the report shows how subsidies have often had few benefits and caused many problems.

53 Total factor productivity – TFP – is the ratio of the outputs produced and the inputs (such as land, labour and capital) used. I did not use this term in this book because its measurement in developing countries is imprecise and problematic, but you'll come across it in many of the publications listed in this *further reading* section.

3

THE COMMONS

With Fiona Nunan

> ***Common property, commons, common lands, common goods, common resources and common-pool resources***
>
> *All these terms refer to natural and manmade goods that are (1) not in private or government ownership; (2) renewable, maintainable, or fixable if they are managed wisely; but often (3) sub-tractable in the short term, which means that I cannot consume it if you have already consumed it. This sub-tractability could pose a problem because common-pool resources are (4) non-excludable, which means that it is difficult or impossible to prevent people accessing them, should they choose to do so.*
>
> *A few examples include fishing grounds, forests, grazing lands, and water sources that are not in private or government ownership; communal irrigation systems or toilets; air quality.*

Prologue

When the fishing boats dock along the shores of East Africa's Lake Victoria, fish buyers rush to meet them and examine the catch. Sometimes fish is sold to the highest bidder. Sometimes, it is sold to the person who lent the boat owner money or paid for his fishing gear.

In these shoreline settlements, relationships are crucial. They help people get work, find somewhere to live, and cope with problems. Seniors teach youngsters how to catch, trade, transport, or process fish or how to service the boats. Crucially, they also teach them the norms and taboos, the do's and don'ts, the rights, the limitations, and the obligations that individual fishermen have in relation to this rich but ultimately limited resource – the lake and its fish. Without a common normative framework, and the compliance with the rules that come with it, the fishing grounds would soon lose their economic value because of overfishing, as many men and boys find the industry's 24-hour income cycle much more attractive than the longer cycles associated with agriculture. Lakes small and large are at risk, and even

FIGURE 3.1 Lake Antobo

An example of a customary system for the sustainable management of a common resource: Lake Antobo in Mali, just before the annual fishing frenzy starts. Photo: Matteo Bertolino.

the oceans aren't exempt: in 2015, a third of the world's marine fish stocks were being overfished.[1]

Ways in which fishing communities worldwide manage their fish stock are diverse. Customs and traditions often limit direct access to fishing grounds to men, which cuts the number of potential fisherfolk by half. Some fishing communities fish in seasonal cycles, do not fish in breeding grounds, use nets that only catch larger fish,[2] and return small fish back to the water in time for their survival. Lake Antobo in Mali provides a particularly vivid illustration of a 'common property regime' that combines a number of these rules. In this lake, men of the Dogon compete for fish, but only once a year, when the new generation of fish is alive but still too small to be caught, and when the removal of bigger fish gives the younger generation the space they need to grow. On the picture, you see the men waiting for the starting shot. They'll then rush into the lake for a ten-minute fishing frenzy, after which all but the smallest fish will have been caught.

Common property regimes, such as the one for Lake Antobo, have existed for a long time, and descriptions of some longstanding ones go back to at least the 13th century.[3] In recent times, two things have changed. First, such techniques were never stationary, but in today's volatile world, they are evolving faster than they were before. Second, the extent of the preservation challenge is new. The recent past has seen destruction at an unprecedented scale and speed, and many of the common goods are in grave danger or no longer exist at all (see Box 3.1).

BOX 3.1 A FEW QUOTATIONS ABOUT THE DESTRUCTION OF OUR NATURAL ENVIRONMENT

"Global deforestation continues at an alarming rate: 7 million hectares of forest are destroyed every year, an area roughly the size of Portugal" [UNEP (undated)].

">40%: amphibian species threatened with extinction. Almost 33%: reef forming corals, sharks and shark relatives, and >33% marine mammals threatened with extinction" [UN (2019)].

"Since 1993, the global *Red List Index* of threatened species [indicates] an alarming trend in the decline of mammals, birds, amphibians, corals and cycads. The primary drivers of this [decline] are habitat loss from unsustainable agriculture, deforestation, unsustainable harvest and trade and invasive alien species" [UN (2018)].

Sources: United Nations Environment Programme (undated) *Forests*, accessible from *unenvironment.org/explore-topics*, selecting the 'Forests' topic page, accessed on 10 October 2019. United Nations (2019) *UN Report: nature's dangerous decline 'unprecedented'; species extinction rates 'accelerating'*, 6 May 2019, online. United Nations (2018) *The sustainable development goals report 2018*, page 11, online.

The world is struggling to find ways to preserve these common goods. We are not doing a very good job yet, and for many common goods, we are still far from reaching a turning point where destruction stops and rejuvenation starts. But we are learning, and there are a few success stories. This chapter covers some of the options for the management of local common goods and takes a look at the future.

What are we talking about?

Many rural people in low-income countries rely on common goods for at least part of their income (see Box 3.2). People farm land that they do not legally own and graze livestock on common grassland. Mangrove forests and coral reefs provide breeding and nursery grounds for fish, crabs, shrimp and scallop, and forests provide fuel wood, timber, leaves, seeds and fruit. These are all *direct* benefits that people enjoy: they use the common goods as inputs for their farming activities and to gather products they may consume or sell.

BOX 3.2   A POOR HOUSEHOLD'S LIVELIHOOD

Ask rural people about their source of income, and the answer will be straightforward.
   I farm. I repair bicycles. I am a teacher.

Then ask this:
   Oh, OK. Thanks. What else?

Do so repeatedly, and wait patiently for the answers, as they often don't come right away. But they do in the end, and you'll find that people in poor rural households are likely to spread their bets.
   Sometimes my uncle sends us money. I also work on the cotton farm down the road. Sometimes I go fishing. I get fruits and mushrooms from the forest. I collect firewood and burn and sell charcoal. I hunt for bush rats. I dig for gold sand and quarry stones.
   Rural households use a range of common goods, and this use increases when times are hard. When the rains come late or an income disappears because of illness or a death in a family, the forest and river provide a safety net of sorts, and people turn to them for marketable products and consumption.

Common goods also bring *indirect* benefits, in the form of protection. Trees may break the wind or waves or prevent landslides by binding the soil.[4] You may only notice such benefits when they are no longer there. The massive tsunami of 2004 hit two small towns in Sri Lanka's southern lagoon. In one, a healthy mangrove forest shielded the town from the waves, and only two people died. In the other, there was no such protection, as local communities had cut down their mangrove forest. The waves submerged the town, and 5,000 people lost their lives.[5]

So what's the problem?

The wonderful thing about mangrove forests is that they are resilient. They have the capacity to grow new trees, and life within them is able to regenerate. This is a feature of common goods in general: over a period of time, they have the capacity to replenish themselves. They are *renewable*. But renewability is a long-term game. For species that mature and reproduce slowly, it may take decades, or even longer. In the shorter term, common goods are *subtractable*: if someone uses something, there will be less left for others. This subtractability is painfully obvious on a very large scale. Many of the world's mangrove forests have been destroyed, for example.[6] Even worse, people using too much of something sometimes leads to natural resources disappearing altogether and forever. The dodos? They're *gone*.

The often-expressed fear is for a vicious circle to occur:

- The subtractability principle means that consumption reduces the common resource, at least in the short term.
- This problem of subtractability is compounded by the problem of the *non-excludability* of common goods: people can take and eat or otherwise use them, even if this reduces the resource to dangerous levels.
- This reduction in the resource increases the competition among its users. They compete for ever-fewer trees to cut down, game to hunt, or fish to catch.
- This competition accelerates the decline of the resource, until it might reach the point of no return.
- Once the resource is no longer useful to its users, these users will move to another part of the commons. They will exhaust the resources on that part as well, and so forth.

This fear of a vicious circle, in which all commons eventually decline and all their users face poverty, was given a theoretical underpinning in 1968, when a biology professor named Garrett Hardin wrote a six-page essay titled the "Tragedy of the Commons".[7] He argued that this combination of subtractability and non-excludability *inevitably* causes common goods to deteriorate. He used the example of herders who graze their livestock on a piece of common land. Each herder wants to benefit to the greatest extent possible, and every additional cow he[8] brings to the commons adds to his benefits in the short term. In the long term, this behaviour leads to degraded, overgrazed land, and all those using it eventually have to reduce the number of cattle to avoid their starvation. So, the availability of common land led to its deterioration, causing short-term gains but long-term losses. Hardin concluded that this process could not be stopped as long as the commons remained

Sometimes, human behaviour causes irreversible harm

THE SOLE REMAINING DODO MAY HAVE PERFORMED HIS MATING SONG FOR 25 YEARS, WITH NO FEMALE LEFT TO HEAR IT

FIGURE 3.2 The sole remaining dodo

accessible to all, and he advised that such lands are privatised or brought within state control.

Privatisation, nationalisation, and common property management

Hardin's notion that common goods will be damaged beyond repair or eaten to extinction added credibility to the process of privatisation and nationalisation of common goods that had long been part of colonialism's approach. In North America, large swathes of previously common land were registered as the property of colonists, and as soon as somebody invented barbed wire that could be mass-produced (which Joseph Glidden did in 1874), these now-private lands were rapidly fenced off. In Kenya, large plots were expropriated from Maasai and other communities and allocated to colonists. The colonial power in Kenya also used a 'fences and fines' approach to park management, which meant that local people were fenced out of government-claimed national parks. People were no longer allowed to graze their livestock on land that had been communally owned for as long as their collective memory stretched, and they were fined and imprisoned if they violated the new rules.[9] By 2017, some 73% of forests worldwide were government owned; the rest were roughly equally divided between local community and private ownership.[10]

Hardin ignored two major drawbacks of privatisation and nationalisation. First, fencing off commons with whichever legal justification means that communities suffer the loss of their livelihoods, or chunks thereof. Second, the privatisation and nationalisation of forests and other common lands do not necessarily, or even usually, preserve them. Instead, natural resources often suffer roughly equally from medium- and large-scale activities (which typically take place on privately owned land and under government concessions)[11] and from small-scale activities (which are typically households overusing the commons). Much of the rainforest that has been cut down over the last few decades was under government control – and concessions to logging, mining, and agricultural companies have filled government coffers and lined the pockets of corrupt civil servants and their leaders. It's the same with private property: the tropical world is full of large stretches of former rainforest that private owners have turned into commercial farmlands.[12]

Thankfully, Hardin was wrong: the deterioration of common lands is *not* inevitable. His underpinning assumption was that individuals operate in isolation – but this is not actually true.[13] Instead, people talk to each other and collaborate, agreeing on and enforcing rules that maintain the health of the common resources their livelihoods depend on.

The late Elinor Ostrom researched the management of common goods in a range of countries; many of today's researchers still build on the foundations she laid. In 1990, she concluded that there are eight 'design principles' that must hold to ensure the commons' sustainability.[14] This is part of 'common property theory', which is the main counter-theory to Hardin's. The principles are as follows:

1   The commons have clear boundaries.
2   Rules governing the management of the commons can take very different forms, which is fine as long as they're appropriate to the context.
3   The effects of these rules are monitored.
4   There are sanctions that increase if non-compliance is more serious or keeps occurring.
5   There are arrangements in place about the way the system will work. This includes clarity on entitlements of different groups and individuals.
6   There are agreed-upon mechanisms in case conflicts occur.
7   The users see the system as legitimate, and they therefore respect the system and rules.
8   There is a multi-layered system with connections between structures and rules in cases where the commons are large.

There is a ninth principle that Ostrom considered so fundamental that she didn't list it:

9   All effective management approaches involve the users of the commons in the management of these commons and in the decision-making about both the entitlements of various people and groups, and the sanctions that are imposed when rules are broken.

These principles are relevant to a range of management systems, developed world-wide for commonly owned forests, fisheries, grazing lands, and other natural resources. We will discuss two broad types: 'customary systems' and 'community-based natural resource management systems'. Both tend to have flaws, and the result-ant use of the common goods is rarely truly inclusive as well as truly sustainable. Still, there are lessons to be learned from the trials, errors, and modest successes of the past.

Customary systems: an ancient type of system that is full of flaws but can be learned from

Customary systems are steeped in history. They are *socially embedded institutions* (as opposed to *bureaucratic institutions* that are formalized in writing and 'official' in the eyes of government). Customary systems consist of structures, rules, values, beliefs, and everyday practice that groups of people have developed and live by, often for many years already. Part of the customary systems is directly related to the manage-ment of common resources – such as the rule not to catch small fish. Wider expecta-tions regarding the appropriate behaviour of women and men and the roles different groups should play are important as well. If 'killing' is something exclusively associated with adult men, then, by implication, women and children won't add to the hunting pressure.

That annual fishing festival in Mali's Lake Antobo (see pages 76-8) is a good exam-ple of a customary system that has ensured the sustainable use of a common resource – in this case a fishing ground – for a long time. Many pastoralist communities still have customary systems as well. Such systems reflect knowledge about grazing land, water sources, and their status throughout the annual cycle, and about corridors through which livestock can be herded. People pass on norms and rules about care of livestock and use of land from one generation to the next, and this prevents overgrazing of pastureland and maintains practices that make the most of available water.

Customary systems may have existed for centuries, but they evolve over time. They evolve because of changes in the physical environment, such as shifts in animal migration patterns or conversions of grazing lands into farmland or highways that cut through forests. They also change when other systems of governance come up and encroach upon their operating space – such as colonial rule and local and national governments.

In the 21st century, very few customary systems still operate on their own. Instead, most rural people in developing countries now live in a context of 'legal pluralism', where a system of customary law – with rights, rules, and justice systems – exists alongside a local or national government system. This can be complex and confusing. First, it needs awareness of multiple sets of rules. People who want to graze their cattle need to be aware of the government policy on the lands they can and cannot move through to reach the grazing land; the community rules on how many livestock they can graze in a certain area; and the government and community rules about the conditions under which they can use water sources. Second, the systems overlap. As both are potentially authoritative, this is troublesome but may provide opportunities too, as people can choose the system that seems to be better-functioning, cheaper, faster, or friendlier. You might go to the customary system to resolve a land dispute and to the state system for an issue related to inheritance (albeit in both cases with the risk that the other system interferes).

Within this pluralism, the power and authority of many customary systems are declining. In part, this is the consequence of the deliberate action of governments that want more control over communities, land and other natural resources. In Ethiopia, for example, pastoralist communities were encouraged to settle down, and the powers of customary authority over land and water eroded after the introduction of government-initiated village committees. It's also an image thing: pastoralists all over the world are portrayed as being 'backward' and responsible for overgrazing and the desertification of land. Their customary systems will gradually lose their appeal and authority if you say this often enough and combine it with the establishment of alternative systems, competing committees and suchlike.

Where this happens, the last and most persistent features of customary systems are their norms and taboos. Long after a government has taken over, these norms and taboos determine what is and what is not possible. Their link with sustainable management may not be obvious, as good practice is often swaddled in myths, local deities, and notions of bad luck. 'Do not fish there or you'll upset the spirits.' 'Do not enter that part of the forest, or you'll disturb our ancestors.' Taboos often limit access to common goods by excluding certain groups. It brings bad luck if women fish on Lake Victoria or even just board a fishing boat prior to a fishing expedition. Boys are only ready to hunt after they've gone through puberty. Some tribes traditionally have cattle – but other tribes do not and it would upset local norms if they tried.

All in all, it's a mixed picture. On the one hand, customary systems are on the losing side of history. In today's terms, they're also often deeply sexist, ageist, and discriminatory in many other ways. They are not always peaceful either, and some include elements of perpetual conflict. Pastoralist communities of the Karimojong in Uganda traditionally expect young men to prove themselves through raiding cattle from other communities, for example. And they cannot always cope with forceful new developments. In the Solomon Islands, the customary justice system was overwhelmed by the new phenomenon of widespread drug abuse amongst youngsters. In Afghanistan, the local systems could not cope with the arrival of new strongmen who had no standing in the community but were obviously powerful.

On the other hand, there is much to learn from customary systems. In recent history, the world has violated all the ground rules of such systems in the ruthless exploitation of our living planet. This contributed to incredible human progress, but it put other life at risk – and has, in many cases, killed it. To avert catastrophes, the way we engage with our living planet must change, and some serious lessons can be learned from the world's past and remaining customary systems. What, for example, enabled pastoralists to adapt to changing conditions, including drought, for so long? And what of this might still be relevant and could possibly even be a matter of life and death for communities, and for animal and plant life in the commons?

Sometimes, such lessons are already being learned. The ways customary systems resolve conflict, for example, have informed local peacebuilding and forgiveness processes after the Rwandan genocide and many other conflicts. Such processes are often more appropriate, effective, and affordable than the formal justice systems – with the costly and drawn-out processes of the International Criminal Tribunal for Rwanda serving as the world's most vivid illustration of the formal systems' failure to play a timely reconciliatory role in the aftermath of conflicts.

Community-based natural resource management: a newer type of system that is also far from perfect

By the 1980s, there was strong evidence that nationalisation and privatisation had not stopped processes of decline – and had indeed often accelerated them. It had also become increasingly clear that the nationalisation and privatisation of common lands and goods caused great harm to the communities using them. Many of the customary systems for the commons that remained were seen as backward and sexist, and they were losing their authority for the reasons just discussed. The world needed something new.

This was also the era of 'participatory approaches', which asserted that efforts to improve poor communities' lives and livelihoods required their active involvement. Participatory approaches would lead to sensible and locally appropriate plans and to a sense of ownership that would increase the chance of them being realised. The approach enthused many donors and organisations and led to experiments with 'community-based natural resource management', which we will, incorrectly but conveniently, simply call 'community management' (see the *further reading* section for other terms used for broadly the same thing).

The aims of the community management of common resources are threefold: first, to ensure that common resources are conserved, by avoiding usage beyond immediate renewability; second, to improve the livelihoods of those who use them; and third, to cut government costs – another very popular theme in the 1980s – by transferring part of the responsibilities from government to communities. Because of the use of participatory approaches, there would be a widespread sense of ownership of and support for these aims, and this would enhance compliance with the rules that regulate usage.

The idea caught on, and there are many community-based management systems today. Some of them work reasonably well. The 'community conservancies' in Namibia are a good example (see Box 3.3).

BOX 3.3 NAMIBIA'S COMMUNITY CONSERVANCIES

Namibia's community conservancies were formed in the late 1990s, in response to local people's demands for more access to the riches offered by Namibia's natural environment. They follow Ostrom's design principles, such as clear boundaries and agreement on how income is distributed. They are meant to recognise and formalise local people's roles in wildlife management, and to ensure that they benefit from the conservation effort.

By 2017, there were 83 conservancies, covering lands on which over 200,000 people were living. Each conservancy has a game management plan that includes the local communities' hunting rights and a compliance monitoring system. Income generated by tourism goes to the conservancies, and elected committees decide how it is used.

The system did indeed strengthen the protection of common resources and is generally seen as one of the most successful community management systems in the world. This is a sobering qualification, as the system is far from perfect. Specifically,

- After 20 years, most conservancies are still not financially viable and continue to depend on donor and government support.
- The system is vulnerable to 'elite capture', which means that people in privileged positions use the conservancies to pursue their individual interests.
- The community game hunting entitlements had to be reduced in 2017, following several years of drought, and this showed the system's fragility, as the reduction was not supported by all and led to friction.

There are quite a few examples of reasonable success, but failures are also common. There are two reasons for this.

First, community management systems operate in an imperfect world. The management of commons requires trust, for example, but people often have good reason *not* to trust each other. Research on fisheries in Lake Victoria, Benin, and Costa Rica all found that mistrust reinforced non-compliance, and non-compliance reinforced mistrust. After all, why would I stick to the rules if you don't? Similarly, governments and international donors lose their enthusiasm for the community-based management of forests when they find that illegal loggers are using community paperwork to make their timber look legal.[15]

Second, the development and operations of community management systems have been affected by the origins of these systems, which have often been short-term, donor-driven, project-shaped initiatives, designed and implemented with only fleeting participation of unrepresentative segments of communities. Systems have been developed and implemented under the watchful eyes of government authorities who are reluctant to give up power and politicians who may support or break these systems, depending on their interests. Let's take a look at each of these shortcomings.

1 of 6: these community-based management systems are often pushed by donors – and the push is full of flaws

A few years ago, I evaluated the results of a programme that, in part, focused on community-based forest management in West Africa. It was implemented by a consortium of organisations, and financed by the European Union and the British DFID. The terms of reference of this evaluation required me to visit a range of countries, but there were no plans for me to leave their capitals. This meant I assessed the results of community-based forestry management without ever being close to any such community or setting foot in a forest. Instead, I based my findings (and I hang my head in shame and promise I won't do this again) almost exclusively on interviews with a limited range of stakeholders, including 'community representatives', during forums and training events in fancy hotels. In my report, I wrote the following:

- The forums are led by a British company. They are part of a project that is funded by two European donors and led by a British university.
- The proportion of Europeans on the podium far exceeds the proportion of Europeans in the audience. This might make sense from the point of view of international sharing but does not create a sense of African ownership.
- The prominence of the European involvement is reinforced in other ways. In Cameroon, four of the five logos on the paperwork were of European organisations, and the logos on the distributed USB stick were of the European donors. The EU placed its own large banner on the podium, and the forum's

first speech was of the British university's Project Director rather than, say, a community representative.

This illustrated two problems that many community-based management systems have to deal with:

- Donors push for them, and talk a lot about community engagement and ownership, but don't lead by example. Instead, much of their money goes to organisations that are headquartered in the donors' home countries and to workshops in big cities, where the donor branding is prominently visible. This is generally not a choice made by the implementing organisations but a contractual obligation imposed by the donor. The participants are people who speak English or French and who generally receive a financial incentive for their participation.
- Such projects operate in the heroic assumption that insights shared and discussed at such events naturally trickle down to, and are then utilised by, actual communities. There is little evidence that this is happening. (See Box 3.4 for an extreme example of the common disconnect between event participants and local communities.)

BOX 3.4 LOTS OF TRAINING, LITTLE CHANGE

A Liberian organisation specialising in community-based forestry management is based in Monrovia, Liberia's capital city. I visited the organisation as part of an evaluation of a sustainable forestry training programme.

The people in this small organisation had received an astonishing amount of training in the UK, Australia, Nigeria, Kenya, and locally. All very useful, they said – especially the stuff abroad. There was lots of learning, and there were now lots of plans to use it to promote and improve the community-based management of Liberia's remaining forests.

I was keen to learn about the organisation's recent achievements with such communities, preferably with a link to all that learning. I asked for this in different ways, for over half an hour or so, until it eventually dawned on me that there *were* no achievements, as they had not left Monrovia for over a year (other than for training abroad). This was because "our only vehicle broke down last year, and we don't have the money to fix it". This organisation was a group of people in an office in the country's capital, pretty much earning a living by getting trained all over the globe.

This was an extreme example of a common problem: donor-funded training is often not actually useful because the participants work for organisations

that lack most elements of 'organisational capacity' – such as clear plans, processes and policies and the money to operationalise them, a strategy, relations
with other stakeholders, or, in this particular case, even just the ability to leave
the city.

Such training programmes are a waste of money, but their evaluations are
often positive. This is because the programmes are typically assessed against
learning (so *potential* usefulness) and action plans (so *intentions* to do useful
things) rather than against the results of actual action. The feeble excuse for
this is timing: 'we use learning and action plans as proxy indicators for usefulness, because most of the results will be achieved after this programme has
come to an end.'

2 of 6: donors tend to fund projects rather than ongoing efforts, and this places the work outside the core operations of governments and community groups

The work is *additional*: it is something you do for the duration of the project.
Generally, there is a superficial pretence of 'sustainability' – a claim that project
stakeholders repeat without actually believing it. This pretence is generally part
of the initial project documentation, in a section titled something like 'sustainability' or 'exit plan', which explains that, somehow, miraculously, the government or organisation will be able to absorb whatever the project did or achieved
into its core work, not right away but when the project comes to an end, using
money generated through some sort of unlikely revenue-creation mechanism.
Here is a representative example of what such 'plans' look like (and I've not corrected the English to illustrate another drawback of donor-led projects, which
is the need for community organisations to communicate in a language that is
not their first):

> ***Exit plan:*** As the project will link the DDP with government service pro-
> vider department to support the DDP so that they can stand on their own
> strength. With the support of local government and service provider bodies
> and agencies a workshop will be arranged and detail plan will be place there
> how future this DDP will rum (<u>sic</u>).[16]

These exit plans almost never actually work. Instead, in most cases, the project is
extended or followed by a successor project, or terminated. When the latter happens,
the organisation or government agency looks for alternative sources of finance. If
this does not work out, then slowly, or not so very slowly, the lights go out.

3 of 6: because of this 'projectification', interventions are generally short-term, pretending to achieve something they cannot realistically deliver

Just imagine the challenges. After a long period in which communities gradually lost control over their common lands and goods, they are suddenly back in the picture. But they need to work with the local government. And the donor says that gender equality is crucial – though the notion is alien to many cultures. And there's a need for financial reports. Rules need to be formalised and written down (often in a language people do not understand), and there must be formal monitoring processes and reports. People must feel true ownership of all this.

None of this is impossible, but turning it into a new everyday reality takes a *long* time – and projects don't have that long. Formally, they typically have a three- to five-year time line. This is far too short to achieve meaningful change of the nature required and, in reality, the period is often shorter still, because of initial delays and the time it takes to get community committees ready for community management to actually begin.

4 of 6: genuine community participation is really, really hard to achieve; fleeting consultations and elite capture are common

When have you 'engaged' enough? How do you get to know and meet the concerns, desires, expectations, needs and rights of different stakeholders? How do you make sure you maintain genuine engagement during the establishment, implementation, and review of projects? How do you assess and seize the opportunities they might see? To what extent do you need to be accountable to communities (and to whom, in these communities), in the sense that *your* action is subject to *their* scrutiny and approval? How do you handle people's complaints, conflicts among stakeholders, issues of non-compliance to the rules set in order to ensure the sustainability of the commons? How do you ensure that all men and women (and perhaps children) are able to engage – *also* if they are living with disabilities, are illiterate and belong to ethnic and other minority groups that are often ignored? In the world of participatory approaches, there are many shades of grey. It is possible to go too far: I recall an organisation being chased out of an Indonesian village when, after a year of endlessly inclusive engagement, no actual work had been done. This is rare, though, and the more common scenario is that the engagement occurs at certain points in the project life cycle rather than continuously, and is more focused on providing information than on deeper forms of engagement.

Even project implementers who make a concerted effort to ensure meaningful community engagement throughout the project cycle might not be successful, as they are at risk of unwittingly engaging with only a few unrepresentative members of the community. After all, communities are very diverse. They consist of individuals and households that have interests, objectives, types of livelihoods, and levels of power that are wide apart.

FIGURE 3.3 John is visiting Fragilistan for a bit of community engagement

In a 1983 book titled *Rural Development*,[17] Robert Chambers, the trailblazer for and beacon of participatory development approaches, presented a simple table that looked a little like Table 3.1:

TABLE 3.1 Where development professionals *should* go, and where they *actually* go

Where they should *go*	*Where they* actually *go*
Rural	Urban
Modest	Prestigious
Homes	Offices
Side streets	Main streets
'Normal' children, women, and men	Leaders and 'representatives'
Wet season	Dry season
In 'remote' areas	In or close to capital

Development professionals believe that the left-hand column is very important in theory but focus on the right-hand column in practice. I recognise this in my own work as an evaluator. In principle, I really want to know more about, and learn from, the illiterate disabled rural girl who dropped out of school. In reality, I don't have time to travel to her village and wouldn't know how to find her once I got there. Even if I did have time to make the trip, the rains will have left the roads inaccessible or a security officer won't allow me to travel because of security issues. So I settle and meet with a few vaguely relevant people I can get easy access to (see Box 3.5). So do other development practitioners, and the result is that their engagement with 'communities' is often really an engagement with their generally male-dominated multilingual elite. In the worst case, such flawed participatory approaches reinforce gender disparities and leave marginalised groups of people even worse off.[18]

BOX 3.5 'REPRESENTATIVE MEMBERS OF THE COMMUNITY' IN CENTRAL MALI

In 2017, I reviewed a few community-based projects in Mali. Much of the work was done in the rural central and northern parts of the country. I couldn't go there, said the donor's security officer, as these regions were unsafe and foreigners like me were specifically targeted.

So we negotiated, and the compromise was that I would meet a group of 'representative members of the community' in a safe riverside hotel in the centre of Mali, to which I travelled in a convoy of three armoured vehicles. Upon arrival, the security officer checked the hotel while I remained in my bulletproof safe zone, from where I saw a foreign woman getting out of the river.

Dressed in a towel, she casually walked along the hotel walls and disappeared through its gate. Maybe it wasn't *that* unsafe around here.

After forever, I was let into a meeting room where I met with six people, with whom I talked for a few hours. They were helpful and knowledgeable about these projects and indeed about every other project implemented in that region.

The reason they were so knowledgeable was that this little group of 'representative community members' consisted of a locally prominent woman, her son, her nephew, his wife, her sister, and the mayor of one of the larger villages. They all played key roles in all aid projects in the region.

There are two things to learn. First, 'community participation' is at risk of 'elite capture': a small group of powerful people who monopolise aid flows and decision-making. Second, my armoured convoy and the bathing foreigner illustrate that donors are very, *very* risk averse when it comes to the safety of their staff and associates. An implication of this overly cautious behaviour is that donors often don't really know what's going on.

5 of 6: governments don't like giving up power

Community committees, or whatever name these groups adopt (or, more likely, are given) will always have to work with some sort of government counterpart – such as the district forest officer, the district environment office, the district planner, or a local branch of a central authority. In some cases, there is genuine power sharing between such authorities and the community groups. Nepal provides a good example: in very visible 'handover' processes, government authorities transferred extensive rights to local 'Forest User Groups', to both manage and use large chunks of forest.

There are a few such countries (check Google Scholar for case studies on Madagascar, Mexico, and Tanzania, for example) – but they are exceptions. The more general pattern is that government authorities are not enthusiastic about sharing power. Sharing power on issues that involve money – such as issuing licences and collecting fees – is particularly unattractive, and the police and security forces often feel strong attachment to their monopoly on the enforcement of rules. Governments, therefore, often only transfer the poor, degraded, and smaller forests to community groups. Or they opt for something called 'collaborative forms of management', rather than a community-based approach. Collaborative management helps governments that are unable to effectively manage common resources by themselves (as they lack money, sufficient local presence, or equipment), and it has a degree of power-sharing in name, but the government maintains its power to set rules, allocate licences, and punish those who don't stay within whatever limits the government has set to the various user groups.

6 of 6: politicians can be helpful or obstructive

Politicians can support initiatives through legislation, budgeting, and negotiations with donors. They also pose challenges, as they might turn a blind eye to illegalities so that members of their constituency vote for them again. Their obstruction is sometimes quite pro-active, with local councillors stopping government officers from carrying out enforcement in forests and fisheries and getting people released from custody.

That is disappointing, no?

Well, there is certainly no easy way forward. There's a lot to learn from customary systems, but they won't regain their past position. And as long as community-based resource management systems are driven by short-term foreign-funded projects that struggle to engage meaningfully with truly representative members of communities, these trials will often fail. At the same time, *without* foreign donors, there would have been little money to test this community-based model at all because, at least until now, local and national governments have often been more inclined to milk common resources than to invest in their sustainable management.

All in all, community-based approaches to the management of the commons will not stop their process of deterioration unless the next generation of donor and government decision-makers creates more truly empowering, long-term conditions for such approaches to succeed. It is now clear that this needs more than 'just' meeting the principles that Ostrom formulated in 1990 – credible as they still are. Research and practical experience built up since then suggest that the following list more fully reflects the conditions that must be met for commons to stand a chance.[19]

- The commons have clear boundaries, and if they are large, they have nested structures, with easy-to-manage local-level groups as the foundation.
- Local forest users are adequately identified – *so not just the elite!* – and meaningfully involved in forestry planning, management, and review.
- Resource users trust each other, and they more or less trust the other stakeholders as well. This is crucial because suspected non-compliance is likely to lead to (more) non-compliance.
- There are clear, negotiated and widely agreed-upon rules on forest aims, use, replanting, and other responsibilities, rights, costs and benefits sharing, dispute settlement, and sanctions. There is some sort of reciprocity in the system: I get this or do this for you; you get that or do that for me.
- Rules are widely publicised, using methods that also reach illiterate people and other groups that are often overlooked. They are confirmed in a formal legal transfer of authority from government to community groups. The government sticks to its word.

- Dispute settlements are accessible, swift, and cheap, and sanctions increase in case non-compliance is serious or keeps occurring.
- Community committees (or whatever they are called) have clear internal governance rules that ensure that there is no capture of resources by elites. This is tough, and the threat is continuous. Transparency of rules and the decision-making that resulted in these rules reduce this risk of elite capture.
- The results of the management systems are monitored, and the monitoring findings are available to all stakeholders (and people *know* this). Regular, widely accessible meetings take place to review the activities, results, and plans of the forest users themselves and the committees that represent them. As such meetings quickly deteriorate into platforms where elites share their insights (which must be avoided), they need to be very carefully designed and pro-actively managed (and the obvious question then is *by whom?*).
- Technical support is available. Community knowledge can be mightily insightful but communities may have not seen much of the rest of the world. Without access to knowledge about what good and really bad practice look like, communities are at risk of making serious and entirely avoidable mistakes.
- Donor-driven, project-shaped, short-term initiatives are unlikely to lead to community-based management systems that adhere to these conditions.

Future experience will no doubt add to this list but probably won't take anything out of it.

Why is all this relevant, and what does it mean for you?

The commons are crying for help. Some years are worse than others (and 2019 was a *particularly* bad one for wildfires, in Brazil and elsewhere), but *every* year, the commons in the world shrink a little, and many of the remaining ones deteriorate. This affects people's cultures and livelihoods, strips away layers of natural protection, reduces biodiversity and tourism appeal, and accelerates climate change.

It seems clear that the users of these commons *must* have a role in their sustainable management – but it is not yet clear how this could best be done, and there are still far too few stories of common resources being successfully and sustainably maintained. We have a list of conditions, or 'principles' as Ostrom called them, and this list is evolving on the basis of cumulative experience. But it's obviously not yet good enough.

So if you work in this field, don't just replicate what you've seen elsewhere, but build upon what worked well, and then innovate a little. If you do so successfully, please publish a paper or find another way to share the insights you gained and help refine the evolving list of good practice principles. Also, please think creatively about ways to reduce governmental reluctance to give up power, donor reluctance to move beyond projects, and the reluctance of politicians to think long-term and their inclination to make exceptions for their respective voter groups. Think of ways to reduce elite capture and of ways to increase opportunities for 'captured elites', where social relationships and expectations drive leaders to instigate or support collective action driven by collective interests.

If you are active in a community committee, then you probably won't read this book but just in case you do,

- Try to make decisions and decision-making processes as transparent as possible, as this reduces the risk of elite capture. If you are 'elite' yourself, and you have it in you, redistribute the power within the committee and community.
- Consider technical advice, so that you don't reinvent the wheel and can avoid an unnecessary repetition of mistakes.
- Once equipped with both localised knowledge and insights gained from elsewhere, hold your ground, in relation to your engagement with government and donors. Ultimately, they need you just as you need them, and negotiating with the one who holds the purse strings really *is* an option.

If you work for a government and on the issue of your country's remaining common lands and resources,

- Do not assume that Hardin's 'tragedy of the commons' is inevitable, and resist the temptation and ongoing corporate pressure[20] to nationalise and privatise the remaining common lands. This includes the privatisation of 'minor forest products' in otherwise common forests, which is really just a sneaky version of wholesale privatisation.[21]
- If you can, take the risk of a transfer of power to user communities – *if* the plans seem truly sound, support seems truly widespread, and the other conditions are or can be fulfilled. If this is not yet the case, try to work towards the point where it *is* the case. This needs courage, but you are not alone and would contribute to a trend that is already happening: between 2002 and 2017, forests owned by local communities increased from 10 to 13% of the total.[22]
- If you feel able to pursue such a transfer of power, make sure to turn agreements into formal legal rights. There are many cases where companies could turn community forests into palm oil plantations because the community's legal rights were not sufficiently clear.[23]

If you work for a donor,

- Please do what you can to move away from short-term project cycles. If this is impossible, try to design your projects as part of a longer project chain, where projects are several years each and follow on from each other so that, say, three sequential projects span a total period of 15 years. If this is what you're going for, do what you can to avoid time gaps between your projects. I say this with some frustration as I looked at many project chains in a recent review of DFID's work with civil society organisations and found that there were very nearly *always* gaps between projects. These gaps often exceeded a year, and they caused a significant loss of previous gains.[24]

- Some of your work is likely to be in 'capacity building'. If so, don't assume that training solves the current capacity deficit in this field. To fulfil their mandates, governments, community organisations and advocacy groups need policies, processes, systems, relationships and a sense of direction, as well as predictable, reliable, and timely sources of money. (And yes, sometimes an organisation's staff lacks skills and competencies, in which case a training course might be useful.) If you do finance training, make sure it is evaluated appropriately. This means that you don't just assess skills and plans but also what *actual* change this training has contributed to. As change takes time, this means that training programmes require (but almost never yet get) *ex post* evaluations: evaluations that take place a few years after the training has ended.

For all involved in the management of common lands and resources,

- While the overall track record in the management of common resources is poor and innovation is needed, you should also keep in mind that 40 years of experience with community-based forestry have shown that "in general, the knowledge needed to improve outcomes for forests and people is available. What is missing in most cases is a 'level playing field' and the political will to make it happen."[25] This applies to other types of commons as well.
- Practice what you preach. Take community engagement seriously, and make sure that you carefully identify all relevant stakeholders, and that marginalised groups really *do* have a voice. Too many token minority representatives have sat in meetings in silence.
- Learn from customary systems. They are often ignored or presented as backward and yesteryear's solutions, but they may be more appropriate, socially and ecologically, than more recent systems, and they often reflect knowledge that was gained in the course of centuries. That said, don't be dewy-eyed about them, as they are not just on the losing end of history; they also often *are* backward and *do* present yesteryear's solutions. They invariably discriminate on the basis of gender, age, and other features that differentiate people into groups with very different levels of power, and their solutions sometimes include an element of violence.
- Consider the 'multiplier threat' of climate change (see Chapter 9). It adds complexity and urgency to everything related to the commons. Even if the customary system that still maintains the fish stock in Mali's Lake Antobo continues to work flawlessly, there won't be any fish left if the lake dries up because of global warming.

Further reading

For recent research

Check the last few issues of the biannual, open-source *International Journal of the Commons*. Not yet published at the time of writing but probably also interesting: the

Journal of Business Ethics has announced a special issue on "The ethics of the commons", which will have been published by the time you read this.

If this chapter was a downer and you need some good news stories

The reports, country case studies, and videos of the 'knowledge resources' section of the UN's Poverty-Environment Initiative are about ways in which poverty reduction and environment protection and restoration could go hand in hand.

About the state of and trends in global natural resources

Choose a type of common resource, and a 30-second web search will get you recent reports on global and regional trends for that particular resource. For example,

- For fisheries and suchlike, check FAO (2018) *The state of the world fisheries and aquaculture; meeting the sustainable development goals*, online.
- For forests, your best bet is FAO again: check FAO (2018) *The state of the world's forests*, online. Competitor organisations such as CIFOR also have good reports on forests and agroforestry, but these tend to combine text on the bigger picture with a lot of talk about their own work.
- For mangrove forests in particular, check Bochove, J.W. van, Sullivan, E. and Nakamura, T., editors (2014) *The importance of mangroves to people: a call to action*, UNEP, online.

As always, be aware of the nature of the agencies that write such reports: they employ the world's finest experts, but UN organisations are *not* independent research bodies, and they have political agendas that may colour what they write. Alternatively, but generally a bit harder to read, you could go to more academic publications. Measurements of trends in deforestation and their causes are particularly sophisticated because of the power of detailed satellite imagery. Recent findings are reported in

- Austin, K.G. et al. (2017) "Trends in size of tropical deforestation events signal increasing dominance of industrial-scale drivers" *Environmental Research Letters*, volume 12, number 5, online.
- Curtis, P.G. et al. (2018) "Classifying drivers of global forest loss" *Science*, volume 361, issue 6407, pages 1108–1111, online.
- Dang, D.K.D. (2019) "An analysis of the spatial association between deforestation and agricultural field sizes in the tropics and subtropics", *PLoS One*, volume 14, issue 1, online.

Different publications come to different conclusions, but they share a key one: notwithstanding all the international declarations and good intentions, deforestation continues, at speed.

For insight into the role of common lands and resources in the lives and livelihoods of poor rural people

Again, the *International Journal of the Commons* reports on research efforts from around the world, which focus on a wide range of common lands and goods and often zoom in on the livelihoods of user groups. Or for a powerful bedtime read, take Kizito, A. et al. (2012) *Strength, creativity and livelihoods of Karimojong youth*, Restless Development Uganda and the Institute of Development Studies, online. This is an unusual and energising piece of action research, conducted by people from the Karamoja region in northern Uganda. Some of the researchers have a university degree, some are illiterate; together, they have produced a text that conveys deep messages in the most casual of styles. It also covers the cattle raids mentioned in this chapter.

About the indirect benefits of the commons

Common goods and resources offer various types of protection – benefits you often only notice when things go wrong after the resources have been damaged. The annual publications that cover the state of particular kinds of commons (discussed earlier) cover the protective roles of these commons as well, as part of their explanation as to why their deterioration is a bad thing. For example, for more about the way mangrove forests protect against hurricanes and tsunamis, see pages 52–58 of the aforementioned mangrove publication: Bochove, J.W. van, Sullivan, E. and Nakamura, T., editors (2014) *The importance of mangroves to people: a call to action*, UNEP, online.

Frameworks that help the understanding of relationships between people and the environment

For an overview of often-used frameworks in 'common-pool resources' and 'ecosystem services' research,[26] with plenty of examples and an exploration of a number of cross-cutting issues such as power, property regimes and social capital, read Nunan, F. (2015) *Understanding poverty and the environment*, Routledge.

About the 'tragedy of the commons' and the subsequent discourse

The foundational paper arguing that the 'tragedy of the commons' is inevitable is Hardin, G. (December 1968) "The tragedy of the commons", *Science*, volume 162, pages 1243–1248 (and see Box 3.6 on how to progress from there).

The foundational paper arguing against this and proposing 'principles' that community management of common resources need to adhere to is Ostrom, E. (1990) *Governing the commons: the evolution of institutions for collective action*, Cambridge University Press. If you search for "ending the tragedy of the commons" on YouTube,

---

BOX 3.6   REFINING A SEARCH FOR PAPERS, STARTING WITH A SEMINAL PAPER

If you use Google Scholar: click on the 'Cited by. . .' button underneath the link to an important book or paper, and you get all the publications referencing it. You can then click 'search within citing articles' for a more limited search on the basis of key words that you are particularly interested in or by limiting the year of publication. This way, you quickly get an idea of the way recent research has evolved, since that milestone publication.

---

you could hear the late Elinor Ostrom cover a few key issues, in just a few minutes, only a few months before she passed away. You could also search for the 'social-ecological systems' (SES) framework, as this is where Ostrom's principles continue to be refined.

Customary systems

Search for "customary systems" and commons, and you'll find lots. Understandably, most recent publications that cover customary systems discuss their deterioration, or their survival within a context of legal pluralism. To give but two interesting examples,

On legal pluralism: Benjamin, C.E. (2008) "Legal pluralism and decentralization: natural resource management in Mali", *World Development*, volume 36, issue 11, pages 2255–2276. This paper looks at the way three Malian customary systems (called 'community institutions', in this publication) have developed very different ways of interacting with formal government institutions.

Brocklesby, M.A., Hobley, M. and Scott-Villiers, P. (2009) *Raising voice – securing a livelihood*, Pastoralist Communication Initiative, online (choose the version with the many pictures, which enliven the text). This is a very readable publication that (1) describes elements of a few customary systems (*busaa gonofaa, dagu,* and *gadaa*); (2) shows how location, gender, age, and status amplify or mute the voices of different types of community members; (3) shows the way systems that are meant to provide support, settle disputes, and dispense justice are in fact sometimes reinforcing the discrimination suffered by poorer and marginalised groups within pastoralist communities; and (4) explores how government influence is on the rise and how the pastoralists feel that the systems for land use and pasture and water management are "no longer as effective as [they were] in the past".

Participatory approaches

The champion of careful, simple, but sophisticated participatory development is Robert Chambers, who wrote 1983's *Rural development: putting the last first*, Longman (now Pearson Education). For a warning issued after participatory approaches turned out to be far more difficult and risky than originally assumed, see Cooke, B. and Kothari U., editors (2001) *Participation: The New Tyranny?*, Zed Books. Follow the steps listed in Box 3.6 to explore how the discourse evolved since these two seminal works were published.

Community-based natural resource management

When searching for 'community-based natural resource management' (which is often simply referred to as 'community management' in this chapter), also search for 'CBNRM', 'community-based conservation', 'community forest management', and 'community-based fisheries management'.

For an overview of the results of 40 years of community-based forestry, see Gilmour, D. (2016) "Forty years of community-based forestry; a review of its extent and effectiveness", *FAO Forestry Paper number 176*, FAO, online.

For research on the way and extent to which the participation of women, as well as of different age groups, castes, and classes in forest user community groups shape forest management and the products the rules focus on, see Agarwal, B. (2010) *Gender and green governance: the political economy of women's presence within and beyond community forestry*, Oxford University Press.

In 2002, the *European Journal of Development Research* published a special issue on land and water rights. It contains a number of interesting papers about the interplay between bureaucratic and socially embedded commons management systems. At least read Cleaver, F. (2002) 'Reinventing institutions: bricolage and the social embeddedness of natural resource management', *European Journal of Development Research*, volume 14, number 2, pages 11–30. You could also read her book from 2012, which is rich in engaging stories from Tanzania, Zimbabwe, India, Pakistan, Nepal, and Sweden: *Development through bricolage: rethinking institutions for natural resource management*, Routledge.

Elite capture

If you read a few papers assessing customary systems or community-based management systems, the issue of elite capture will appear – simply because it is a common problem. For a particularly interesting comparative study, read Warren, C. and Visser, L. (2016) "The local turn: an introductory essay revisiting leadership, elite capture and good governance in Indonesian conservation and development programs", *Human Ecology*, volume 44, pages 277–286, online. It's called "an introductory essay", as it's the start of a special issue, and it may inspire you to read some of the subsequent papers. These papers look at a number of initiatives in Indonesia and assess them against *elite capture* (where the elite use their position to pursue self-interest) as well as *captured elites* (where social relationships and expectations drive leaders to instigate or support collective actions that are driven by collective interests). This special issue is interesting because of the wide variety of findings, from elite behaviour being straight-up predatory to it being strongly committed to conservation and community development goals. The introductory paper also makes valuable observations about the ways government decentralisation affects community-based management.

Other issues mentioned in this chapter

For recent research about the fishery regimes in East Africa, Benin, and Costa Rica

I don't know of any published research on Lake Antobo in Mali. For the other fishery regimes mentioned in this chapter:

- Lake Victoria: Nunan, F. (2018) "Compliance, corruption and co-management: how corruption fuels illegalities and undermines the legitimacy of fisheries co-management", *International Journal of the Commons*, volume 12, number 2, pages 58–79, online.
- The lakes in Benin: Sonneveld, B. et al. (2019) "Tragedy of the inland lakes", *International Journal of the Commons*, volume 13, number 1, pages 609–636 (or 1–28, depending on where you get it from).
- Costa Rica: Carrillo, I.I.C. et al. (2019) "Do responsible fishing areas work? Comparing collective action challenges in three small-scale fisheries in Costa Rica", *International Journal of the Commons*, volume 13, number 1, pages 705–746, online.

About the relatively successful community-based management systems in Namibia and Nepal

- Namibia: MET/NACSO (2018) *The state of community conservation in Namibia – a review of communal conservancies, community forests and other CBNRM activities (Annual Report 2017)*, MET/NACSO, online.
- Nepal: Oldekop, J.A. et al. (May 2019) "Reductions in deforestation and poverty from decentralised forest management in Nepal", *Nature Sustainability*, volume 2, pages 421–428. It concludes that "CFM [common forestry management] has, on average, contributed to significant net reductions in both poverty and deforestation across Nepal and that CFM increases the likelihood of win–win outcomes" (abstract). Or, for an older and more critical account, see Nagendra, H., Karmacharya, M., and Karna, B. (2005) "Evaluating forest management in Nepal: views across space and time", *Ecology and Society*, volume 10, number 1, online. This paper acknowledges that "Nepal was an early leader in initiating innovative programs of forest management aimed at involving local communities" (page 2) but also concludes that "user groups are not allowed to make significant changes to management policies" and that "user groups have limited decision-making authority over their forests" (both on page 12).

About the erosion of customary systems in Afghanistan and the Solomon Islands

- Afghanistan: Dempsey and Coburn (2010), "Traditional dispute resolution and stability in Afghanistan", *PeaceBrief 10*, United States Institute for Peace (USIP), online.
- The Solomon Islands: Allen, M. et al. (2013), *Justice delivered locally: systems, challenges, and innovations in Solomon Islands*, World Bank, online (not every link to this paper works but the one through *researchgate.net* does).

About the undue dominance of training in capacity building work

The man who first coined this notion was South African Alan Kaplan, and he has published a number of papers on the issue. One that proposes alternatives is Kaplan, A. (1999) *The development of capacity*, Community Development Resource Association, online. His and another model of what organisational capacity really means are best summarised in Chapter 1 of part 1 of Ubels, J., Acquaye-Baddoo, N-A., and Fowler, A., editors (2010) *Capacity development in practice*, Earthscan.

Exercise

You are a group of three people:

1 An advisor to the regional governor of Stabilistan.
2 A staff member of the UNHCR, here to inspect a nearby refugee camp.
3 A project officer who works for a donor agency and is keen to identify a new opportunity for a useful project.

You are on a jungle hike and on your way to a waterfall. Your guide meets her aunt, who invites you all for a meal. You gratefully accept, only to discover that, in this part of the world, preparing a meal takes forever. She's chatty, and your guide translates. This is what she tells you.

> I, my husband, and the extended family have always lived here. It's a forest, but it's walking distance to the road that leads to town. We don't have a piece of paper that says that we own our farm, or any of the land around us, but within our community it's always been clear what we can and cannot do. Until recently, at least. Then three things happened:
>
> 1 – Some time ago, refugees arrived from neighbouring Fragilistan. There are quite a few of them, and they live in a camp. They get their firewood and a range of other products from the forest as well. I understand that they need this, but it does mean that an expanding circle around the camp is getting

empty. Some of my relatives are already affected, and the circle is coming ever closer to where I forage.

2 – A logging company has come to our region. It's not close to where we live yet, but it is scary: I've heard that they only take certain types of trees but that their big machines also damage everything else.

3 – The government never really bothered us, but they have now opened a school, not far from me, and said that my children must go there. Even worse, they must wear a school uniform, which costs money, which I don't have. People living elsewhere told me that the government *starts* with a school and then gets involved in other parts of our lives. I fear they'll take away my plot of land.

After the meal, you continue your hike to that waterfall, and you discuss what you've just heard. Is any of this information useful, for any of you? Might there be scope for a project, a policy, or a little bit of research to find out more? Possibly something that might reduce the risk that your guide's aunt loses her natural environment, farm, and livelihood?

Notes

1 Compared to only 10% in 1974. See FAO (2018) *The state of the world fisheries and aquaculture; meeting the sustainable development goals*, pages 39 and 40, online. 'Overfishing' is a level of fishing that causes a fish stock to move below the level that is in the world's long-term economic interest (in formal terms: the level that provides 'maximum sustainable yield'). It's a human-centric criterion, which is the standard in this field and reflected in the terms we use: we talk about common *resources*, for example, implying that we see them as being of value for humans, rather than of *intrinsic* value.

2 The first known mention of a sustainable management principle of common property is about the design of fishing nets. Mencius (also written as Mengzi or Meng-tzu) wrote, more than 2,000 years ago, that "if you do not allow nets with too fine a mesh to be used in large ponds, then there will be more fish and turtles than they can eat". Quoted in Hughes, J.D. (1989) "Mencius' prescriptions for ancient Chinese environmental problems", *Environmental Review*, volume 13, issue 13–14, pages 15–27, with the quotation on page 18.

3 Some such systems are described in Chapter 3 on "long-enduring, self-organized, and self-governed common property regimes" of Ostrom, E. (2015, and originally 1990) *Governing the commons: the evolution of institutions for collective action*, Cambridge University Press. The reference to the 13th century is taken from page 62, which is part of a section on an ancient set of rules for community-owned property in Törbel, Switzerland.

4 This is generally because of the binding effects of networks of roots, but there are also trees that excrete soil-binding chemicals, such as cashew trees – which is why you sometimes see them growing on the sloping sides of roads.

5 These small towns are Kapuhenwala and Wanduruppa, and the story is told in IUCN (December 2005) *South Asia: mangrove forests saved lives in 2004 tsunami disaster*, International Union for Conservation of Nature, online.

6 The 'International Partnership for Blue Carbon' says it's 50%, over the past 50 years, but it is unclear what this figure is based on (one of the many examples where you follow a reference trail until it stops, without ever reaching the root data). See International Partnership for Blue Carbon (2017) *Coastal blue carbon: an introduction for policy makers*, online.

7   Hardin, G. (December 1968) "The tragedy of the commons", *Science*, volume 162, pages 1243–1248.

8   In Hardin's world, all herders are male.

9   A fine not exceeding five hundred shillings or imprisonment for the term not exceeding two months, or both such fine and imprisonment, according to Act 48 of 1962, article 11, online.

10 Ginsberg, C. and Keene, S. (2018) *At a crossroads: consequential trends in recognition of community-based forest tenure from 2002–2017*, Rights and Resources Initiative, online, figure 4 on page 12, based on a sample of 41 countries (with slightly different figures on page 9, which are based on a lower-quality sample of 58 countries). In this context, 'government ownership' means that the government claims legal and administrative control, even if this control is contested.

11 A concession is a legal act by which an authority grants somebody or something the rights to take something from something – such as wood from a forest or oil from a well.

12 The latter is mostly a Latin American phenomenon: "Commercial agriculture accounts for almost 70 percent of the deforestation in Latin America but for only one-third in Africa, where small-scale agriculture is a more significant driver of deforestation." FAO (2016) *State of the world's forests*, online, page X and page 20 (figures for 2000–10). For an overview of the contribution of small, medium, and large-scale activity to deforestation, and how this changes over time, see Austin, K.G. et al. (2017) "Trends in size of tropical deforestation events signal increasing dominance of industrial-scale drivers", *Environmental Research Letters*, volume 12, issue 5. (If you read this, you'll see that the title is a little misleading.)

13 Hardin seems to have based his analysis on the common grazing lands of medieval and post-medieval England, but his understanding of the 'free for all' dynamics of these commons is historically inaccurate. Access to the English commons was in fact highly regulated, and sanctions on violations were severe. See Cox, S.J.B. (1985) "No tragedy on the commons", *Environmental Ethics*, volume 7, pages 49–62.

14 The original source of the principles is Ostrom, E. (1990) *Governing the commons: the evolution of institutions for collective action*, Cambridge University Press.

15 This was a problem in Cameroon, West Africa's first country to experiment with community-based forestry management, in the 1990s. It is mentioned in Karsenty, A. (2016) *The contemporary forest concessions in West and Central Africa: chronicle of a foretold decline?* FAO, online.

16 This is an actual and broadly representative quotation, which I then anonymised. The addition '*(sic)*' means that the quotation's grammatical or spelling errors are copied from the original text.

17 Chambers, R. (1983) *Rural development: putting the last first*, Longman (now Pearson Education).

18 For more on this, see Cooke, B. and Kothari, U., editors (2001) *Participation: the new tyranny?* Zed Books, London and New York.

19 This is an amalgamation of Ostrom's principles and what practitioners and papers say most commonly. I'm grateful to the Centre for International Development and Training (CIDT) for enabling me to talk with a wide range of stakeholders in community-based forest management from around the world.

20 Because this pressure is ongoing, there continues to be a steady trickle of papers that are repeating the point that privatisation and nationalisation are not inherently superior to managing common resources as *common* resources. For a recent example, see *The Economist* (12 September 2019) "The alternatives to privatisation and nationalisation; more public resources could be managed as commons without much loss of efficiency", online.

21 A number of states in India, for example, have nationalised tendu leaves, gum, mahua, and sal seeds and flowers that people used to gather in community-owned forests. See Mahapatra, R. et al. (March 2018) How government is subverting forest rights act, *Down to Earth*, online.

22 Ginsberg, C. and Keene, S. (2018) *At a crossroads: consequential trends in recognition of community-based forest tenure from 2002–2017*, Rights and Resources Initiative, online, figure 4 on page 12, based on a sample of 41 countries.

23 This is the case for 59% of what used to be community forests in West Kalimantan in Indonesia, for example. See Stevens, C. et al. (2014) *Securing rights, combating climate change: how strengthening community forest rights mitigates climate change*, World Resources Institute, online, page 3.

24 "Delays were the norm for . . . the next phases of longitudinal series of projects. . . . DFID's weak handling of disruptive events, and the poor process management of both DFID and most of its funding intermediaries, led to unreliable and unpredictable donor behaviour in the stages before project implementation, with insufficient communication around timelines and an inability to stick to them. This . . . has affected the results of many DFID-funded projects." ICAI (2019) *DFID's partnerships with civil society organisations*, Paragraphs 4.49 and 5.5, online. This review also discusses the projectification of DFID.

25 Gilmour, D. (2016) "Forty years of community-based forestry: a review of its extent and effectiveness", *FAO Forestry Paper Number 176*, FAO, page xic, online.

26 'Common-pool resources' research originates in the social sciences, and 'ecosystem services' research is rooted in ecology. For the way these two interdisciplinary research fields relate to and influence each other, see Rodela, R. et al. (2014) "Intersections of ecosystem services and common-pool resources literature: an interdisciplinary encounter", *Environmental Science & Policy*, volume 94, pages 72–81.

4

TRADE

Prologue: trade and the positive sum game

A few months before the elections, the Ethiopian government connected a small town in Afar, one of the country's nine states, to the electricity grid. This offered a host of new opportunities, and one of the NGOs there had seized some of them. They had paid for the school to 'get connected'. They had installed a pump, to pump river water to fields and houses. They had donated refrigerators to a health clinic to store vaccinations. Then, unfortunately but not uncommonly, the electricity supply was cut again, shortly after the elections. Water could no longer be pumped, and the refrigerators no longer worked.

The NGO had done lots of other things, under the umbrella of an 'integrated rural development programme'. They had established a farmers' cooperative next to the river, but the river had swallowed most of the land the following year, when heavy rains caused flooding. The organisation had constructed a few 'model latrines' to improve sanitation, but nobody had replicated the idea, and most people still relieved themselves in the open. They had built and furnished a few classrooms, but there was no system or budget for maintenance, and at the time of my visit, most windows had shattered, and most of the furniture and equipment had broken down.

All in all, the work of this NGO had not been very effective. But there was one thing that *had* worked: the organisation had invested in the establishment of a weekly livestock market – and it was flourishing. Looking at the impact of this market shows just how beneficial trade can be.

The pastoral families in Afar had traditionally valued their livestock as an important indicator of wealth and status, only selling their animals in <u>distress sales</u>.[1] In recent years, though, this had changed. More than before, people now valued education, health services, and consumer goods – and for those, they needed money.

Therefore, people occasionally walked to a faraway market to sell some of their animals. The trip lasted a day, and the animals were tired towards the end of it. This affected the prices, but the owners almost always sold the animals anyway. Sometimes the prices were good; sometimes there was an oversupply of livestock, and the prices were low. As there was no phone coverage in this part of Afar, it was not possible to get an indication of the average prices beforehand.

This new local livestock market had made life easier and profits higher. The sales volume increased every week, and buyers and sellers were willing to travel increasingly long distances. Indeed, some meat factories from other regions now sent their representatives, who arrived on the Friday and left on the Sunday. When I visited this market, only a year after it had opened, it already featured more than livestock. You could now buy agricultural produce and animal derivatives, like sheep wool and camel fat (which people use as hair gel), as well as textiles and a range of other manufactured products. The surrounding service industry had also benefited: a restaurant owner now had more customers *and* spent much less time searching for the sheep and goats she needed for her dishes, because she could buy them at the market.

New businesses opened. Somebody bought a few mattresses, called his house a 'hotel', and offered the traders a good night's rest. Somebody else took to tanning and selling hides. An entrepreneurial football fan bought a solar-powered battery, a satellite receiver and a television, and was making money by inviting traders and others to watch the English Premier League in his yard.

Because of the obvious success, people felt ownership of the market and were keen to keep it going. When floods washed away a short stretch of road, a group of men fixed it, without any payments from anyone, to make sure the traders could reach the market a few days later.

This market had only required some initial advertising and a bit of infrastructure to turn into a massive 'positive sum game' – it benefited everybody, and the benefits grew over time.

But trading is not always quite so easy and beneficial.

Common trade problems and bottlenecks

An Indian NGO specialising in education had wanted to help alleviate poverty in a particularly poor group of villages.[2] It had identified the most vulnerable people and had given them goats. The idea was that these goats would eat the region's scrubs and produce milk and meat for their owners' own consumption and for the market.

The project had been a disaster. The NGO had taken a so-called <u>dump-and-run</u>[3] approach to development: it distributed the goats, and that was the end of its involvement. The owners had no prior knowledge of goat-rearing and hadn't received any training. The goats did not get vaccinated and were not dewormed. The assumption had been that the goats would eat scrubs, but this region's scrubs were largely inedible, so the goats needed fodder too. Unsurprisingly, most of them died.

A few of the goats did survive, but even they did not provide a meaningful income, because their owners traded in poorly functioning markets. Here are some of the problems they faced.

First, you can't always buy what you need

If you are poor and live in a remote community, you may know a great deal about the local context and traditional production methods – but you're probably not aware of good practice from elsewhere and therefore probably produce less than you could. Even if you do have that awareness, you're likely to encounter three problems when trying to get the inputs you need:

Unaffordability

If the goat owners had known about the need for vaccinations and deworming tablets, they would probably not have been able to afford them. They were, after all, the poorest people in these remote villages. And, frustratingly, the general rule is that *the poorer and more remote you are, the more you pay per unit of almost anything* (see Box 4.1).

BOX 4.1   ABOUT THE PRICE OF SUGAR

My hotel in Khartoum was next to a depot that sold imported sugar in bags of 50 kilograms each. The trip from there to a refugee camp passed by a number of shops that sold sugar as well, in ever-smaller bags and at ever-higher prices per kilogram. The smallest units were sold in the camp, where people sold sugar per teaspoon, at the side of the road, on small pieces of paper, for a single cup of tea. The price per teaspoon was small, but per kilogram, the refugees paid many times the wholesale price.

The sad reality is that, unless it is produced locally, everything gets more expensive the poorer and more remotely located you are.

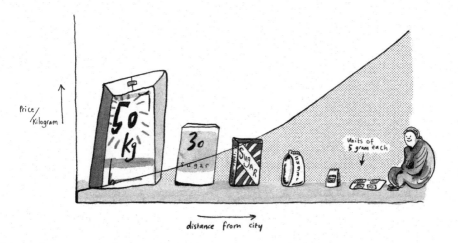

FIGURE 4.1   The price of sugar

Unavailability

If the goat owners had been able to afford these vaccinations and deworming tablets, they might not have found them, as both goats and vets were rare in the region. This is the second general rule: *the poorer and the more remote you are, the less likely it is that you have access to the things you need to produce sellable products.*

Quality

The third general rule is that *input quality and remoteness are inversely correlated.* In part, this is because inputs are often perishable. The vaccinations mentioned in the prologue, for example, quickly lost their power after the electricity was cut. In part, it is also the consequence of immoral business practices: if you produce something that isn't good enough, you could either throw it away or you could dump it in a remote area, without much risk that anybody outside this area will ever know. An example just presented itself as I'm writing part of this chapter in a hotel room in

RECIPIENTS OF A GOAT-DISTRIBUTION PROGRAMME

FIGURE 4.2 A problem distribution programme

a small town in Bangladesh. I've bought a razor here, but it is unusable because the sharp ends of the cutting blades point the wrong way. The producer could never sell this faulty product in Dhaka but can get away with it in this small town close to the Burmese border, where consumers have no rights and are invisible to the rest of the world.

Second, you can't always sell what you produce, and if you can, you can't control the price you get

Unattractive offer

A few of the goats that survived got offspring and produced milk, which the owners could drink but not sell. There was no local market for goats' milk, and the nearest milk-processing factory was a long way away. They had tried transporting the milk, but it had not worked out: the costs were high, the revenue was low, and the milk wasn't always fresh upon arrival. Even when the milk did arrive fresh, the factory wasn't really interested, because – by that factory's standards – the volume was small and the villagers were argumentative.

Being small and scattered is not just a problem for farmers. The *buyers* of agricultural produce, too, struggle to make a profit if the farms are small or hard to reach. To make money, they need a predictable volume of produce of reliable quality, at a reasonable cost. Small local farmers may not be the ones able to deliver this, even if the geographical distance to the factory is short. A juice factory in Bosnia is getting most of its apples from far-away Poland, for example, because the produce of the local growers is of varying quality, the growers are unable to organise themselves and are therefore fragmented, and they transport their fruits over slow and bumpy roads. Moreover, they tend to sell only their *surplus* to the factory: the portion of the production they do not need for their own consumption and cannot sell directly to consumers, at higher prices than the factory can offer. In good years, such surplus can be voluminous. But when there has been little rainfall, flooding or a fungus, the quantity of surplus production may drop to zero. Factories cannot cope with this unpredictability: they have contractual obligations and need to run their machines all the time in order to generate a profit.

Little negotiating power

If the factory had been closer to our goat owners, and if the villagers had been able to organise themselves, a useful buyer-seller relationship might have developed. Even then, the goat-owners would probably have received relatively low prices for their milk. This is partly where the bad image of 'big business' comes from: when there are many sellers and there is only one buyer (this is called a 'monopsony'), then the buyer can pretty much pay whatever he or she wants, as the seller has no alternatives. And if there are only a *few* buyers of produce (an 'oligopsony'), then these buyers often agree to buy within a predetermined price range – a practice that is generally illegal but nonetheless common. The longer-term prospects are the only real limitation to the exploitation of small producers: if prices are unattractive, farmers may change their crops, or move out of rearing goats and into government employment. This risk often ensures that buyers offer reasonable prices. Even then, though, 'reasonable' is a relative term: we live in a world where poor people's time and efforts are worth little, and their 'added value' to value chains[4] is small. Peanuts are the most important component of a bag of peanuts, but the Senegalese farmers who grow them only get a small portion of the price you pay.

Price volatility

Some people sold their goats almost immediately after they had received them. This was wise, as they would have been unable to truly benefit from them. However, they probably made less money than the NGO had spent on them because

- They were inexperienced sellers who were unfamiliar with the goat market.
- There were suddenly a lot of one-time goat sellers in the region, and this probably caused the price per goat to drop.

This price volatility is one of the biggest vulnerabilities in the agricultural sector. Price volatility affects smallholders but also affects large farms (and therewith the employment of many rural labourers),[5] buyers, and consumers. The effects can be grave, or *very* satisfying. Rainfall, shifting consumer preferences, floods, pests, wonderful seasons, increases in the global acreage dedicated to a crop, and NGOs that hand out free goats all influence market prices. It is possible to have the best-ever harvest without earning any money because everybody else has had a great harvest too, and all this produce floods the market. This may cause the supply of a crop to exceed the demand for it, and this typically reduces trading prices. If you grew tomatoes in Kenya, in 2018, you probably had a bumper harvest, but you probably made little money because of the region's overproduction of tomatoes that year. This is one of the big risks of mono-crop farming, and the main reason that poor people often make sure they have multiple sources of income. Without this, they may end up with nothing if their potatoes get a fungus or if the potato market collapses.

All in all, trade is a positive sum game – if everything goes well. This sometimes happens, but we live in an imperfect world, and things are difficult and go wrong. Therefore, the production and trading choices farmers make are partly informed by expected prices but partly also by the risks and obstacles that they are facing. We will now discuss a hierarchy of markets that shape rural livelihoods. The way these markets function is not inevitable or natural. Economic history shows that other market mechanisms have existed, sometimes for much longer periods of time than the mechanisms that are most common today (see Box 4.2).

BOX 4.2 A PAIR OF SHOES

In the old city of Sarajevo, there is a string of shoemakers. When, shortly after the Bosnian war, a friend of mine ordered a pair from one of them, the old shoemaker apologised. "I am sorry, dear stranger," he said, "but I have already sold a pair of shoes today. Please buy a pair from my neighbour instead."

In today's economy, this is an uncommon response, but at other times, this may have been the standard. In a 1944 book that has withstood the test of time, Karl Polanyi describes how industrialisation and government regulations have changed people's economic mentality and behaviour. Over time, land, labour, and products came to be sold at prices set by demand and supply. This was new: before industrialisation, markets were far less strong, and the allocation of products and labour was steeped in traditions that were based on social norms rather than market dynamics.

A hierarchy of markets

1 of 4: local markets

It is hard to get a good price selling local produce on the local market to local consumers – but this is nonetheless how many millions of small farmers make their money. In part, and for reasons described in the previous section, small and isolated producers may just not be sufficiently attractive for larger buyers who need a reliable source of a minimum volume of products of predictable quality, of which the costs, including transport, are competitive.

Even if it *is* possible to link up to larger markets, the risks might be too high. In a diversified economy, production networks tend to be secure because there are backup systems and alternative providers. If a truck breaks down, there will be another truck to transport the produce. If a producer stops operations, there will be other producers. For small, remote farms in undiversified economies, the risks are higher. Here, the truck is more likely to break down because the roads are bad, and there are far fewer spare parts and qualified mechanics available. As the production network is only as strong as its weakest link, and as this link cannot be replaced, trading may stop because of something as simple as a flat tire or rains that have made the only access road impassable.

Local markets pose fewer risks. In addition, transport and storage costs are low, access is easy, perishable goods can be sold quickly, and you may have known the buyers for years. But there are big disadvantages as well. The number of products for which there is a local market is small. Prices tend to be low, and supply often outstrips demand, as everybody is harvesting the same crops around the same time. There are some tricks that prolong the marketable lives of your produce. You could

FIGURE 4.3 The local market, after the tomato harvest

pickle your cabbage, for example, or use your unsold tomatoes to make a sauce and sell it with cassava in the evening. But the options are limited, and you often see rotting tomatoes and suchlike on the wayside – even in regions with chronic malnutrition.

Catering for the local market while female

A Chadian micro-finance organisation gave two women a loan to start their small town's first-ever bakery. They found it easy to buy grain and produce and sell their bread. Then the local chief heard about their initiative. He felt a bakery was unsuitable for women. He confiscated the grain cleaning and milling equipment and the oven, all of which now stand in his house, unused. The women were left with a loan to repay and no income.

2 of 4: larger markets

One way of accessing larger markets, even if a farm's production volume is too low for independent access, is through a cooperative that brings the produce of several farmers together to achieve <u>economies of scale</u>.[6]

Cooperatives exist in many forms. They often provide seeds, tools, and fertilisers. They may also operate machine rings that allow you to use equipment without having to buy it. They may offer veterinary services, maintain irrigation systems, and give technical advice. On the output side, cooperatives arrange crop collection, processing, and transport, and they secure their members' access to markets. Cooperatives have lower 'transaction costs' (the costs related to a buying or selling process), and they fetch higher prices than their members could fetch individually, because they bulk small producers' harvests, which adds to the attractiveness of their offer. They are likely to retain some of the profits and use the money later to cope with price swings, demand fluctuations, or expenses in relation to maintenance or the purchase of new equipment.

One step up from cooperatives are marketing boards (or 'marketing organisations'), which also facilitate the buying and selling of agricultural produce. They sometimes work with *groups* of cooperatives to further reduce costs and maximise returns. The boards do not limit their activities to buying and selling: they shape and implement national agricultural strategies and sometimes conduct research and maintain buffer stocks to dampen price fluctuations and to help ensure a country's food security.

On paper, cooperatives and marketing boards are great, and they sometimes compete successfully with large-scale farms over long periods of time. But many cooperatives fail, and many marketing boards require ongoing government spending. There seem to be three major challenges:

- **Artificial successes.** Often, governments subsidise cooperatives to prove a political point, and NGOs invest in pilot cooperatives meant to 'show the local community how it's done'. Such support creates artificial success, and such cooperatives often collapse shortly after the support is terminated. Maintenance stops, machine rings collapse, irrigation canals get clogged up, farmers withdraw, and once that starts happening, the cooperatives implode.
- **Disappointing volumes.** Unsubsidised cooperatives and marketing boards will survive only if they create economies of scale that outweigh the costs of staff and bureaucracy. If the total trading volume is insufficient to create such economies of scale, the institutions lose their advantage, simply because they compete with all other marketing options and will only attract farmers if the profits they generate are higher than the profits achievable through other channels. Cooperatives that do not offer low-cost inputs and buy well-priced harvests only get a farmer's 'residual sales' – the part of the harvest for which farmers cannot find another market. Most cooperatives are unable to survive on that basis.
- **Inefficiency and corruption** used to be common in both cooperatives and marketing boards. In cooperatives, this problem is far smaller now than it has been in the past, as so many of the inefficient and corrupt ones have gone bankrupt. However, these problems have stigmatised cooperatives in countries that were previously socialist, because of their history of forced participation in cooperatives that were exploitative and associated with dictatorial regimes. Marketing boards are still often inefficient. That's because many of them are (semi-)governmental bodies that are playing a partly private sector role, without having the strong focus on efficiency that profit-driven companies tend to have.

So cooperatives and marketing boards still exist, many thrive, and some governments still promote and support them (such as is the case in China, where there are close to two million registered cooperatives)[7] – but they are no longer 'the obvious choice' they once were, in socialist countries in particular.

Joining a cooperative while female

A new cooperative in Ethiopia was looking for members. Women applied but only men were selected. In protest, three women visited the decision-maker's office every day for a month, until he finally allocated plots of land to them – but not to any other women.

3 of 4: global markets

Even if you trade locally or through cooperatives, your products may be consumed by people living anywhere in the world. There are local cotton markets that cater for middlemen who sell in bulk to the global textile industry, and a cooperative's tobacco harvest may well end up in cigarettes smoked halfway across the globe. Where local markets and cooperatives produce for consumers across the ocean, it is likely that large international companies play a key role.

Some international companies control the value chain from the farm to the final packaged consumer product. This has historically been true of a portion of 'colonial' products in particular: coffee, tea, rubber, fruit (and especially bananas and pineapples) and palm oil, for example. Alternatively or in addition, companies may buy crops from individual producers or cooperatives through contracts or auctions or buy-at-the-gate systems. They then sell them to factories that turn, say, cocoa, sugar, and other ingredients from around the world into chocolates.

Whatever the model used, such international companies can be major forces in local, regional, and even national economies. They are often the sole buyer, or one of only a few buyers, of certain crops – and they are often criticised for exploiting people and the environment. Accusations of price fixing at low levels, tax avoidance, and a reluctance to invest are common. In response, these companies do two things. First, they point to the international bulk market's low or volatile price level of the products they trade in. Second, they state they take their corporate social responsibilities seriously. 'We run schools and a reforestation project'; 'we work with the local community to improve local people's lives'; 'we donate to UNICEF'.

The benefits of these long value chains depend, in part, on the policies and behaviour of such companies, but probably more on the specific country you are in.

The movement of agricultural products is subject to global trading arrangements (though truly global companies deploy some circumvention techniques). In Chapter 1, we saw how the world has been moving to lower trade barriers and towards an emerging consensus that 'trade is good'. Still, though, the arrangements are complex. First, imports are often subject to tariffs, which are not the same for all countries. For example, the least developed countries[8] often impose high tariffs on their imports,[9] but none of them face import tariffs when exporting sugar to the European Union, while Cuba and Brazil pay €98 per ton. Second, products often face 'non-tariff barriers'. These are obstacles that take the shape of cumbersome product standards, lengthy import procedures, or import quotas beyond which a country's products may no longer enter another country. For example, that sugar export from Cuba and Brazil to the EU incurs an import tariff of €98 per ton, *and* the combined export volume of these two countries is capped at 85,000 tonnes.[10]

Some of these globally traded crops are risky crop choices because of subsidies that may make it impossible for unsubsidised farmers to generate a profit. The USA and a number of EU countries have long paid their farmers massive export subsidies; much more recently, China, India, and a few other upcoming countries have followed suit. The result of such subsidies is that domestic crop production in the subsidising countries is artificially high and export prices are artificially low. This distorts the worldwide market prices, and NGOs and many others have long advocated against these export subsidies, as they have the potential of destroying farms in non-subsidising countries.[11] They have had dramatic consequences for small-scale Mexican farmers, for example, because the free trade agreement with the USA and Canada caused subsidised North American crops to outcompete them on Mexican markets. It took decades, but the advocacy work has had some level of success: in December 2015, the WTO facilitated an agreement that may prove to be the start of the end of agricultural export subsidies.[12]

4 of 4: the fair trade market

Fair trade at a scale that matters is a relatively recent phenomenon. When I was growing up, it was still a fringe market in which quality was of little relevance to the highly ideological consumers. (I recall a large dead spider in a pack of coffee, when I opened it, back in the early 1980s.) But it has grown rapidly in size and product range, and fair trade coffee, tea, chocolate, bananas, sugar, and several other products can now be bought in regular supermarkets in an increasing number of countries.

Fair trade products reach your kitchen with the help of sophisticated global logistical systems and use the same marketing techniques that a supermarket's other products use. They are also subject to the same legislation and taxes as all other trade. When the EU recently changed its rules relating to the import of sugar, for example, the EU's beet sugar replaced some of the imported cane sugar – including fair trade cane sugar. The only difference between fair trade and other products is, or is meant to be, the compensation and treatment of small-scale producers in the Global South and the level of care for the environment in which these producers live.

The concept of fair trade is roughly based on the assumptions that

- Free markets lead to unreasonably low and volatile prices for small-scale producers in developing countries.
- This is aggravated by monopsonistic (only one buyer) or oligopsonistic (only a few buyers) markets and by the location of the processing industry, which is only rarely in the country where the crops are grown.

- Smallholders often lack the knowledge and inputs required to produce high-quality crops.
- Environmental degradation must be stopped.

The answers are almost obvious:

- Create a market for consumers that would like to be 'fair'. In this market, prices are stable and reasonable.
- Provide farmers with the training and technical support required to produce quality crops in a sustainable fashion. There is often an empowerment dimension that goes beyond the technical side of farming and ultimately aims to help women or other disadvantaged groups get their voices heard.[13]
- Where possible (and often the conclusion is that it is *not* possible), processing takes place in the country in which the crops are grown.

To make it all happen, fair trade companies buy, transport, process, and sell farmers' produce. They also provide training and support to farmers, and arrange certification for their products. Ideally, everyone benefits: the farmers and their workers earn more, children get better education, the consumers have a better conscience, and authorities get additional taxes and foreign currencies.

On the side of Western consumers and parts of the retail industry in a few European countries, it seems to work. The product range is still small, but within this range, the fair trade market share has been rising for decades. In some quarters – in the coffee shop industry, for example – *not* being part of this movement has become a liability. Major chains highlight their Fairtrade certification in their marketing material and feature posters of happy farmers in their outlets, with texts explaining how your daily cups turned their lives around. Nowadays, some supermarket chains sell *only* fair trade coffee and bananas, and YouTube is full of clips showing the impact this is having on farmers in developing countries.

But these clips are typically produced by fair-trade companies. They are marketing tools, and they are misleading. The reality is that fair trade does not work altogether well, from the perspective of the producers. First, fair trade is bureaucratic and cumbersome and often does not pay that much more to the farmer. Second, most people engaged in the production of fair trade crops are farm workers, not farm owners. Farmers have to commit to fair-trade codes but often ignore them in practice. They often pay far below living wages, create debt bondage,[14] do not provide the facilities (toilets, electricity, safe drinking water) they promised, and only get the protective gear out of storage on the days the fair-trade inspectors are visiting.[15] If fair trade is ever to fulfil its objectives, it needs an overhaul at the farm level.

Work at the start of global value chains, while female

Fair trade typically seeks to promote gender equality, but on-the-ground realities are hard to change.

In Ghana, the man generally owns the cocoa farm and what grows on it, and he may or may not grant his wife or wives a plot. Gender norms and the gender-based division of labour are such that women will work far more hours a day, as they combine farming with time-consuming child-care and household duties, . . . but they are not the ones who take the bean bags to get weighed and sold or decide what to do with the profits made.

There's a new kid on the block, and its name is ICT

In this chapter's prologue, I mentioned that there was no phone coverage in most of Afar. As coverage expands into new regions every day, this may well be a temporary problem. This is good news, as mobile phones open up a world of opportunities. Apps and text messages complement radio shows, posters, and plays that inform farmers and pastoralists about micro-insurance products that could protect them against climate-related and other shocks. Farmers get daily information about prices of crops in the various markets in the regions to help them decide when and where to sell their produce. Many millions of rural men and women use mobile banking to send and receive money, and phones enable people to increase the efficiency of the marketplace ('yes, I am going to the market and could pick up a few of your goats on my way'). Even the physical livestock market, which is such an important asset to that town in Afar, may soon face real competition from virtual auctions. One day soon, the woman who owns that restaurant could either go to the nearby market or simply inform her virtual network that she needs a new goat.

The opportunities that ICT offers, and the challenges it poses, are covered in a separate chapter, as ICT is fundamental to the future of the rural world and its influence extends far beyond markets and trade.

Why is all this relevant, and what does it mean for you?

Much of the rural economy depends on the efficiency of markets. This chapter focused on markets for agricultural inputs and outputs, but the same principles apply to, say, the fishing sector, where improved handling, storage, processing, transportation, and trading places would all increase the value of fish and the income of fishing communities.

Increasing trading efficiency is a good place to start if your aim is to reduce rural poverty and you have a regulatory or infrastructural role or have money to invest in rural development or agricultural value chains. Streamlined regulation and investments in rural transport could improve the affordability, availability, and appropriateness of inputs and increase trading opportunities and the stability and level of prices paid for small-scale farmers' outputs. Such investments may require a reversal of common practice in your country, as many countries focus their investments on urban areas, not on hard-to-reach rural regions with high concentrations of poverty. As you improve local markets, keep an eye on global trade rules, tariffs, and subsidies for the crops you focus on. This seems remote and outside your scope of control, but the effects of changes are almost immediate and often significant.

Ideally, your market improvements are pro-poor, in the sense that poor people (and possibly poor women in particular) not only benefit in absolute terms but also get a larger portion of the overall value generated. This is unlikely to happen unless you deliberately plan for it. (The people who do this refer to their work as M4P, or sometimes MMW4P, which stands for 'making markets work for the poor'.) You could do this by focusing your work on equipping poor producers with market knowledge and access. You could also focus on the efficiency of the marketplace for labour in particular, as this increases the appeal of labour-intensive production methods, which are typically to the benefit of poor communities. Think of the sustainability of the results of your work, and think of possible resistance and counter-moves from wealthier farmers, if more income for poor farmers means less income for them.

Interventions should not just be based on the maximisation of small farmers' profits but also on the mitigation of market risks and uncertainties. If you influence farmers' crop choices, then keep in mind that mono-cropping is risky and could turn out disastrous, and that perishable and niche crops may have relatively high value, but selling them is easily affected by market obstacles. Speciality mushrooms can be profitable, but their market may be small and uncertain. Onions can survive transport delays, but strawberries cannot (see Box 4.3 for an extreme example of the benefits of a crop that easily turns into a non-perishable product).

BOX 4.3   COLOMBIA'S COCAINE INDUSTRY

Colombia is the world's largest cocaine producer. Cocaine's core ingredient is the coca leaf. The coca leaf is an ideal crop: the plant produces multiple harvests per year for up to 40 years, and the first harvest comes less than two years after planting. The coca leaves are grown in mountainous jungle regions, and they are bulky (less so if you dry them first), but they only need to reach one of thousands of simple laboratories that use a thousand kilograms of bulky leaves to produce a little over a kilogram of easy-to-transport, imperishable bricks of cocaine.

In areas with few and barely navigable roads and poorly developed fruit and vegetable markets, there are no other crops that generate as much profit as coca leaves (in 2017, a hectare of Colombian coca plants would generate an average of some $3,000).[16] This is why none of the attempts to persuade farmers to substitute their coca production with other crops has been successful and why even the extensive aerial spraying of poison that has done massive damage to Colombia's environment and human, animal, and plant health has not stopped the country's cocaine industry (search for 'Plan Colombia' if you want to know more about this).

If you work for an NGO, it is probably unwise to set up farmers' cooperatives. It sounds good, and they are pro-poor by design, but unless you are true specialists and sure to stay in the community for at least a decade, your cooperatives are unlikely to survive your departure. Similarly, do not be naïve about fair trade: it is a hugely complex industry, and it is really difficult to maintain truly 'fair' standards.

Lastly, regarding the failed initiatives in the prologue: depending on the country, it may be unwise to base your programming decisions on a government promise or even on government action, if this promise is made or this action is taken in election time. Once the elections are over, the new electricity network may lose its power, the connecting road may never be completed, and the anti-corruption drive may lose its momentum.

Further reading

Schools of thought on trade

Few fields of research have sparked as much tension and conflicting analyses as the field of trade, and international trade in particular. For a brief and wonderfully clear summary of the various schools of thought and their stance on free trade, see Exploring Economics (2016) *Free trade in economic theories*, online. This three-page text covers classical, neo-classical, institutionalist, Marxian, world system, developmentalist, and ecological theory. Then, if you want to know more about any of them, run a Google Scholar search.

Making markets work for poor rural people

A good exposé on the effects of the various forms of trade on poverty is Stiglitz, J.E. and Charlton, A. (2006) 'Free Trade, Fair Trade', *World Ark*, March/ April 2006, pages 9–17, online. (You have to download the entire magazine to get to the paper.) These few pages show that, to achieve pro-poor rural development, smoothly functioning markets are necessary but are not in and by themselves sufficient.

In fact, smoothly functioning markets sometimes cause economic growth without improving poor people's lives. For an example, read Dauda, R.S. "The paradox of persistent poverty amidst high growth: the case of Nigeria", in Shaffer, P., Kanbur, R. and Sandbrook, R. (2019) *Immiserizing growth: when growth fails the poor*, Oxford Scholarship Online. You may want to read the book's introduction as well, to see if any of the one-paragraph chapter summaries tickle your interest. Or run a Google Scholar search on key terms like 'jobless growth' and 'immiserisation'.

Recognising that trade could either harm or benefit poor communities, many programmes and policies are specifically designed to 'make markets work for the poor', or 'M4P'. Most M4P efforts are naïve. They implicitly assume that buyers will tolerate extra effort or extra risk just for the benefit of poor producers and that the competing suppliers will not adapt to win their buyers back. Most M4P papers and manuals use illustrations from such programmes – but fail to mention that achievements are often temporary and collapse quickly after the end of the programmes. Still, M4P-related initiatives that work well could contribute to the livelihoods of many households. Moreover, if the results 'stick', such initiatives may help change the attitude of the market's buyers. If the results instil a sense that, for example, "gender equality is smart economics,"[17] the result may be a gradual change in gender patterns.

- Better than most papers, and very readable, is Thorpe, J. (June 2017) *Market system approaches and 'leaving no one behind'*, the BEAM Exchange, online.
- This chapter's blurbs on *trading while female* illustrated a few of the additional obstacles many women face. These additional obstacles are common, and unless you assess these obstacles and keep them in mind, your work is likely to disproportionately benefit men – and quite possibly harm women, as was the case for the loan to the Chadian women. This nine-page guide is a practical analytical starting point: Rüegg, M. and Carter, J. (2016) *Mainstreaming women's economic empowerment (WEE) in market systems development*, SDC, online.

Daily life while female and living with a disability

NGOs have lofty goals on disability inclusion, but on-the-ground realities are hard to change.

An NGO in Malawi had helped a blind woman navigate her surroundings with the help of a cane and had trained her to grow crops. I interviewed her, hoping for a story of resilience, empowerment, and victory.

She could now fetch water, she said, but on her way home, kids would sneak up on her and spit in her bucket. She could now grow vegetables in her garden, she said, but her husband would sell her harvest and drink it away.

Types of markets

In this chapter, we explored (a) selling to nearby markets, (b) selling through cooperatives and marketing boards, (c) being part of global agricultural value chains, and (d) being part of a fair trade value chain. There is ample research on each of these options, and if you are interested in a particular country, region, or sub-topic, a Google Scholar search will probably give more interesting results than the following suggestions.

Nearby markets

This chapter started with a prologue about a small-town market in Ethiopia. For a far more thorough account of the positive development spiral (or 'virtuous cycle', as Hanna Karg and her colleagues call it) that nearby markets may create, see Karg, H. et al. (2019) "Small-town agricultural markets in northern Ghana and their connection to rural and urban transformation", *The European Journal of Development Studies*, volume 31, issue 1, pages 95–117.

Other recent research on local agricultural markets tends to focus on two particular elements: the importance of rural infrastructure and the role of ICT.

Papers about rural infrastructure often assess the link between poor farmers' access to nearby markets and the quality of rural infrastructure. They tend to find that better roads lead to better access; the better availability of goods, including fertiliser and suchlike; and better integration between the local market and the more remote and larger markets in the value chain. See, for example, Aggarwal, S. (July 2018) "Do rural roads create pathways out of poverty? Evidence from India", *Journal of Development Economics*, volume 133, pages 375–395, online. But the effects on poverty are not straightforward. For a rich one-page text on the complexities, see Table 5.1 on page 120 of World Bank (2008) *World development report 2008; agriculture for development*, online. Then follow the references for details.

ICT is playing an increasing role in local market dynamics. Chapter 6, on ICT, talks more about this and suggests a few papers. This is obviously a rapidly evolving field, so don't read anything that is more than a few years old.

Cooperatives and marketing boards

To get an overview of the history, theory, and practicalities of agricultural cooperatives, a good start is Ortmann, G.F. and King, R.P. (2010) "Agricultural cooperatives I: history, theory and problems", *Agrekon*, volume 46, issue 1, pages 18–46.

To understand just how vastly the usefulness of cooperatives differ even within countries, read Liu, H. et al. (2018) "Emerging agricultural cooperatives and the structural change of crop production in China", *30th International conference of agricultural economists*, online. This paper is also interesting because of its sensible policy recommendations to the Chinese government. This government has a track record of following up on such advice (which is part of that 'crossing the river by feeling for stones' approach explained in Chapter 1), and this helps explain why China's agricultural production has been expanding so significantly: after the last decline in 1980, the growth pattern has been nonstop and averaged 4.5% per year, between 1981 and 2018.[18]

If you run a Google Scholar search for the countries that interest you, make sure to look for recent papers, as the nature and dynamics of cooperatives are changing, and in many countries the cooperatives of the turn of the century are different from what they are today.

Long agricultural value chains

- Staatz, J.M. et al. (June 2017); "Linking smallholders to profitable markets in West Africa: case study synthesis", chapter 12 of Staatz, J.M., Diallo, B. and

Me-Nsope, N.M. *Strengthening regional agricultural integration in West Africa: key findings and policy implications*, Syngenta Foundation for Sustainable Agriculture and Michigan State University, online. This chapter is not a very easy read. However, it is interesting and covers different ways in which West African small-scale farmers are included in value chains. It also explains *why* arrangements are the way they are, using the sensible lens of 'transaction-cost economics', which is a school of thought that, as the name suggests, focuses on the costs related to the various transactions along the value chain. The chapter refers to several other chapters in the same book, which are worth reading as well.

- For a reflection on big business and their impact on rural sustainability, read Elder, S.D. and Dauvergne, P. (2015) "Farming for Walmart: the politics of corporate control and responsibility in the Global South" *Journal of Peasant Studies*, volume 45, number 5, pages 1029–1046, online.

- For a comparative study, you could read Brunori, G. et al. (2015) "Are local food chains more sustainable than global food chains? Considerations for assessments", *Sustainability*, volume 8, issue 449, online. It comes to the somewhat dissatisfying conclusion that, essentially, 'we don't know, it depends'.

- For research on the extent to which a selection of 320 European multinational companies take their corporate social responsibility seriously, see Lock, I. and Seele, P. (2016) "The credibility of CSR [corporate social responsibility] reports in Europe. Evidence from a quantitative content analysis in 11 countries." *Journal of Cleaner Production*, volume 122, pages 186–200. The credibility of reporting (which was assessed along the criteria of truthfulness and sincerity) was found to be "mediocre rather than good". There are also country studies that look at particular types of behaviour that explain some of the resentment vis-à-vis multinational companies, such as Otusanya, O.J. (2011), "The role of multinational companies in tax evasion and tax avoidance: the case of Nigeria", *Critical Perspectives on Accounting*, volume 22, number 3, pages 316–332.

Fair trade

At the time of writing, a Google Scholar search on the term *fair trade* gives 356,000 hits. It will be more by the time you read this, and a new biannual publication entitled *Journal of Fair Trade* was launched in February 2019 (though the second issue had not yet been published by October 2019, so perhaps the journal was short-lived). The issues covered in this vast amount of literature are diverse. For example,

- There are endless country-specific studies, such as Wilson, B.R. (2010), "Indebted to fair trade? Coffee and crisis in Nicaragua", *Geoforum*, volume 41, number 1, pages 84–91. (Nicaragua is not a random choice: it is possibly the most extensively researched country, when it comes to fair trade.)
- There are many studies on what does and does not qualify as 'fair trade', such as Bacon, Chr. (2010), "Who decides what is fair in fair trade? The agri-

environmental governance of standards, access, and price", *Journal of Peasant Studies*, volume 37, number 1, pages 111–147, online.
- There are studies about mainstreaming fair trade concepts, such as Macdonald, K. (2007), "Globalising justice within coffee supply chains? Fair Trade, Starbucks and the transformation of supply chain governance", *Third World Quarterly*, volume 28, number 4, pages 793–812.
- And there are many gender-related studies, such as Doherty, B. (2018) "Gender equality and women's empowerment through fair trade social enterprise: case of divine chocolate and Kuapa Kokoo", in Apostolopoulos, N. et al., *Entrepreneurship and the sustainable development goals (contemporary issues in entrepreneurship research, volume 8)*, Emerald Publishing Limited, pages 151–163. Or watch a sobering 17-minute video on Vimeo, titled "Gender and Fairtrade – the stories of women cocoa farmers in Ghana", of the University of Bath.

The one recent report that I have found truly shocking is LeBaron, G. (2018) *The global business of forced labour; report of findings*, SPERI and University of Sheffield, online. In essence, it asserts that modern forms of slavery are common, on cocoa and tea farms, and that "standards are routinely violated by employers" – even in fair-trade-branded farms.

Other issues

The link between electricity provision and elections, mentioned in the prologue

Baskaran, T., Min, B. and Uppal, Y. (2015) "Election cycles and electricity provision: Evidence from a quasi-experiment with Indian special elections", *Journal of Public Economics*, volume 126, pages 64–73. It's about India instead of Ethiopia, but the principle is the same. Check out Figure 4.1.

The EU reform programme on agricultural export subsidies

WTO (undated) *Export competition/subsidies*, online (accessed on 10 October 2019). For a brief and readable account of the history and current status of the EU's agricultural export subsidies in particular, read this blog post (and perhaps a few of its references): Matthews, A. (25 November 2015) *The EU has finally agreed to eliminate export subsidies . . . three cheers!*, online.

Cocaine production

Mejía, D. and Posada, C. (2008), "Cocaine production and trafficking: What do we know?" *IDEAS Working Paper Series*, RePEc, online. Do a web search for "Plan Colombia" if you want to know more about the way in which the USA and the Colombian government have used aerial spraying to reduce Colombia's cocaine production and about the consequences this has had on human and other life. Or read Mejía, D. (2016) *Plan Colombia: an analysis of effectiveness and costs*, Foreign Policy at Brookings, online.

If you liked box 4.2 about the pair of shoes

Karl Polanyi's "The Great Transformation" of 1944 and his "Trade and markets in the early empires" of 1957 are both fascinating reads for anybody who feels that today's global economic system is in any way 'natural'.

Exercise on trade and markets

Background

You are part of a household that consists of six people:

- Two grandparents. Both are healthy and able to work.
- Two parents. Both are living with HIV. Both take medication and are relatively healthy.
- Two children. Both are 15 years old and attending a form of schooling that allows time for agricultural activities.

The harvest season is over, and the harvest of your rain-fed plot of land has been good. In addition, the local market prices of your crops (cassava, onions, tomatoes, and peppers) are higher than normal. This is because of flooding earlier this year, which has affected the crops of the riverside farms.

You are all in good spirits! Unlike last year, none of you will be hungry this year, and you will be able to save some money. Without investments you expect to have some 100,000 *quasi* (Qs 100,000) left by the time the next harvest season starts. In addition, you have livestock that, if sold, would generate another Qs 100,000.

Options

You wonder if it might be wise to invest this money into the household's economic base. You are considering six options:

Option	Investment required	Expected revenues in a normal year
1. Continue without any modifications.	No investment required.	Qs 100,000. In addition, you produce your own food. Buying this food on the local market would cost Qs 100,000.

Option	Investment required	Expected revenues in a normal year
2. Focus on tomatoes only.	No investment required.	Qs 250,000.
3. You could swap your rain-fed plot of land for a plot of land three kilometres to the west, which is next to the river and could be irrigated. In most years, that would mean larger harvests.	Qs 100,000.	Qs 300,000.
4. Join the local mango cooperative, or swap to mango production and sell to the national mango marketing board. In the case of either option, the trees do not bear much fruit in the first two years.	Qs 150,000 for a total crop swap, or Qs 75,000 for a 50% crop swap.	Qs 400,000 in case of a total crop swap, or Qs 250,000 for a 50% crop swap. In case of a 50% crop swap, you would still produce some of your own food, with a market value of Qs 50,000.
5. Join a new project, initiated by an international NGO. This NGO uses model farms to show how farmers could sustainably increase production. The model farmers – who are locals who joined this project two years ago – have produced impressive crops, using manure instead of fertilisers, and the NGO is offering free courses to replicate these farms' success. Next year, the NGO intends to set up its own cooperative.	Qs 50,000 registration fee. Everything else is free.	The model farms, which are the same size as your plot of land, generated Qs 350,000 in the past year, and Qs 200,000 in the year before. The NGO says that further growth might be possible.
6. Sell everything, move to the city, and try to make a living there. A big advantage: health care is better in the city.	You could sell your farm for Qs 400,000, and bus tickets to the city are cheap. Initially, you could stay with family.	Some people 'make it', and some people end up in the most horrific slums, living in dire poverty.

Your assignment

Please discuss the various options, and present your plan. This plan should be based on expected income for the years to come *and* the risks related to each of the options.

Notes

1 A 'distress sale' is the urgent sale of a household's key asset(s), made because money is needed *now* to avert disaster. Because distress sales are made in a hurry, and often at times when many other households are also struggling, prices fetched are typically low.

2 This is often a bad starting point: organisations that are specialised in one sector will not necessarily succeed in another sector.

3 The 'dump-and-run' approach to development is a derogatory term for the approach taken by development initiatives that pay insufficient attention to the requirements for an initiative to achieve sustainable results.

4 A value chain is the chain of activities that are required to produce and sell (and then maintain or dispose of) something. The value chain of a plane is longer and more complex than the value chain of a cauliflower, but even the latter can be long and complex, if you really and truly consider everything that is needed to bring it to your table.

5 For internationally traded crops, such as coffee and tea, large farms face a little less risk than smaller ones, because they may have access to 'futures contracts', in which two parties agree to trade a crop for a pre-determined price at a pre-determined volume that's typically larger than what small farmers are able to produce. This offers both parties some protection from price volatility.

6 You achieve 'economies of scale' if you are able to decrease your costs per unit of production by increasing the size of your production or if you manage to fetch higher prices by selling larger volumes of produce.

7 Liu, H. et al. (2018) *Emerging agricultural cooperatives and the structural change of crop production in China*, 30th International conference of agricultural economists, online, with the fact mentioned on page 1.

8 The EU follows the UN's online list of least developed countries (online).

9 Developing countries tend to impose these tariffs in part to protect their own production (which often cannot compete on the global marketplace) and in part as a source of income – which is important for countries that do not have a meaningful system of income tax. For a map that colour-codes countries on the basis of the level of their import tariffs, see the online WTO database at *data.wto.org*.

10 EU (June 2006) *Sugar*, online but hard to find, as it's buried deep inside the EU website.

11 There is a flipside though: without these subsidies, food would be more expensive in urban areas.

12 See the section on "Export Subsidies" of the WTO Ministerial Decision of 19 December 2015 (WT/MIN(15)/45 – WT/L/980), online.

13 The assumption is that this would then result in governments providing better services in the fields of education and health and suchlike, not in governments responding with aggression and suppression. This assumption is not always correct.

14 Debt bondage: I work for you, and my child gets sick, so you lend me money at a high interest rate, but I am unable to pay off my debt; therefore I, and possibly my children, have to continue to work for you.

15 For a sobering account of realities in India and Ghana in particular, read LeBaron, G. (2018) *The global business of forced labour: report of findings*, SPERI, online. It has an excellent summary.

16 The calculation was done on the basis of production estimates of Keefer, P. and Loayza, N. (2010) *Innocent bystanders: developing countries and the war on drugs*, World Bank, in combination with the 2017 crop price estimates of UNODC (online, page 2).

17 I think the phrase was coined in World Bank (September 2006) *Gender equality as smart economics: a world bank group gender action plan (fiscal years 2007–2010)*, online.

18 From *data.worldbank.org/indicator*, indicators China and 'Agriculture, forestry, and fishing, value added (annual % growth)', accessed on 6 October 2019, and then use the 'download data' button that gets you a spreadsheet, from which you can make whatever tabulation you are interested in. (In this case, I selected China, looked for the last year of negative growth, and then took the average growth between the following and the most recent years.)

5

MICROFINANCE

This chapter also makes a few observations about other levels of finance, and has a prologue about the sustainable livelihoods framework.

Prologue

If you're an urbanite who travels to rural areas for some sort of poverty reduction purpose, take a printout of the 'sustainable livelihoods framework' with you, and read a bit about its use as an assessment tool. Using this framework reduces the risk of returning to town with simplistic notions of what is needed to bolster liveli- hoods, or naïve conclusions about the achievements of the programme you went to visit. The framework can be visualised as a simple flowchart – see Figure 5.1. Table 5.1 lists its components.

Households often combine activities, which may include farming, paid work, cottage production, foraging, fishing and small-scale trading. Government support, charitable handouts and gifts from relatives may add to the income.

The aims of these various livelihood elements may evolve. Initially, the overall aim might be to increase income or to even-out consumption over the year to minimise hunger in the lean season. This aim may change into strengthening the household's ability to cope with shocks by building reserves or buying insurance, or into something related to the next generation's prospects.

People's livelihoods are shaped by a complex constellation of ever-changing and interrelated issues, and many of them are outside their own control. Because success depends on so many things, interventions that focus on only one of them - such as financial capital - are unlikely to lift many households out of poverty.

So why is this chapter about microfinance? Because rural households do need financial products and services, and more so now than in the past. Moreover, the nature and role of financial products and services are evolving, and they are likely to have much more impact in the future than they have to date.

FIGURE 5.1   The sustainable livelihoods framework

TABLE 5.1   The components of the sustainable livelihoods framework

Issue	Explanation or examples	Really bad case scenario
Vulnerability context		
Shocks	Death in the family, war, earthquake, price hike, failed harvest.	You face multiple shocks and trends of different types. Each one reduces your ability to deal with the next. Collectively, they cause you to lose your reserves and your ability to make a living.
Trends	Gradual soil degradation, climate change, migration trends, ICT trends.	
Seasonality	The months without job opportunities or before the harvest, the cold winter months, the season in which people get sick.	You skip meals or sell your assets at low prices to meet urgent needs ('distress sales').
Household assets		
Human capital	Skills, competencies, and other qualities. Ankita is strong and can read. Afaafa knows all about forest products. The voice of Umm Kulthum moved her out of rural poverty and into stardom.[1]	You are illiterate, undernourished, unskilled, in poor health, and living with a serious disability.

Issue	Explanation or examples	Really bad case scenario
Social capital	All people who help you out in times of trouble, or may do so in the future, because of family ties, kinship, or friendship.	You have relied on social capital so much that nobody wants to help you anymore. Now you owe people.
Natural capital	Forests and the other resources that are covered in Chapter 3, on 'the commons'.	These resources have deteriorated, or you no longer have access to them.
Physical capital	Yours: your home and everything you own that may be useful or sellable (including livestock). Not yours: roads, school buildings and such.	You never had anything or now sold everything. You have no access to a school, electricity, roads, or a mobile network.
Financial capital	Savings in whatever form (gold earrings count), as well as loans, wages, and cash transfers from the state, your aunt or anywhere else.	You have no regular income or reserves to invest or to deal with adversities. Or worse (and very common): you are indebted.
The operating environment		
Laws, rules, norms, and values	Official laws and rules, ranging from international trade laws to local rules about market access. This also includes religious and social norms and values. Rules are not the same for everybody! See the cross-cutting issue of intersectionality.	You aren't permitted to borrow, buy, collect, produce, or sell certain products because you can't get the right permit or because you are a woman or belong to a certain caste or group.
Institutions	Government and its bureaucracy, but also all sorts of companies and organisations that can be helpful or make life extra difficult.	
The cross-cutting issue		
Intersecting discrimination because of all sorts of personal identifiers (also called 'intersectionality')	Power structures and perceptions about your multiple identities compound (or ease) the challenges you face. These are not *inherent* weaknesses but *imposed* weaknesses: they are weaknesses only because people say and think they are.	You are unlikely to develop to your full potential if you are a poor rural child bride from an ethnic minority, who follows a minority religion and lives with the stigma of a disability.[2]

The potential of financial inclusion

'Financial inclusion' means that people and small businesses have access to useful, affordable, and understandable financial products and services, whenever they might need them. Financial inclusion is important. Consider the potential impact of financial inclusion on the lives of our remotely located heroes: Ankita and her child (see Table 5.2).

The second Ankita strengthened her livelihood by investing in her production capacity. She also smoothed her consumption by taking a consumer loan when times were tough, by investing in a pension and insurance, and by saving money to

TABLE 5.2 Ankita's life story, in worlds with and without financial inclusion

The issue	Ankita 1, in a world without financial inclusion	Ankita 2, in a world with financial inclusion
A piece of land next to Ankita's farm is for sale.	Ankita has no money. The only loans offered by the village's microcredit office require the first repayments to be made almost immediately. Ankita would not be able to make these initial repayments because it will take months to get the first harvest. So she can't buy the land.	Ankita has no money but takes an ***agricultural loan*** that won't have to be repaid until she has a harvest to sell. She buys the piece of land and the necessary inputs for that extra land. As a result, her annual income goes up. She uses part of the extra income to repay the loan, and another part of it to ***insure against harvest failure*** and to invest in a ***village saving scheme***.
A bad harvest means lean months before the next one.	Ankita gets support from a neighbour.	Ankita takes a ***short–term consumption loan*** to bridge these lean months.
A few years later, Ankita's cow dies, and extreme weather destroys the harvest.	A relative gives Ankita food and a new cow. This depletes her social capital. She now owes her neighbour and her relative a favour.	Ankita's insurance compensates her for the harvest failure. She buys a new cow with the money saved in that village saving scheme.
After another few years, there is another disappointing harvest.	Ankita has no social capital left. She and her child skip meals, and she borrows money from a wealthy farmer who doubles as a loan shark.	Ankita does not face problems, as she has a bigger field and therefore a larger harvest and because her insurance compensates for part of her losses. She starts investing in a ***micro-pension***.

The issue	Ankita 1, in a world without financial inclusion	Ankita 2, in a world with financial inclusion
Ankita's child gets sick.	Ankita sells her cow to cover treatment costs.	Ankita covers the treatment costs with the savings she has accumulated in that village saving scheme.
Years go by. Climate change makes the harvests increasingly unpredictable.	Ankita is unable to cope with shocks, the gradual deterioration of her plot of land and the effects of climate change. She gets more loans from the wealthy farmer. She sells her farmland, but that's not enough to repay the wealthy farmer, and she and her child are forced to work for him to pay off her debts. These debts have grown because of high interest rates and her failure to make timely repayments.	When the internet came to her region, she used **peer-to-peer lending** to move to profitable multi-year crops. The extra income allows her to invest in the ongoing fertility of her land. As Ankita gets older and loses some of her strength, she **leases equipment**[3] to ease her workload. To ensure she has enough to last until the next harvest, she deposits the money she earns after the harvest into her bank account and withdraws one-twelfth every month. Ankita is no longer poor and regularly supports friends and relatives in their times of hardship. This builds Ankita's social capital.
Ankita passes away.	Ankita dies at 60, in abject poverty. She and her child were unable to pay off all her debts, so the child – now an adult – is forced to continue as a debt slave for the wealthy farmer and his offspring.	Ankita dies at 70. Until the end, she used her social capital to get occasional care and her pension to cover her increasing medical costs. Her child – now an adult – inherits what remains of Ankita's wealth.

bridge income gaps. The first Ankita did nothing of the sort. Instead, she depleted her social capital and fell prey to a loan shark, resulting in the loss of her land and 'debt slavery' that her child continued to suffer from after her death.

So, potentially, the differences between a life lived with and without microfinance are very significant. However, most of today's poor rural households don't yet benefit from any financial products. The reason is that microfinance faces three problems.

Financial inclusion in practice

Problem 1 of 3: most poor farmers worldwide don't have access to financial products

The reason that poor farmers have less access to financial products than wealthier farmers[4] is that it is hard to reach them and lend them money without taking high risks and incurring high costs, compared to the size of the loans.

About these risks

In some cases, microfinance is not feasible at all. In fragile environments, for example, or in the case of highly mobile populations, few institutions will lend Ankita money, as she might be untraceable when it's time to repay the loan. They won't insure her against adversity either, as the risk of adversity is simply too high.

Even if Ankita stays where she is, she might <u>default</u>[5] on her repayments. Her harvest may fail, or she may not have access to markets where she can turn her produce into money. Or perhaps she *does* have the money to repay the loan but lives in an area where people have low repayment discipline.

To cover defaulting risks, traditional banks secure 'collateral'. This is some sort of fixed asset, like a house or piece of land, which goes to the bank if the loan is not repaid. But poor people often do not *have* collateral – and poor women even less, as land is often registered in the names of men (see Chapter 2). If Ankita does have a fixed asset, it will probably be something small and remote, which the lender will not be able to turn into meaningful money. And suppose that she *does* have a sellable piece of land, do you really want to take that away from her? If you do, you effectively gave her a loan that did not increase her income (or else she would have repaid it) and then take her sole property, leaving her worse off than she was before you lent her the money! Then again, if you *don't* claim your collateral, you implicitly tell other borrowers that it's OK to default. These are the tricky dilemmas microfinance institutions have to deal with.

Microfinance institutions have found ways to reduce default risks. Some are based on cruelty. I once interviewed a woman who told me that "when I couldn't pay, they took my second sari to punish me, and now I only have what I'm wearing." Some of the creepier lenders shame defaulters by yelling at them in public or forcing them to sit in front of their office. More humanely, microfinance institutions have created 'lending ladders' that allow people to borrow ever-increasing sums of money, provided they repaid all their previous loans. 'Yes Ankita, we can lend you $1,000, as you've previously borrowed $100 and $500, and you repaid both loans on time.' Institutions also lend to people (mostly women) who form groups and serve as each other's guarantors. 'We promise that we will repay Ankita's loan if she does not do this herself.' Other microfinance institutions are using harvests as collateral, instead of the more traditional houses and plots of land. And lastly, some institutions check their clients' credit history and current loans, through a governmental credit bureau or community leaders, or by linking their client databases with the ones of other microfinance institutions.

None of these solutions is perfect. Agricultural loans are particularly tricky. If the harvest fails, Ankita can't repay her loan because she has no harvest to sell. Her group members can't repay the loan on her behalf either. *Their* crops are likely to have failed too, as crops typically fail across a whole region rather than just on an individual farm. The lending institution can't take Ankita's harvest as collateral, as there *is* no harvest to take. Even that very cruel option – taking poor Ankita's only other item of clothing – does not actually help the microcredit provider, as a poor woman's secondhand sari won't fetch much money.

Where the lending risks are very high, a combination of microcredit and crop insurance might be a way forward (see Box 5.1). Another option: governments and NGOs sometimes subsidise loans or act as guarantor. 'We will repay these loans in case the rainfall remains below level X, or in case the temperature exceeds level Y.' Such guarantees are risky and often costly affairs for the guarantors, in part because they tend to lead to careless lending: 'It's no problem if Ankita doesn't repay her loan. We'll just claim it back from the government.'

All these risks exist if the bank issues loans to people who live right next to the bank. In reality, poor rural people do not live right next to the bank at all, and reaching them requires additional risk-taking related to their remoteness. This is because the uncertainty under which you agree on a loan is higher if you operate in an environment that you don't know very well. If this is unclear, imagine a phone

---

BOX 5.1   MICRO INSURANCE

Micro insurance provides people with compensation in case of a predefined type and extent of loss. The two most common types are (1) health and accident insurance, which is often offered as an add-on option to loans, and (2) insurance against rural income shocks, offered to farmers, pastoralists, and fisherfolk. In this box, I use harvest insurance to illustrate the key points.

Harvest insurance is generally 'index insurance', which means it uses easily verifiable criteria that are specific to a *region*, rather than a particular farm. This works better than insuring the specific harvests of individual farms, which would require costly inspection and runs the risk of fraud and of farmers not trying hard to get a good harvest. Index insurance pays out if the weather is too hot or cold, or there has been widespread flooding or too little rain or a cyclone, or if satellite imagery shows widespread crop failure in a farmer's wider region. Because insurance pays money when things go wrong, it may reduce people's harmful coping behaviour in case of a crop failure, such as distress sales and skipping meals, and risky behaviour like sex work, begging, and illegal economic activities.

To encourage the expansion of micro insurance products and coverage, governments and donors often give insurance providers grants for rural product development and rollout. To encourage subsequent uptake of these products, they subsidise micro insurance premiums.

Like other forms of microfinance, micro insurance is evolving and expanding rapidly. Already, there are schemes with hundreds of thousands of subscribers and, collectively, the national index insurance programmes in India are reaching over 30 million people.[6] The number of schemes is increasing every year, and providers have increasingly fine-tuned design and links to other microfinance products. Some companies are developing competing products that serve roughly the same purpose. Already, there are guaranteed credit lines that become available once adversity kicks in (so that you know you'll be able to get credit in case you encounter problems), and there is the beginning of peer-to-peer 'weather immunity tokens', where investors and farmers both contribute to a fund that pays out to either one of them after the harvest season, depending on what the weather has been like.

call in which an unfamiliar voice tells you in an unfamiliar dialect that she lives far away but has a very good idea and if you lend her $1,000, then she'll pay you back double – honestly!

So there are challenges, and those mentioned here are merely the tip of a small iceberg. However, they can be overcome with creativity, and the microfinance sector is one where institutions test things out and adopt each other's good practice. The group guarantee and lending ladder principles, for example, were among the earlier innovations, and both are now used all over the Global South.

About these costs

Irrespective of loan size, a lending operation requires several steps. As steps take time and time costs money, each loan incurs a minimum cost. Bigger loans take more time but not proportionally so, which means that small loans are relatively expensive to agree on and manage.

Some of the costs are related to the time and effort it takes to get somewhere. Double the distance incurs much more than double the costs, because the general rule is that locations further from urban centres have worse and fewer roads and more dispersed populations. The costs go up a little more if you restrict your loans to certain groups, as microfinance programmes often do, such as women, people living with a disability, or demobilised soldiers.

Here, too, microfinance institutions have found ways forward. They reduce their work by relying on local groups to do much of their group members' administration. They link up with NGOs that have better outreach capacity, are better able to find people who fit the lending criteria, and are willing to promote the uptake of microfinance products and take responsibility for some of the paperwork. Phone apps further reduce administration and the need for face-to-face contact.

Problem 2 of 3: most people who use microfinance products don't end up with significantly stronger livelihoods

In 2015, the *American Economic Journal* had a special issue that reported on microfinance impact research. The overriding finding was a "consistent pattern of modestly positive, but not transformative, effects".[7] Other research came to similar conclusions. Sometimes the borrower's income composition changed after using microcredit (with more farming income and less labour income, for example) but without increasing the overall size of income, leading to the conclusion that "facilitating access to credit without addressing other constraints may not be enough to increase investment and profits".[8]

Perhaps further design tweaks will improve outcomes. Microcredit could usefully focus more on the agricultural cycle and offer grace periods[9] that don't end until there's a sellable harvest, even where this takes a few years. There is also no widespread venture capital equivalent in microfinance, for initiatives that are high risk but could possibly result in high rewards.[10] More concerted efforts to improve financial literacy among borrowers would help people choose appropriate loans and avoid unserviceable debts.

But design tweaks will only help a little, as the biggest problems are unrelated to the microfinance products themselves. Instead, they have to do with the limits of

ANKITA GOT A MICROLOAN!

FIGURE 5.2   Some training might be useful

undiversified rural economies where <u>markets are quickly saturated</u>[11] and with the 'poverty trap' that poor people find themselves in. If everything works against you, a bit of extra money won't help you lift yourself out of poverty.

Microfinance institutions often deal with disappointing results by complementing microfinance products with other support that might give poor people the push they need to escape poverty. A common addition to microcredit is training that teaches borrowers technical and business skills. The logic is simple: "micro-credit enables the fisherman to buy a net [but if he] doesn't know how to use the net, he will return to his old way of doing things . . . with the added burden of having to pay back the debt."[12]

More recently, microfinance organisations have been combining their loans with add-ons such as health-care services, support to get more education, and business coaches (who are typically more established entrepreneurs who volunteer their time). Notwithstanding all these additional products and services, for now, the results of microfinance operations are disappointing, and sometimes microfinance even causes people harm.

Problem 3 of 3: microfinance causes people harm

An evaluation of a Bangladeshi microcredit programme that focused on <u>tenant farmers</u>[13] found that only a fifth of the eligible households had acquired loans two years after the programme's launch.[14] Other assessments report similar findings: in microfinance programmes in Morocco, Mexico, and Ethiopia, for example, only 17, 19, and 31% of the people who *could* take a loan actually *did* take one.[15]

Part of the explanation is that the obstacles people face cannot be overcome with a bit of money. Another important reason is that many people find loans too risky and therefore unattractive (this behaviour is called 'risk rationing').[16] They have a point, and, paradoxically, the risk of harm is highest in the areas where microfinance aims to achieve the greatest benefits. Specifically,

- Consumer credit is meant to smooth consumption by providing money in times of hardship, to be repaid in times of relative plenty. In reality, such credit is often used to reduce hardship today – but without reasonable expectations of better times tomorrow. In such cases, and over a period of time, the net result is that total consumption is lower than it would be without microcredit, because of the fees and interest payments. People end up "eating leaves and salt"[17] in order to repay their loans. Mobile credit services make it easier for this to happen, as it's quick and prone to borrowing on the basis of impulse (to gamble, for example) rather than sound thinking, and because annualised interest rates may go into several hundred percent.[18]
- Business-focused microcredit is meant to increase business income, but the obvious risk is that the results of investment fall short of expectations. If this happens, your gains may be insufficient to cover the interest payments, and repayments

may require you to sell more assets than you bought. Borrowing costs may further increase if you incur new debts in order to repay old ones or if your repayments are late and fines and interest-on-interest are added to what you owe.[19] That said, you may end up defaulting on your loan altogether and lose your collateral or standing in your community. In the worst-case scenario, this leads to death: in India and Bangladesh, there are many documented cases of people's inability to repay their loans causing such despair that they chose to end their lives.[20]

- Microfinance was hoped to increase people's sense of well-being, as it would reduce hardship and open up opportunities. But some research found the sense of well-being to be *reduced* because of microcredit, as the opportunities cause restlessness and the loans induce repayment stress.[21]
- Especially in non-profit institutions, microfinance streams often prioritise or exclusively target women.[22] The underpinning thoughts are that

1 Women are often poorer than men and therefore a particularly worthy focus of poverty-alleviation efforts.
2 Women have less access to other forms of financing.
3 Women are easier to monitor because they stay closer to their homes and are more likely to repay their loans, as they're more sensitive to peer pressure, make more conservative investment choices, and are less likely to misuse the money they borrow.
4 Microfinance empowers women. Training and other support activities equip them with knowledge and stronger social networks, while their increased control over finances increases their status and authority to make

FIGURE 5.3   Microfinance might be harmful

decisions within their households and in relation to their businesses. This enhanced status also reduces the chance of domestic violence.

5   The empowerment of women is good for the next generation as well, as women tend to use their decision-making power to ensure the nutrition, health, education, and well-being of their children.

All these are true and valid points – except the fourth one. There is little evidence of microfinance empowering women. In fact, there is evidence that microfinance sometimes *dis*empowers them. Women often don't actually control the money they borrow (instead they borrow the money for the men in the household to use) but are left extra vulnerable if they are unable to repay their loans. Occasionally, women-focused microfinance even *causes* domestic violence, if men feel a need to reconfirm their authority (though to my knowledge no research has ever found this to be a systematic and longer-term problem).[23] It may also reduce men's contributions to household expenditures, forcing women to use their loans for consumption rather than investment. And then there's the issue of the types of investments made by women: in many conservative rural areas, women use these loans to invest in traditional, home-based work – duck-rearing, food processing, tailoring and suchlike. Does this empower women and enable them to make the most of their limited set of options, or does it entrench gender patterns that keep women poor and subservient?

Village saving groups perform better than other types of microfinance. Informal saving groups have existed for a long time. In 1991, an NGO called CARE developed a standardised version of such groups, piloted it in West Africa, and called its groups 'Village Savings and Loan Associations' (VSLAs). Like the informal savings groups, VSLAs help poor people build savings that they can use to invest in business or well-being or spend in times of hardship or celebration. VSLAs are designed to ensure they cause no friction, that all is clear to everybody, and that no money disappears. Their results tend to be positive, and they don't suffer the indebtedness risks of microcredit.

Financial inclusion is likely to have more impact in the future

Microfinance in its modern form didn't exist until the early 1980s. It started with microcredit – small loans to poor people. It then expanded into saving schemes and from there to things like insurance and mobile banking services.

Microfinance rapidly grew in turnover and geographical coverage and got recognition in the form of a Nobel Peace Prize in 2006. However, already at that time, an emerging body of research showed that the biggest part of microfinance – the loans – didn't actually have much of a positive effect and had the potential to do grave harm. This research did not stop the sector's growth but did show that microfinance needs a serious upgrade for it to be of real help to large numbers of people.

It is likely to get such an upgrade. Microfinance is rapidly evolving. Every year, microfinance products and services innovate a little more, penetrate more remote and poorer rural areas, and offer more appropriate and appealing products. With fast-evolving ICT solutions, new possibilities are about to be unlocked, also for organisations and companies that do not see themselves as microfinance institutions but that spearhead financial inclusion – such as mobile app developers and companies that transfer migrants' remittances. Even individuals with a bit of money to spare are playing an increasingly important role (see Box 5.2).

BOX 5.2 ONLINE PEER-TO-PEER LENDING

The first online peer-to-peer lending platforms started in 2005, in Canada and the UK. These platforms match individuals who have money to invest with borrowers who struggle to get loans through conventional banking channels. The idea caught on, and the sector now issues billions of dollars in loans every month. It's a volatile sector. New models are being tried all the time, and, in China in particular, many platforms suspend operations soon after they've started.

Most platforms are commercial and lend only within a single country, but there are also some non-profit crowd-funding platforms that link lenders from anywhere to poor borrowers in the Global South. These charitable platforms cover their costs through donations and government grants and tend to charge little or no interest or fees (though their intermediaries generally do and not necessarily low ones either).[24] Some of these non-profit platforms have grown large already, continue to grow more, and seem robust – check out kiva.org and lendwithcare.org, for example.

Such charitable peer-to-peer lending platforms face all the challenges covered in this chapter. But they did manage to generate a whole new flow of money, and there are some seriously creative minds behind them, so watch this space, as they'll probably come with innovations that nobody has thought of yet.

The pace of change will accelerate because ICT makes every next step a little easier, and only a few years from now, a wide range of products and services will be available wherever there is a minimum of stability. Where illiteracy, malnutrition, discrimination, bureaucracy, corruption and other challenges that keep people poor are being resolved, this next generation of financial products really *does* have the potential to reduce short-term hardship and improve long-term prospects.

Microfinance will never help the very poorest people, as they need grants instead of loans, as well as other forms of support. But it *will* help millions of people who are poor but not hugely constrained.

Financial products and services in Ankita's wider environment

Rural development needs at least three levels of financial products and services, and at each level, the landscape is changing.

Microfinance

Lessons of past failure and new ICT opportunities are changing the nature of microfinance products and services. But whatever the changes, microfinance will only ever serve the financial needs of households and very small businesses, with some local spill-over benefits if a loan is spent locally or an investment creates jobs.

Larger-scale financial products and services

Rural economies need bigger companies as well. They run larger shops and farms that employ people, provide affordable inputs, produce and maintain equipment, set up trading networks, and provide mobile phone services, to name just a few of their roles. They, too, need financial products and services – and this is a problem in large parts of the Global South, where the products and services such companies need are the financial sector's 'missing middle'.

At this level, products and services are also on the move. Some microfinance institutions morphed into financial institutions that also issue larger loans, in recognition of the employment-generation potential of such loans; banks that used to cater for big businesses only are now considering smaller clients as well. Both microfinance institutions and banks are supported by donor programmes that typically have aims such as these:

> to increase the availability of finance to the rural economy by expanding credit for rural micro, small, and medium enterprises with a strong focus on women and marginalized areas. . . [and to deepen] the capacity . . . of the participating private sector financial intermediaries . . . to offer sustainable finance, including piloting innovative financial solutions, towards activities that promote inclusion, job creation, and poverty reduction in key sectors like agriculture, livestock, forestry, and fishery.[25]

The long-term hope is that banks get *so* good at doing things that reduce poverty, empower people and grow rural economies, that they will eventually do so with their own resources – just because it makes good business sense.

Financial products for governments

Neither microfinance nor the somewhat larger financial products and services will finance roads and electricity networks, dikes and free education. For those things, *governments* need to invest. Here, too, the donor community is active. Donor countries lobby quite hard for rural investments, partly because they fear that a failure to create massive employment in poor rural areas with young populations will add to migration pressure on, ultimately, their own countries. They also provide technical advice, grants, loans, and, in the case of China, thousands of workers who fly in and out to build things.

There is a lot of progress at each of these three levels, but not everything is working well. For example, and taking the three levels in turn,

- Microfinance is still expensive. The sector's average annualised rate is probably around 40% per year, and there are plenty of companies that charge more than 100%.[26]
- There is little evidence that donor investments in financial institutions have had the catalysing effect they were aiming for. A related aim, the 'blended finance' efforts in which donors provide funding for investments that are meant to inspire the private sector to follow with larger investments, has not yet been successful either. Few private investors have *actually* followed, and almost none of them invested in poor rural communities in low-income countries.[27]
- The level of indebtedness of poor country governments is worsening and is starting to remind people of the debt crisis of the 1970s. In many low-income countries, public debts have become, or will soon become, unserviceable.[28] These governments will have to change their borrowing tactics, or they won't have the money to maintain what they're now building (or, in a recent development, they'll end up transferring key infrastructural assets to China, to compensate for defaults).[29]

Far more important than these various risks and disappointments is the one risk that could wipe out the world as we know it. In 2008, the world financial system was close to a total collapse. The root causes for that financial crisis have not yet been addressed.

The global financial system

The global financial system very nearly collapsed in 2008 because too many banks had taken too much risk. Global economic activity and trade took an immediate hit. Some senior bank employees feared a collapse of the world economy and hoarded food and water. Even in relatively isolated and poor rural communities in developing countries, the banks' excessive risk-taking in the USA housing market had repercussions. Because of the recession that followed, many rural migrants lost their jobs abroad and in the cities, and could no longer send the remittances needed to keep their home villages afloat. Many people working in informal jobs could no longer sell their products, as consumption declined and competition got fiercer.

This financial crisis compounded the effects of the food and fuel price hikes of the years preceding it. These price hikes weakened many people's food intake and led to harsher workdays and negative coping behaviours, such as asset sales and children swapping school for work to supplement their household incomes. Community saving associations collapsed, as participants needed their savings back to buy food.

Together, the price hikes and financial crisis formed the 'triple F crisis' of food, fuel and finance. For most adults, it led to extra but temporary hardship and stress. Some of this hardship arose after the global economy had resumed its growth, as people had sold their productive assets to buy food or had incurred debts that were hard to repay. The effects were worst and most permanent for many children. Kids who drop out of school don't automatically return to it in better times, and you can't reverse stunted growth by eating more a few years later. One estimate, based on interviews with a random sample of 26,000 African mothers, came to the conclusion that the triple F crisis had led to the deaths of an additional 28–50,000 infants in Sub-Saharan Africa alone. Most of them were girls.[30]

In 2008–09, trillions of dollars in government support enabled the global financial system to survive the shock, and the financial crisis itself had brought down food and fuel prices. But these won't have been the last shocks. We live in an interconnected and volatile world, and the next multifaceted global crisis may be around the corner. It may hit unexpectedly, as the triple F crisis did, and would add to the challenges posed by local shocks and trends. It is possible to prepare for such crises by expanding and fine-tuning social assistance, including cash transfers, free education, and school meals (see Chapter 6), and by investing in microfinance products that bolster poor people's resilience. If you're in the position to help set government priorities, these are good ones.

Why is all this relevant, and what does it mean for you?

In the contract for this book, Routledge stipulated that it could not exceed 100,000 words. So why spend almost 10% of it on microfinance, after research found that microfinance had not been making *that* much of a difference?

Two reasons. First, because of the impressive growth pattern, size and appeal of the microfinance sector. The growth of global microfinance has been non-stop since its birth in the early 1980s. This growth path continued even after all that critical research was published a few years ago.[31] As a result, microfinance is now big business: in 2017, microfinance institutions collectively issued loans to the value of US$114 billion, spread over loans issued to an estimated 139 million people.[32] The attraction of microfinance is obvious from my students' choice of essay topics as well: every year, it's one of the top themes (and every time, students are disappointed when their literature research shatters their optimism). Second, microfinance may not be the silver bullet it was once thought to be, but it, and the world around it, is changing, and in all likelihood the best of microfinance is yet to come.

So:

If you're a microfinance practitioner, continue trying out new things, *within* microfinance and by *combining* microfinance with other interventions that address things that keep people poor ('credit-plus'). Realise that these trials are most useful if you link up with researchers who carefully assess the results – or else your costly innovative work won't have much of a footprint beyond the usefulness of the programme itself. And also,

- Don't get into microleasing unless you've made sure you understand your country's tax and banking rules, as they are not always lease-friendly. Also keep in mind that there is a fine line between helpful leasing and exploitation: there are too many rickshaw drivers and garbage collectors that spend far too much leasing rickshaws and pushcarts without ever being able to afford buying one. Lease-to-buy schemes tend to be less exploitative.
- Don't use microfinance instruments to reach the very poorest people in communities – it won't help and may well harm them.
- Do not use non-transparent fees, and consider ways in which you could avoid a situation in which small loans lead to large repayments because of hidden charges and interest-on-interest. For inspiration, take a look at Islamic microfinance principles.
- Be aware that there are massive differences across microfinance institutions. Many are well-intentioned, and your work could help them enhance the impact they have. However, some are sophisticated, large-scale equivalents of the local loan shark, there to make a profit irrespective of the harm this may cause. Please don't work for the latter type.

If you are a researcher, the three biggest research gaps are (1) the impact of microleasing, (2) the impact of micropensions, and (3) the extent to which microfinance has better results if the borrowers are poor but not burdened by many of the other factors that *keep* people poor (so if they are literate, healthy, and living in a cash-based environment with a reasonably diverse rural economy, without being subject to all sorts of discrimination).

If you work for a government, keep in mind that

- State-owned agricultural banks tend to be or become inefficient, overstaffed, and political, and it is generally better to provide strategic support to market-driven private sector banks and microfinance institutions with a local presence. There are limits to that, too. If you serve as a guarantor, for example, you may well be encouraging careless lending and might end up footing huge bills and contributing to a lacklustre repayment discipline among borrowers. I once interviewed a group of women who listed the conditions under which a loan did not need to be repaid, concluding that the borrowers in their village 'will be fine as long as they make sure to meet one of these conditions'.

- Microfinance won't achieve much without basic infrastructure and a meaningful local economy, as people will not have sufficient trading opportunities in such circumstances. This is where governments come in. They need to build and maintain rural infrastructure, including physical marketplaces. They should also ensure that an easy, transparent, and effective regulatory framework facilitates entrepreneurial behaviour and the work of the financial sector. Chapter 2 on agricultural production practice and Chapter 4 on trade cover these issues.
- To deal with shocks, such as the triple F crisis, your country's government should ideally save in times of plenty[33] to be able to continue essential investments and to expand social safety nets or school meals in times of crisis. Failing that, the World Bank and the EU have international crisis facilities that could possibly help with grants and easy loans, in case your country cannot handle a crisis without external support.

Lastly, and returning to the sustainable livelihoods framework mentioned in the prologue: if you're new to this field of work and are planning to visit rural areas for some sort of poverty reduction purpose, you'll need an analytical framework to direct and frame your observations. The sustainable livelihoods framework is a good one, as it reduces the risk of tunnel vision – such as thinking that all poverty can be resolved with a microloan.

FIGURE 5.4 Beware of bias

Further reading

Introductory word of warning

This is a polarised field (see Table 5.3). Don't spend much time on promotional websites of microcredit providers, as they tend to be uncritically positive. The bias is particularly strong if they depend on private donations, such as the non-profit peer-to-peer lending platforms. Similarly, be wary of vocal microcredit critics: they've often made up their minds and only consider evidence that supports their criticism. Instead, look for independent evaluations and academic research.

Microfinance in general and microcredit in particular

The most comprehensive and up-to-date publication on financial inclusion (including but not limited to microfinance) is Duvendack, M. and Mader, P. (2019) "Impact of financial inclusion in low- and middle-income countries: a systematic review of reviews", *3ie Systematic Review*, number 42, 3ie, online. The book is very critical of the quality of the research conducted to date, as well as of the impact microcredit has had so far. It concludes that "the more rigorous and lower risk of bias studies become, the less likely they are to find effects" (page v).

Duvendack's book only considered publications written in 2010 and thereafter. A book that covers the literature *until* that year is also still a very worthwhile read: Armendáriz, B. and Morduch, J. (2010), *The economics of microfinance*, MIT.

TABLE 5.3 Microcredit is a polarised field

"In our careful assessment, meeting the credit needs of the poor is one of the most effective ways to fight exploitation and poverty. I believe that this campaign will become one of the great humanitarian movements of history. This campaign will allow the world's poorest people to free themselves from the bondage of poverty and deprivation to bloom to their fullest potentials to the benefit of all – rich and poor." **Prime Minister of Bangladesh, 1997**, quoted in Banerjee, A., Karlan, D. and Zinman, J. (2015) "Six randomized evaluations of microcredit: introduction and further steps", *American Economic Journal: Applied Economics*, volume 7, number 1, footnote 1.	"Nothing can stop an idea whose time has gone. And micro-finance [he means microcredit in particular] is a discredited model. It has raised more questions than it has answered. To think that we are going to alleviate poverty is a tall claim. Microfinance has promised more than it has actually delivered, created more problems than [it] actually solved and continues to promise much more than what it actually puts on the ground." **Rural Development Minister of India, 2012**, quoted in, among many other papers, Ullah, A. and Haq, M.N. (2017) "Micro financing management and prospects: a case study analysis on Bangladesh perspective" (this really is the title), *IOSR Journal of Humanities and Social Science*, volume 22, issue 5, page 88. This statement followed a string of microfinance scandals and tragedies in India.

This second edition is an updated version of the original of 2007, which had taken ten years to produce and captured all there was to know until then.

Only a year after her 2010 book, Beatriz Armendáriz published a book about "the enormous gap between the limited number of clients that are currently benefiting from microfinance services, and the huge number of potential clients that are not": Armendáriz, B. and Labie, M. editors (2011) *The handbook of microfinance*, World Scientific. It's worth scrolling through the table of contents of this 700-page brick, as it covers important issues like microfinance ethics and the risk of mission drift – the phenomenon of a microfinance institution's gradual move towards larger loans for easier-to-reach, wealthier clients. (This is not the financial 'missing middle' mentioned before – it's just lazy micro-credit, for an easier customer base.)

The next Big Deal was the 2015 special issue on microfinance impact of the *American Economic Journal: Applied Economics* (volume 7, issue 1). The six papers that made it into the issue all report on good, quantitative research, presented in a manner that allows for comparisons across the countries they are looking at (Bosnia, Ethiopia, India, Mexico, Morocco and Mongolia; all except for the India research had a rural and entrepreneurial focus). If you then use Google Scholar to find publications that reference at least the introductory chapter (the one by Banerjee, Karlan, and Zinman) and that focus on rural microcredit in particular, you will find quite a few more recent papers, including one that I quoted in this chapter: Hossain, M. et al. (2019) "Agricultural microcredit for tenant farmers: evidence from a field experience in Bangladesh", *American Journal of Agricultural Economics*, volume 101, issue 3, pages 692–709. Or, if these publications are all too dull and econometric for your taste, read Banerjee, S.B. and Jackson, L. (2017) "Microfinance and the business of poverty reduction: critical perspectives from rural Bangladesh", *Human Relations*, volume 70, number 1, pages 63–91. This paper reflects on research conducted by two researchers who lived in a small group of villages for half a year and includes interview quotations that will make your blood boil.

Recent years saw a few special journal issues on microfinance themes. There is a good 2017 special on the issue of 'microfinance and gender', for example, from the *Journal of Development Studies* (volume 53, issue 5). Within wide themes such as this one, there are systematic literature reviews on sub-themes. On the role of microfinance on women's lives, for example, you now have literature reviews that assess the effects of microfinance on household decision-making, health, and mental health. Respectively,

- Vaessen, J. et al. (2014) "The effects of microcredit on women's control over household spending in developing countries: a systematic review and meta-analysis", *Campbell Systematic Reviews*, online. Sadly, the core finding is that microcredit really doesn't have much effect on women's decision-making authority.
- O'Malley, T.L. and Burke, J.G. (2017) "A systematic review of microfinance and women health literature: directions for future research", *Global Public Health*, volume 12, issue 11.

- Madhani, F.I. et al. (2015) "Participation in micro-finance programmes and women's mental health in South Asia: a modified systematic review", *Journal of Development Studies*, volume 51.

A drawback of these and other literature reviews is that they tend to conclude that more research is needed and that much of the research they reviewed was not very good – which has obvious implications for the quality of the literature reviews themselves.

Micro insurance

This chapter's Box 5.1 on micro insurance said that insurance may reduce negative coping behaviour after adversity hits. For a study about coping behaviours in tough times, read Janzen, S.A. and Carter, M.R. (2019) "After the drought: the impact of micro insurance on consumption smoothening and asset protection", *American Journal of Agricultural Economics*, volume 101, issue 3, pages 651–671. Another potential benefit of micro insurance is that it might encourage more risk-taking entrepreneurial behaviour. For a study on that, read Dercon, S. and Christiaensen, L. (2011), "Consumption risk, technology adoption and poverty traps: evidence from Ethiopia", *Journal of Development Economics*, volume 96, issue 2, pages 159–173.

Or you could read an overall literature review on the issue of micro insurance. The most recent one I'm aware of combines a review of past literature with a good look at current challenges and likely future developments in fields such as quality standards and impact-based targeting: Jensen, N. and Barrett, C. (2017) "Agricultural index insurance for development", *Applied Economic Perspectives and Policy*, volume 39, number 2, pages 199–219. There will probably be a more recent one by the time you read this. About the still-limited uptake of micro insurance products, read Budhathoki, N.K. et al. (2019) "Farmers' interest and willingness-to-pay for index-based crop insurance in the lowlands of Nepal", *Land Use Policy*, volume 85, pages 1–10. Jensen's literature review has a number of other good references for research on this topic as well, but keep in mind that micro insurance is gaining popularity, so research recency is important.

The technical design of micro-insurance programmes is key to their success. See, for example, Shirsath, P. et al. (2019) "Designing weather index insurance of crops for the increased satisfaction of farmers, industry and the government", *Climate Risk Management*, volume 25, online. If you want to know more about design options, keep in mind that recency is important because developments in this field are rapid, so it's best to run a Google Scholar search, limited to the past few years, combining 'micro insurance' with terms like 'remote sensing', 'satellite-based indices', 'weather index', and 'agro-meteorological'.

About guaranteed credit lines as an alternative to micro insurance, read at least the introduction and conclusion of Lane, G. (2018) *Credit lines as insurance: evidence from Bangladesh*, online. And about peer-to-peer 'weather immunity tokens' as an alternative to conventional micro insurance, read Jha, S. Andre, B. and Jha, O. (2018)

ARBOL: smart contract weather risk protection for agriculture, online. Keep in mind that this last publication is a promotional paper – to my knowledge, no academic research has been conducted yet on the issue of peer-to-peer micro-insurance.

Other forms of microfinance

This chapter also mentions three other forms of microfinance: village saving schemes, microleasing, and micropensions.

Saving schemes

For an overview of the basic design principles used in the best-known version of this (the Village Savings and Loan Associations, or VSLAs), see *vsla.net/aboutus/vslmodel*.

The vast majority of country-specific case studies on microsaving are from Africa. Their findings tend to be positive, and so is the overall conclusion from that 2019 literature review mentioned at the start of this *further reading* section. See this Malawian study, for example: Ksoll, C. et al. (2016) "Impact of Village Savings and Loan Associations: evidence from a cluster randomized trial", *Journal of Development Economics*, volume 120, pages 70–85. You may also want to do a web search for 'Rotating Saving and Credit Associations' (ROSCAs) and 'Accumulating Savings and Credit Associations' (ASCAs) – both of which are comparable to VSLAs, but less standardised.

Microleasing

A microleasing agreement is about the lease of a productive asset like a plough or a rickshaw and often includes a bit of training and insurance in case the asset gets damaged or stolen or in case the equipment causes injuries or death. Under some leasing agreements, the asset's ownership eventually swaps to the person who uses the asset. Some 2,800 years after the Chinese invented the concept,[34] BRAC rolled out the modern world's first large-scale microleasing programme in the early 1990s, in Bangladesh. Other organisations copied the concept, and by now, microleasing is fairly widely offered by microfinance institutions around the world. They tend to do this for commonly used types of equipment only, so that it's easy to sell the assets after the end of the lease period or in case the user defaults on the payments. For an overview of the common design options and the challenges and opportunities of microleasing, see Goldberg, M. (2008) "Microleasing; overcoming equipment financing barriers", *en breve*, number 119, World Bank, online. If you're going to conduct a good impact assessment on microleasing, please publish it: to my knowledge you'll be the first to do so. (If you search for relevant publications, you will find a 2012 'systematic review' on micro-leasing, from Ruth Steward et al., but it doesn't really count, as it merely comes to the conclusion that no published research on the topic exists.)

Micropension funds

Micropension funds are funds that people who work in the informal sector contribute to, voluntarily, to get a pension later in life. They are not to be confused with non-contributory government pensions or with corporate pensions from the formal labour market. To my knowledge, there are also no good publications on the effects of micropensions yet.

About larger financial products and services

The chapter quotes a World Bank rural financing project paper. There are papers on many such projects, and you'll find several if you do a web search for papers published in the past 12 months (in Google: go to *Tools* and select the period, and use a combination of terms such as "World Bank rural finance loans"). Reading through one of them gives a good idea of the things that today's financing projects are focused on and concerned with (spoiler alert: there tends to be a lot on women entrepreneurs, climate change adaptation, and the strengthening of the banking sector's ability to reach deep into rural areas). The full paper for the project referenced in this chapter is World Bank (March 2019) *Project paper on a proposed additional loan and restructuring in the amount of $400 million to the Financiera Nacional de Desarrollo Agropecuario, Rural, Forestal y Pesquero for the expanding rural finance project with a guarantee of the United Mexican States*, online. It's best to initially skip the technicalities and start reading on page 6.

On the failure of blended financing, read Attridge, S. and Engen, L. (2019) *Blended finance in the poorest countries: the need for a better approach*, ODI, online. Or do a web search for either 'blended finance' or, probably better, for 'billions to trillions', which is the blended finance crew's slogan.

On the unsustainability of the debt burden of developing countries, see UNC-TAD (2019) *Current challenges to developing country debt sustainability*, online; or, for a few brief and snappy analyses, read the ODI blogs of Jesse Griffiths. At the time of writing this chapter, he had written two of them: in October 2019, it was "Low-income country debt: three key trends", and in November 2019, it was "Solving the low-income country debt crisis: four solutions", *ODI Insights*, online. If you are interested in the debt sustainability of one or more specific countries, search for 'IMF debt sustainability analysis' – and then the countries you're interested in, or go to *imf.org/external/pubs/ft/dsa/* and go from there.

About the 2007–08 global financial crisis and the 'triple F crisis' that this was part of

There are lots of publications about the causes of the financial crisis of 2007–08, about its impact on global production and trade and, in the past few years, about the lack of meaningful reform of the financial sector in the decade after this financial crisis. The most readable of the lot is probably Luyendijk, J. (2016) *Swimming with sharks: inside the world of bankers*, Guardian Faber Publishing.

However, there has not been much research on this crisis's impact on poor communities in the rural areas of developing countries. An exception is De Velde, D. W. et al. (2009) "The global financial crisis and developing countries: synthesis of the findings of 10 country case studies", *Working Paper 306*, ODI, online. For the effects of the three crises combined, read about two research initiatives from the World Bank and the Institute for Development Studies (IDS), both of which are covered in Heltberg, R., Hossain, N. and Reva, A., editors (2012), *Living through crises; how the food, fuel and financial shock affect the poor*, World Bank, online.

And about the prologue's sustainable livelihoods framework

For guidance on how to use that sustainable livelihoods framework, read DFID (1999) *Sustainable livelihoods guidance sheets*, online. On Google Scholar, you will find hundreds of publications that applied this framework, focusing on all sorts of sectors all over the world. This includes themes covered in other chapters of this book. To just give one example, if you liked this book's chapter on 'the commons', you may want to read Pokharel, B.K., "A critical reflection on the sustainable livelihoods approach and its application to Nepal's community forestry", Chapter 6 of Upreti, B.R. and Müller-Böker, U., editors (2010), *Livelihood insecurity and social conflict in Nepal*, Swiss National Centre of Competency in Research (NCCR), online. I suggest this particular one because it has a very good summary of the sustainable livelihoods framework, which it then compares with a few other analytical frameworks, and only *then* does it explore livelihoods in the context of community forestry in Nepal.

Exercise

You're in a team meeting of an agricultural microcredit programme in India. Your organisation committed finances for five years for loans between the equivalent of US$100 and US$1,000 per year, with a grace period of up to 11 months, a maturity of a year, and start dates that are aligned with agricultural cycles. The expectation had been that this microcredit line would be financially self-sustainable after the five-year period.

Spirits are low because the first four years have not gone well. Only a small proportion of the eligible households have used your microcredit facility, and their repayment rate is only 80%. It seems *very* unlikely that this credit line is going to be self-sustainable after just one more year.

There are three items on the agenda.

1 Waiver requests

Four women requested a waiver for the remainder of their repayments. They are unable to make these last few repayments because

- Sharda's cow got sick and died.
- Amrina's harvest failed, as her potatoes got a fungus.

- Ankita's husband took the money and gambled it away. He has done so with two other microloans, taken around the same time from other microcredit organisations.
- Fatima has not been able to find a local market for her biscuits, and the road to the nearby town is nearly inaccessible.

The collateral for these loans was the women's homes and small pieces of land. You could take them to court, where they would not stand a chance. This would not help the organisation financially because court cases are costly, but it would send a clear signal to the wider community that loans really *do* need to be repaid. If you do take their collateral, the women could possibly end up homeless.

You need to make a decision.

2 The programme's past

You want to assess what has gone wrong. Microfinance literature gives you clues about what the most common problems are. Which ones seem the most relevant to your programme?

3 The programme's future

Unless things change dramatically, this credit line will not survive for long after the financial support stops. What to do? A quick email round, prior to the meeting, led to the following suggestions:

- Write a proposal for an extension of the programme for another three years. Because the utilisation rate was so low in the last period, you don't have to ask for new money, just for more time to spend the money you already received.
- Think of ways to increase the uptake and the repayment rates, in a last attempt to make this credit line self-sustainable.
- Instead of re-lending the repayments, invest the money in the improvement of the rural road to a nearby town. Such a Public Work Programme would generate an income for a number of people in the village, *and* it would address one of the key reasons for the failure of this microcredit programme: the lack of access to markets. This is why Fatima was unable to sell her biscuits.
- Instead of re-lending the repayments, invest part of the money to establish and equip an agricultural support centre. You could use the rest of the repayments to run this centre for some two years before it needs money again. This would address another key reason for the failure of this microcredit programme: the lack of agricultural expertise and risk mitigation measures. This is why Sharda's cow died and why Amrina's harvest collapsed.

What do you think of each of these proposals? Do you have better ideas?

Notes

1 Umm Kulthum (or Oum Kalthoum or Om Koltoom – there are many ways to spell her name) came from the Egyptian village of Tammy al-Zahayrah and grew into a megastar. If you are unfamiliar with Arab music, "imagine a singer with the virtuosity of Joan Sutherland or Ella Fitzgerald, the public persona of Eleanor Roosevelt and the audience of Elvis, and you have Umm Kulthum, the most accomplished singer of her century in the Arab world." Danielson, V. (7 January 1997) "Umm Kulthum Ibrahim", *Harvard Magazine*, online.

2 Disabilities may affect one's human capital: if you're blind, there are things that are harder or impossible to do. However, the *stigma* of a disability is part of intersectionality: many doors are closed for people who live with a disability, not because they wouldn't be able to do something, but because people *assume* they wouldn't be able to do something.

3 'Leasing' means that a regular payment entitles you to use, without owning, a piece of equipment.

4 This is a very consistent research finding. See, for example, Ibrahim, S.S. and Aliero, H.M. (2012) "An analysis of farmers access to formal credit in the rural areas of Nigeria", *African Journal of Agricultural Research*, volume 7, issue 47, pages 6249–6253, online; Akudugu, M.A., Egyir, I.S. and Mensah-Bonsu, A. (2009) "Women farmers' access to credit from rural banks in Ghana", *Agricultural Finance Review*, volume 69, issue 3, pages 284–299; Saqib, S.E., Ahmad, M.M. and Panezai, S. (2016) "Landholding size and farmers' access to credit and its utilisation in Pakistan", *Development in Practice*, volume 26, issue 8, pages 1060–1071, online.

5 'Defaulting' means not making repayments according to the original agreement.

6 For more on micro-insurance programmes in India and other countries, see Greatrex, H. et al. (2015) "Scaling up index insurance for smallholder farmers: recent evidence and insights", *CCAFS Report*, issue 14, online.

7 Banerjee, A., Karlan, D. and Zinman, J. (2015) "Six randomized evaluations of micro-credit: introduction and further steps", *American Economic Journal: Applied Economics*, volume 7, abstract.

8 Hossain, M. et al. (2019) "Agricultural microcredit for tenant farmers: evidence from a field experience in Bangladesh", *American Journal of Agricultural Economics*, volume 101, issue 3, pages 692–709, with the quotation taken from the abstract.

9 In the context of this book, a grace period is the period between getting a loan and starting to repay it.

10 This would require a combination of microcredit and micro insurance: you borrow for a high-risk endeavour and insure against failure.

11 Market saturation means that there are no longer any customers for your products. In rural economies, where many people produce a small range of products, you reach this point quickly. Microfinance sometimes causes market saturation by, for example, issuing too many loans for little shops that all sell the same few things.

12 Tonelli, M. and Dalglish, C.L. (2012) "Micro-credit is necessary but not sufficient for entrepreneurs in desperate poverty", *FSR Forum*, volume 14, issue 4, pages 17–21, with the quotation taken from page 17.

13 Tenant farmers are landless farmers who lease their plot from a landowner. They tend to be the poorer type of farmers.

14 Hossain, M. et al. (2019) "Agricultural microcredit for tenant farmers: evidence from a field experience in Bangladesh", *American Journal of Agricultural Economics*, volume 101, issue 3, pages 692–709.

15 These percentages are discussed in the corresponding country studies covered in special microfinance issue 1 of volume 7 of the *American Economic Journal: Applied Economics*; and summarised on page 10 of the introductory paper of this special issue.

16 Widespread risk rationing also means that efforts to register and thereby formalise land ownership (see Chapter 2) may not increase microcredit uptake, even though this is often stated to be one of the objectives of such efforts.

17 This quotation is part of a longer and heart-breaking text from Banerjee, S.B. and Jackson, L. (2017) "Microfinance and the business of poverty reduction: critical perspectives from rural Bangladesh", *Human Relations*, volume 70, issue 1, pages 63–91 (quotation from page 75).

18 For a very concise overview of the problems and possible ways forward, see the *Economist* (17 November 2018) *Borrowing by mobile phone gets some poor people into trouble*, online.

19 This trap of delayed repayments, which leads to interest-over-interest, does not exist in Islamic microfinance. Here, the lender gets compensated for the risk taken, but this does not take the shape of interest payments (called 'riba'). If Islamic microfinance interests you, do a web search for *qard hasan* (or *qardhul-hasan* or suchlike – there are no coherent spelling conventions yet) if there is no profit aim, or otherwise for *salam, murabaha, mudaraba,* and *musharak*. For savings, your key words are *al-wadi'a* and *sukuk*; for insurance, they are *takaful, ta'awun,* and *tabarru'*; and for Islamic microleasing, search for *ijara(h)*.

20 An experiment with microborrowers in rural India showed that group-based microfinance sometimes comes with excessive peer pressure and peer punishment. See Czura, K. (2015) "Pay, peek, punish? Repayment, information acquisition and punishment in a microcredit lab-in-the-field experiment", *Journal of Development Economics*, volume 117, pages 119–133. This paper hyperlinks to a few newspaper articles about the problem of microfinance-related suicides.

21 One of the earliest pieces of research that tested this hypothesis, and came to the conclusion that microcredit caused rather than alleviated stress, is reported on in Karlan, D. and Zinman, J. (2011) "Microcredit in theory and practice: using randomized credit scoring for impact evaluation", *Science*, volume 332, issue 6035, pages 1278–1284 (it's hypothesis 3, discussed on page 1282). If you use Google Scholar to find references to this paper, you will find that subsequent research came to similar conclusions.

22 This is less so now than it was in the past, partly because of the rise of commercial microfinance institutions and partly because programme designs changed after evidence showed that women-focused microfinance might in fact disempower women.

23 A few bits of research came to the conclusion that violence might initially go up when women join microfinance schemes, but that this effect dissipates over time. See page 700 of Orton, L. et al. (2016) "Group-based microfinance for collective empowerment: a systematic review of health impacts", *Bulletin of the World Health Organization*, volume 94, issue 9, pages 694–704, online.

24 The only figure I have seen is from Kiva, from 2014: "Kiva's Field Partners . . . usually charge interest . . . and the average portfolio yield of our microfinance partners is ~35 percent". (You'll find this quotation in *nextbillion.net/kiva-responds/*.)

25 These quotations are representative for a range of lending programmes that the international donor community is currently funding. These particular quotations are from a March 2019 World Bank announcement of a US$400 million facility for "additional financing for expanding rural finance project" in the south of Mexico (project summary online). It is a follow-up of a project of comparable size that spent 15% of its lending on microcredit (defined, in this context, as loans below US$1,000) and 85% on larger loans.

26 This 40% is the average annualised rate in a sample of 405 microfinance institutions in 73 countries. See table 2 on pages 10–11 of Strøm, R.Ø. and Mersland, R. (2012) "Microfinance: costs, lending rates and profitability", in Caprio, G., editor, *Handbook of key global financial markets, institutions, and infrastructure*, Elsevier, Oxford. The book is expensive but, at the time of writing, this particular chapter is available online, free of charge. Note that loans have different durations, fees, and interest rates, but it is possible to compare them by calculating their 'annual percentage rate of charge' (or 'APR').

27 See Attridge, S. and Engen, L. (2019) *Blended finance in the poorest countries: the need for a better approach*, ODI, online.

28 See UNCTAD (2019) *Current challenges to developing country debt sustainability*, online.

29 For a politically motivated but nonetheless convincing documentary about China's long-term strategy to reshape the world's infrastructure to get China in its centre, search for Vox's documentary on YouTube titled *"China's trillion dollar plan to dominate global trade"*.

30 Friedman, J. and Schady, N. (2013) "How many infants likely died in Africa as a result of the 2008–2009 global financial crisis?" *Health Economics*, volume 22, pages 611–622.

31 According to the *microfinance barometer 2018* (online, page 2), the global volume of microloans grew 8.6%, 9.4%, and 15.6% in 2015, '16, and '17 respectively.

32 See the *microfinance barometer 2018*, online, page 2.

33 Financially and through stockpiling. The latter is useful for cases of trade disruptions or large price hikes, such as those seen during the triple F crisis. However, they are only a good idea if you're able to arrange storage facilities that are safe and secure and not vulnerable to mould and mildew.

34 Trager, J. (1995) *The food chronology*, Henry Holt, New York, section on 800 BC.

6

INFORMATION AND COMMUNICATION TECHNOLOGY

At the start of Chapter 1, I said that much of rural Africa looks the way it looked decades ago. This is not true: in today's rural Africa, people have mobile phones in their hands, pockets, or hanging round their necks, and many have a reasonable signal.

Prologue

Some 20 or so rural Malawian kids were sitting on the classroom floor. Each one had a tablet, and the exercises they were doing were meant to strengthen their numerical skills. Their 'edutainment' required no literacy: it was all picture-based, with a woman's voice giving easy instructions in the local language. Some of the children recognised that six corncobs fit on six plates. Others tried it with five or seven. One or two merely moved the corncobs around, patiently but without evidence of learning or sense of enjoyment.

I was standing there, as the evaluator of this pilot programme, and made my observations with a 'business as usual' attitude. The notes I took at the time are a little dry:

- A few kids get it and like it.
- The teacher engages equally with girls and boys,
- but she ignores the kids with learning difficulties, as well as the girl who seems capable of doing far more challenging exercises.
- Two of the tablets do not work. A third tablet is about to break down, as the child is poking it too hard.

I was getting bored. This was the second school I had visited, and I thought the strengths and weaknesses of this little pilot were obvious.

Then I looked up and out of the window. Out in the open, a large group of kids was sitting under the sun, with a single suit-wearing teacher standing in the shade of a solitary tree, legs apart, surrounded by his pupils. Some were trying to get their exercise books into his hands. He took some of them without eye contact, signed them without looking, and threw them back. Others were just sitting there, waiting for the school day to be over.

This woke me up and changed my mind-set. Suddenly, the tablets were fascinating, as *they had the potential to overcome problems that decades of education strategies, teacher training, curriculum development and foreign support had not managed to address.* Even in large classrooms, tablets would allow children to become their best selves, at their own pace. Many of them would be able to do this without the support of a qualified, motivated teacher. Kids would *enjoy* working on these tablets, as e-lessons were more interesting, challenging and interactive than traditional teaching. This might keep them in school for longer and help their speed of learning. The teachers' login, in the morning, could be used to monitor the massive problem of teacher absenteeism.[1] I was sold. These solar-powered tablets had the potential of achieving a step-change in the learning of millions of rural kids.

A few days later, I flew from Malawi to Papua New Guinea, as part of that same NGO's evaluation, and saw the pilot stage of a programme that sent daily text messages to teachers in remote areas, with lesson plans and exercises they could use during that day. An assessment of the results after 100 school days of this pilot concluded that kids had more chance of progressing their learning if they were taught by teachers who received these daily text messages than if they were taught by teachers who didn't.[2] I saw a third ICT project in Cambodia (see Box 6.1) and was impressed once more. I returned home convinced that ICT was going to make a massive difference to education in even the world's most remote schools.

BOX 6.1   IF PEOPLE DON'T UNDERSTAND WHAT YOU'RE SAYING, WRITE IT DOWN

I left my phone on a restaurant table in a small Cambodian town and returned the next day with a simple question: "Did you find my phone?" Blank faces: the staff did not understand what I was saying. I asked the question many times, using different words and ever-shorter sentences, but it remained unclear what this foreigner was trying to ask. Then I wrote it down: "I lost my phone. Did you find it?" It was instantly clear, and I got my phone back. It had been a matter of pronunciation.

At the time, the Government of Cambodia and VSO – an international NGO – were jointly developing a smart phone app, for use by teachers, to help kids learn English. In countries with languages that are very different from the one kids are studying, the audio recordings of this app seem particularly important.

Years later, there are still moments where I am in awe at the way ICT can help kids learn, sometimes without any guidance at all. Check out the results of the *Hole in the Wall* initiative (see the *further reading* section), for example: sturdy tablets, embedded in a wall in the open air that children go to just because they are fun – and they learn things in the process, without any guidance or supervision. Amazing!

Overall, however, I have lost my sense of euphoria. As it turns out, ICT in education is not the silver bullet I briefly and naively believed it to be. Many ICT pilots in the education sector fail. The text message initiative in Papua New Guinea, for example, had good results, . . . yet it collapsed after the first few years. Even positive effects do not necessarily mean that the ICT investments represent good value for money. I now wholeheartedly agree with Julián Cristia, who concluded that

> Governments should consider alternative uses of public funds before implementing large-scale technology in education programs [as] recent work on this topic suggests that technology in education programs that prioritize hardware provision are unlikely to provide a cost-effective and simple solution to educational disparities both across and within countries. In particular, in poor countries where teachers' salaries are low, the opportunity costs of implementing (capital-intensive) technology programs may be substantial compared with alternative labour-intensive education interventions, including reductions in class size and professional development.[3]

This brings me to this chapter's key questions: what are the potential benefits and challenges of ICT, in rural life in the Global South, and what conditions need to be in place for the poorer segments in society to benefit from it?

What is ICT, and why is it useful in rural regions in the Global South?

ICT is the sum total of technologies that are used to facilitate communication or to store, retrieve, use or manipulate information. Radio, television, computers and phones and their hardware and software, and services such as internet kiosks, videoconferencing facilities and satellites: it all counts as 'information and communication technology'.

The effects of ICT are diverse and enormous. Let's look at seven broad areas in which ICT is potentially life-changing.

1   **ICT helps overcome disabilities.** Every now and again, my dear Egyptian wife's phone makes a pling-plong noise. This is the 'Be My Eyes' app. At the same time, several other Arabic-language volunteers hear that same noise. The volunteer who picks up first gets a visually impaired person on the line, from anywhere in the world, who will hover her camera phone above whatever she wants the volunteer to read out loud. It takes less than a minute, and it makes life easier.[4] I don't think many of the app's users are from

FIGURE 6.1 Wind-up radio

rural Yemen or Syria at the moment, but potentially the coverage is global, the service is free of charge, and the support is instantaneous. It is one of many ways in which ICT empowers people with disabilities. Text messages remind chronically ill people when it's time to take their medication. Multiple ICT channels collectively reach people with various disabilities to, for example, warn them that a cyclone is on its way and that there's a need for emergency evacuation.

2   **ICT helps the agricultural production process.** Some ICT applications are not yet within the reach of small farmers in the Global South. They don't get their cows chipped to monitor their health and fine-tune their feeding habits, for example. But the range of ICT applications that small-scale but online farmers do use is already dazzling.[5] Online platforms provide information about technical support programmes and tell you how to turn faecal matter into organic manure and who could vaccinate your livestock (and children). Apps help you build barns and recognise common animal and plant health problems. The extension centre's specialists can be in more frequent contact with you if they are able to do so by phone, FaceTime or WeChat than if contact requires face-to-face encounters. (It costs less, too, and so does a vet if a photo and phone call take the place of a visit.) There have been weather apps for quite a while, but their functionality evolved, and now they tell you, in the morning, how much water your crops require that day, and if local pest risks might be on the rise and how they could be mitigated. Social media discuss local climate change patterns and their implications for crops, planting, and harvesting methods. For some fruits and vegetables, there are apps that use your photos to identify pests and diseases. Local radio and mobile phone networks warn you in case of immediate danger, and enable you to move yourself, your dependents and your livestock to safe places before the storm reaches you. Micro-insurance uses satellite imagery and climate sensors to verify if pay-out criteria are met (because such insurance is 'index-based' – see Chapter 5). New products and services arrive every month. I'm writing this in January 2020, in Bangalore, India, where I just visited Fasal and TartanSense, two agro-tech start-up companies. Fasal is about to launch in-field sensors that link up with farmer smartphones to give real-time information about a particular field's crop and soil conditions. TartanSense is conducting final tests on a robot that will drive around small cotton farms with an eye and a bunch of logarithms that enable it to spray on weeds and diseased cotton plants, while leaving healthy ones undisturbed. By the time you read this, they may have added precision-sowing functionality too. I don't know if they'll make it, but if they do then Fasal's sensors and TartanSense's robots will elevate small farmers' precision farming in India and beyond to a new level, reducing their use of water and chemicals, and increasing their harvests. Transformative technology like this will help solve some of the key problems discussed in Chapter 2.

3   **ICT helps you trade and gets you better prices.** When I studied economics in the 1980s, neo-classical economic theory was still part of the curriculum. We ridiculed this theory, as it assumes that trade is based on equal and

perfect access to information, which was obviously and painfully untrue. ICT makes neo-classical economics look potentially relevant again, and farmers often consider "market information, including daily updates on the prices of agricultural commodities in the local markets of the surrounding district, as one of the most relevant ICT services".[6]

In many parts of the Global South, farmers no longer rely on a single local market or single middleman periodically visiting the farm. Instead, they compare demand and prices across different markets, phone a few other middlemen, and check the prices nearby factories are paying. And it shows: farmers with access to market information are more likely to produce highly perishable crops (see Box 6.2), and for products as wide apart as grain and sardines, studies find that price dispersion and variations across markets have reduced with the introduction of mobile phones.[7] The reason is simple: if the price you offer to pay is too low, nobody is going to sell you their produce, as ICT provides farmers with information about better-paying buyers. In a situation less common, but no doubt increasing in the years to come, groups form on social media to get access to quantum discounts when buying things or a good price when selling things. Farmers used to need cooperatives for this, but ICT solutions are a more efficient and less corruptible alternative.

BOX 6.2   ICT MAKES PERISHABLE CROPS A LESS RISKY CHOICE

My Thai friend's parents grow strawberries – a very perishable fruit. Their window of opportunity to sell their produce is short, and a recurrent dinner table conversation is about the volume of perished harvest. ICT has expanded their market, and this resulted in a much lower proportion of unsold perished fruit.

Saher Asad, of the Lahore University of Management Science, researched the effects of ICT on crop choices by comparing those of Pakistani farmers close to the Indian borders, where mobile phones are forbidden, with the farmers living right next to them. He found that the farmers with access to mobile phones were more inclined to grow very perishable – but also more valuable – crops than their phoneless neighbours. He reports his findings in Asad, S. (March 2016) *The crop connection: impact of cell phone access on crop choice in rural Pakistan*, online. The publication starts with this instantly clarifying farmer's quotation: "Before I had a cell phone I harvested my crops and then had to wait for a trader to buy my crops; now I talk to the trader and harvest my crops when he will buy them".

---

4   **ICT diversifies local livelihoods.** Rural livelihoods are not just about goats and tomatoes. A while ago, I did an online Excel course, given by a man somewhere in India. The background noises suggested he lived somewhere in the countryside, making a handsome income from trainees around the globe. Indeed, in some rural areas, a new elite is emerging: people whose jobs require

the internet rather than a physical presence are moving to well-connected rural regions, because they find life there to be cheaper, cleaner and nicer than in the city. More commonly, rural people make an income by selling ICT products and services. There are open-air street shops all over the Global South, sometimes in long rows, where you can order a smart phone on the basis of paper or plastic replicas of a wide range of models. Small shops sell pre-pay phone cards and <u>dongles</u>;[8] offer computer, printing and phone services – including charging your phone battery; and use an app to pay your electricity bill.

But by far the most important effect of ICT on non-agricultural rural livelihoods is its boost to economic diversification, within households and communities. ICT reduces the costs incurred when buying or selling goods and services (the 'transaction costs') and expands the market for nearly every product and service you may have on offer. The ICT's ability to match demand and supply is great

FIGURE 6.2 ICT facilitates the rural gig economy

for the 'gig economy' that has always been part and parcel of any poor country's rural life. In Western cities, Airbnb and Über were trailblazers in the utilisation of an individual's spare capacity, but poor people in rural areas have always done multiple things to make a living and have used all their assets in the process. ICT has made it easier to do this. 'Hello? Yes, sure, I could come over to fix your bike.'

5   **ICT facilitates payments, saving, and lending.** In the case of mobile payments, poor countries have led the way. Kenya wasn't the first country to launch mobile payments when it did so in 2007 (it was launched in Europe in the late 1990s), but it did have the strongest and quickest uptake: by 2013, 75% of all adult Kenyans were using it.[9] These easy electronic transfers are convenient for everybody but even more so for people in remote locations and countries that are facing war and instability. Indeed, it is *big* in Somalia, where the journey to a Western Union or similar office could be long and dangerous and where, instead, many people use mobile banking to receive money from their families and friends abroad.[10]

These remote electronic payments have also made social assistance pro-grammes cheaper, safer, and easier to implement (see Chapter 8). Eligible peo-ple receive SIM cards or debit cards that sometimes have biometric data like iris scans incorporated into them. Once the SIM or debit cards have been printed and distributed, transfers are done at nearly zero cost. Incomings and outgoings are easy to monitor, and the money arrives without opportunity for programme staff to take under-the-table fees. Robbers cannot steal cash depots because there *are* no cash depots. Vouchers for subsidised fertilisers and school uniforms are also electronic and sent to SIM cards.

Finance-related ICT is not just about easy payments: micro-finance institu-tions and village saving and lending groups use apps to facilitate their lending and saving, and for book-keeping. This saves time and money, and is more secure than the traditional 'group saving' box. But there are limits: ultimately, microfinance requires a lot of human interaction and, while mobile transfers have made operations easier for existing micro-finance users, it has not led to a massive surge in new ones yet.

6   **ICT cuts through bureaucracy and reduces the scope for corruption.** As students, my friend Jan-Kees and I spent six months in India, where we bought a secondhand auto rickshaw and drove it all across the sub-continent. We tried to get a rickshaw driving licence, but after six weeks of queuing, form-fill-ing, and paying small sums here and there (never quite sure if they were bribes or fees), we still had no clue about the process, time lines, exams, and costs involved. Eventually, we typed up a few words indicating that we were the owners of the rickshaw with number plate so-and-so and got it laminated. We occasionally showed this non-licence to policemen who stopped us and got away with it, probably because the sight of two foreigners driving a rickshaw confused them.

Even at a time in which many developing countries suffered from a lack of regulatory transparency, India's bureaucracy was unusual in its impenetrability (as you may recall from Chapter 1). To make things worse, the general rule was that the poorest and least educated groups in society had to travel further and queue for longer, and were less likely to be able to avoid paying bribes to get things done, than any other group.

Since then, the government invested heavily in 'e-governance'. In the initial stages, this was a matter of trial and error. Many initiatives collapsed or failed to reach the poorer segments of communities.[11] The most common reason was the 'design–reality gap': the product did not align well with local realities, in terms of people's needs and abilities, awareness and access. But the govern-ment persisted and learned from mistakes, and by now, India's e-governance is helping rural communities across the country cut through red tape and reduce ambiguity and opportunities for bribery. Paperwork related to land registra-tion and ownership, registering a birth or one's marriage or business, sorting out inheritance: nowadays much of the work can be done online[12] (though the poorest segments of society remain less likely to do so than the wealthier ones). Even the larger-scale corruption is under pressure because of ICT, for two reasons. First, if information portals tell people how much money has been allocated to, say, a village's electrification system, it is more likely that the village will indeed get hooked up to the electricity network. Second, shady deals are less likely if the government uses transparent e-procurement methods.[13]

7 **ICT enables us to monitor the health of and changes in rural life's core resources in real time.** Satellite imagery monitors the size and health of forests and savannahs, the size of lakes, and the state of coral reefs. Meteorological ICT follows the build-up and direction of storms, rain patterns, and temperature. Soil sensors transmit data about the soil's moisture and oxygen levels. There is also ICT that measures air pollution, tracks fish migration flows, monitors the thickness of the ozone layer, and does a million other handy things that could potentially be useful. Collectively, we are not yet smart and decisive enough to use the data generated to actually stop deforestation, climate change, or air pollution – but, at least in some quarters, the detail with which we see things going wrong helps generate a sense of urgency (see Chapter 9).

Clearly, the speed of ICT innovation is dizzying and varied (see Table 6.1), and the collective effects of ICT are enormous. But what drives this super-fast ICT evolution? And how can you make sure that the benefits are widespread and inclusive, and that the risks are mitigated?

TABLE 6.1 Four types of innovation

User-led innovation, supply chain innovation, process innovation – you could slice 'innovation' up into many different types.
Personally, I like the grouping illustrated in the following, but if this does not work for you, just do a web search on "types of innovation", and you will see all sorts of alternatives.

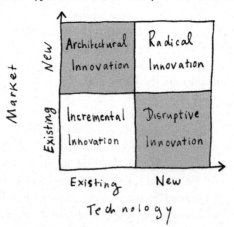

FIGURE 6.3 Types of innovation

Source: This figure is adapted from Lopez, J. (29 June 2015) *Types of Innovation*, Constant Contact Tech Blog, online.

Type of innovation	Example
Incremental innovation. Tweak something that exists already, making it a little better or cheaper.	Next year's technical tweaks will improve the performance of dongles.
Disruptive innovation. Use a new technology to cater for an existing market.	In the past, websites used to provide only centrally gathered information. Then new technology enabled them to become interactive. This was disruptive innovation: this new technology allowed information to be updated in real time by many people. It also allowed people to buy and sell products and services online.
Architectural innovation. Use existing technology in new ways.	Drone technology existed already – and then farmers started using it in their farming effort.[14]
Radical innovation. Make or do something that did not exist before, for a market that does not yet exist.	Mobile phones connected people in ways unfathomable prior to their introduction. They enable people to maintain and utilise far larger networks than ever before. We did not know we needed them … until they appeared on the market.

Over time, successful innovations move towards 'incremental innovation': the next month's mobile phones will be a little better but probably won't use radically new technologies or cater for new markets.

What drives ICT innovation?

A demand for ICT products and services does not appear out of nowhere. At the very least, people need to know that something exists and think it is attractive and affordable.

1 – People need to know that something exists. This requires access to information, which could be through social networks, media, the local school, the market square, and so on. There are many potential information channels, but access to them is unequal. Information about ICT options reaches people in urban areas quicker than in rural ones and will take longest to reach the most remote people, or people who rarely leave the farm or cannot move around independently.

2 – People must think they need an ICT product or service, or at least see its attraction. This depends in part on the inherent qualities and possibilities of a product or service, and on people's previous exposure to other ICT products and services (as this makes any new ones less unfamiliar and scary). However, traditions, fashion, social pressure, the bandwagon effect and belief systems are also important for the perceived desirability of ICT. Such factors can accelerate ICT's spread, but they can also cause a disinterest in things that, to the outsider, seem to be so very attractive. The most dramatic example I have encountered was an elderly lady who rejected an operation that could have reversed her blindness and a smartphone that could help her cope (if only because it would bleep when it was time for her pills), because she would rather 'surrender to the will of God'.

Urban and rural ICT users may not be driven by the same things. In China, researchers found that

> As rural residents have much less income and lower living standard than their urban counterparts, they are more influenced by socioeconomic conditions and living environment, and less affected by their perceptions and feelings, in their adoption and use of new media technologies. [In rural areas,] behavioural factors, including adoption of other similar media technologies, mass media use, and interpersonal communication, play a more important role than psychological factors in the diffusion process.[15]

3 – An ICT product or service needs to be obtainable and affordable. High-speed broadband is largely an urban or rich-country's blessing, and if it did exist in rural Bhutan, it would probably be too costly for most people. A general rule that we discussed in Chapter 4, on trade, applies: the poorer and more remote you are, the more you pay for almost anything that is not produced locally.

4 – And then there's 'triability' and suchlike. You may be familiar with the 'diffusion of innovation theory' (see Figure 6.4). It distinguishes (1) innovators, (2) early adaptors, (3) early majority, (4) late majority, and (5) laggards. This theory presents several adoption facilitators and impediments such as complexity (something is more attractive if it is easy to use), 'triability' (the possibility to try it out), and 'observability' (the ability to see the ICT's benefits). On average, rural people have enjoyed less education – and may therefore perceive something to be 'complex' before the average urban person does. Many products and services are also not widely available in rural areas so, often, triability and observability is low.

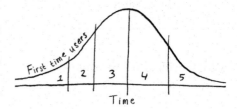

FIGURE 6.4 Diffusion of innovation theory

Even in some of the poorest rural regions in the world, demand can surge very quickly indeed. This was the case for mobile money transfers. But more commonly, ICT adoption is far slower in the countryside than elsewhere (though still faster than other forms of behavioural change – see Table 6.2). This relatively slow adoption contributes to a 'digital divide'.

What is the 'digital divide'?

The digital divide is the gulf between those who easily access modern ICT and those who do not. A 50-year-old illiterate rural woman in the Global South is on the wrong side of five divides: the education divide, the urban-rural divide, the gender divide, the age divide, and the North-South divide. These divides are not independent but reinforce each other. For example, "Women are less likely than men to make use of the internet in most countries, but are *more* underrepresented online

TABLE 6.2 Knowledge → Attitude → Behaviour ('KAB')

Community-wide behavioural change often takes a long, *long* time, and there are many
obstacles on the way. First, people require **K**nowledge. Merely sending messages around
(wash your hands, use organic manure, get your children vaccinated) is not enough: for
people to build up knowledge, they need to actually *absorb* these messages. Secondly, this
knowledge must then change **A**ttitudes: people must see the advantages and importance
of washing their hands (and so on). And finally, this must then translate into actual
Behaviour. Often, it takes years and a concerted, long-term awareness-raising effort for a
community to move from open defecation to using toilets and washing hands.

With ICT, it is different. Mobile phones were adopted, wherever there was a mobile
signal and electricity, in a matter of a few years. Or take the mobile payments in Kenya
mentioned before: the service was introduced to Kenya by M-Pesa, in early 2007, and
reached over five million active users by the December of that same year.[16]

It is easy to see why ICT-induced behavioural change progresses far faster than hand-washing:

Using a phone to be in touch	**Washing your hands after defecation**
Get a phone, and you can talk with people who are far away. The reward is direct and immediate.	Wash your hands, and this might help you or other people to avoid getting sick at some undefined later point in time because of something you can't see. The process is invisible, and the reward is indirect and delayed.

in developing countries than in developed countries, and are *especially* underrepresented in [the least developed countries]."[17]

The poorest, least educated women in the most remote regions could potentially
benefit more from ICT opportunities than anybody else, because travel costs and
other obstacles mean that other methods of communication are difficult and limited. But they are the least likely to actually have *access* to these opportunities, as they
are the least connected people in the least connected parts of the world.[18] Most ICT
products are not designed with them in mind, either. In part, this is because people
involved in ICT product development are rarely uneducated rural women from the
Global South themselves and therefore simply don't have this group in mind when
developing products. Even if they try, the results may not be very good because of
the lack of real understanding of these women's needs – see Table 6.3. And in part,
it is simply because the profit prospects are not great and because of the complica-
tions caused by the absence or unreliability of ICT infrastructure in remote areas.[19]

The problem is not just that the poorest segments of society benefit relatively little from ICT: it is also that ICT may increase inequality. First, ICT sometimes sub-
stitutes labour. Pesticide-spraying drones could cause landless labourers to lose part
of their income, for example. Second, poorer farmers may lose their market share
because the more tech-savvy and literate farmers jump at opportunities before
the poorer farmers know they even exist. Third, the mere availability of real-time
information might help the wealthier farmers and not the poorer ones – even if
both groups have access to that information. For example, if all farmers learn about
an opportunity at the same time, but wealthier farmers have quicker access to use-
able roads (as is often the case), the poorer ones lose out compared to a position

TABLE 6.3 The ladder of inclusive innovation

Level 1: Intention. The intention of
an ICT product or service is to be
of use to a group that is poor and
often overlooked.

Level 2: Consumption. The
innovative product is affordable to,
visible for, and actually adopted
and used by that group.

Level 3: Impact. The innovation has a
positive impact on the livelihoods
or well-being of the group. If you
do not want existing inequalities to
increase, then that positive impact
for the group must be larger than
the impact on other groups.

Level 4: Process. Members of the
group are involved in the design,
development, production, and
distribution of the innovation.
Being 'involved' could mean all
sorts of things, from simply being
consulted to having an actual say in
or even control over an innovation.

Level 5: Structure. The innovation is
created within a structure that is
itself inclusive. The involvement
of members of the normally
excluded group is part of standard
procedures and not merely a
temporary convenience to the
innovators.

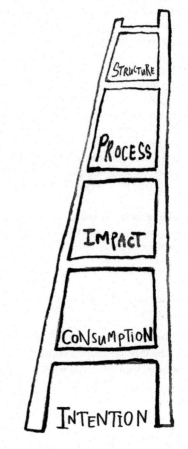

FIGURE 6.5 The ladder of inclusive innovation

Source: This is paraphrased and summarised from Heeks, R. (August 2013) "Understanding inclusive
innovation", *ICTs for Development*, online, with thanks to Richard Heeks for editing this box.

in which all farmers just go to the market and hope for the best. Finally, wealthier
farmers are more likely to use digital soil maps and satellite or drone imagery for
precision farming techniques, leaving the poorer farmers behind with poorer crops
produced at higher costs. I am not generally worried about innovation causing job
losses, as the labour market tends to adapt and seize new opportunities, but for the
poorest rural segments to benefit from these opportunities, literacy and ICT skills
will become ever-more important.

For decades now, development-focused NGOs have sought to address these
digital divides. They have invented many of the products mentioned in this chapter
and often use the higher levels of that 'ladder of inclusive innovation' summarised in
Table 6.3. Their role has been helpful, but NGOs are not specialist ICT developers,

and many of their endeavours have failed. Moreover, NGOs do not generally cover the investments needed for the ICT infrastructure that the use of individual ICT products and services requires (i.e., electricity and connectivity). For that, and to get the powerful private ICT sector to *address* rather than *reinforce* digital divides, government action is needed. To underscore the urgency to this action, part of target 17.8 of the Sustainable Development Goals is to "enhance the use of enabling technology, in particular information and communications technology". The target's success indicator is simply the "proportion of individuals using the internet"[20] (which, admittedly, is not always a good proxy indicator – see Box 6.3).

BOX 6.3 *MANHUNT* AND *BULLETSTORM*

Demand for ICT does not necessarily lead to socio-economic development, empowerment of women, or better and more secure livelihoods. Walk into an internet café anywhere in Egypt, for example, and you're likely to see neither girls nor women. This is the domain of boys and young men, and most are using the computers to play violent games.

This proportion of people using the internet will continue to increase year-on-year, because the growth of global coverage is still going strong, but also simply because one of the most important digital divides is age, and the unconnected older people will gradually be replaced with much better-connected younger ones, who won't stop being online just because they are getting older. To accelerate this inevitable progress, governments could do a mixture of two things:[21]

1   **Facilitate healthy competition.** In 2003–04, I lived in Lebanon and wondered if I really needed home internet and a mobile phone, as both were so very expensive.[22] Such high prices are a big deal because they fortify the digital divide between wealthier and poorer segments in society.

    In some countries, prices are high because ICT products are categorised as 'luxury goods' and are taxed heavily as a result. Another reason is corruption and a cumbersome regulatory environment that dogs the country's other economic sectors as well. More commonly, prices are high because there is no healthy competition. There are three reasons for this. First, some countries have state monopolies that keep prices high because of their inefficiency or because they allow governments to maintain high profit margins. Second, governments sometimes limit foreign companies' market access in an otherwise open marketplace. This is because an open ICT market will often mean that national companies are outcompeted by global players, because ICT's underlying technologies evolve *so* fast that only the world's most versatile companies are able to keep up. Governments do not like this, especially in a sector as sensitive as ICT (I write this just as Facebook is facing a new information abuse scandal, and the USA has just blacklisted a Chinese ICT giant over spying concerns). Therefore, governments are inclined to protect their national industry. Unless their countries are on the cutting edge of ICT, such governments effectively limit their people's and companies' access to yesterday's technology – slower, less user-friendly, and more expensive – because their national companies sell products that are outdated the moment they launch them. Third, governments sometimes limit competition to persuade companies to make the considerable investment required to get the infrastructure in place or develop and launch a new product. 'If you make this investment, we will give you exclusive rights in this region.' The result is costly ICT products, which reinforce the digital divide, which increases inequality.

Open competition is better, if the aim is to keep a country's ICT products current and affordable. However, open competition will not connect the poorest people in the more remote rural regions – unless the government makes it happen.

2   **Engage in public-private partnerships, and issue licenses with coverage obligations.** The key bottleneck for rural phone and internet access is 'the last mile' that links rural people to the regional electricity grid and to phone and internet networks. For profit-driven companies, this last mile is not commercially interesting in a country's more remote regions, as it is expensive to build and operate. Public-private partnerships can help: a government pays a company to build and maintain the infrastructure and stipulates, as one of the conditions, that this infrastructure must be made available to competitors too. Another option is that governments grant licenses that come with coverage obligations (as in, 'yes, you can cover region X but only if you also make the necessary investments to also cover region Y'). This option increased internet access in Nicaragua, for example.

Why is all this relevant, and what does it mean for you?

ICT is massively important for rural development. So be ICT savvy and think of ICT options for whatever sub-field you work in. Do not be the person who 'does not like smartphones' or who thinks that 'small-scale farmers are not ready for this'.

But equally do not think ICT is the silver bullet for all problems. Under repressive regimes, information sharing is problematic and risky. In countries where information exchange is not a problem in principle, it often is in practice. Many rural regions still don't have the necessary ICT infrastructure in place. In regions with the necessary infrastructure, not everybody has access to, and knows how to use, smartphones and other ICT hardware.

If you work in this field, consider how and by whom the results of your work are used and if they might increase inequalities. A climate information service in northern Ghana (which is the poorer part of Ghana), for example, attracted over 300,000 paying subscribers in only two years – but a mere 21% of them were women.[23] If you have or get a relevant position in government or the private sector, please help overcome these digital divides, including the overall urban-rural and male-female divides. Prioritise mobile phone and internet *coverage* (rather than *high speed*) and low-cost accessibility. Help ensure a conducive environment for ICT businesses, so that investments are viable and healthy competition keeps the prices down. Realise that many people do not need much to become increasingly ICT literate but that a bit of support speeds up the learning process and reduces the chance that the internet is merely used for gaming, gambling, and celebrity gossip. If your e-governance is likely to cause civil servants to lose power or the ability to extract bribes, expect and plan to cope with resistance.[24]

Consider your market when you develop your systems. Illiterate people need a local-language text-to-speak and voice recognition system to use online services, for example. But at the same time, be modest about the ambitions and hawkish about your budget monitoring, as most large-scale government-led ICT endeavours fail or end up vastly more expensive than originally envisaged.[25] Lastly, keep an eye on cyber security, as it is going to be the next 'big thing'.

If you work for an NGO, consider ICT options for whatever you do. In doing so, be sure to stay current: the time for distributing community mobile phones, for example, is over. However, unless you work in partnership with specialist ICT companies, do not try to develop ICT solutions from scratch, as they rarely work well. Instead, use easy-to-use existing products and templates, and then localise them by adapting them to whatever the local environment might require. For NGOs, the only truly viable niches are probably replication (recognise success and apply it somewhere else) and *architectural* innovation (taking something that exists and applying it to something new – see Table 6.1). As you innovate, keep in mind that – for years to come – the biggest gains ICT will achieve will probably be efficiency gains: ICT can help people achieve more yield per acre, lower their transaction costs, get better prices per unit of produce, and enable people to utilise their ploughs, storage space, motorbikes – and indeed drones – more fully.

Further reading

Resources that keep you current

This is a fast-moving field, so take an occasional look at recent journal issues of *Information Technology for Development*; *Information Technologies and International Development*; and *Technological Forecasting & Social Change*. Or go to the digital library of *IEEE Xplore*, or the World Bank's *Information and Communications for Development* series. The *Journal of Rural Social Sciences* also regularly publishes ICT-related, rural-focused papers. For more journalistic articles that are based on sound research, check out the 'agriculture' category of *ICTworks.org*.

This is just the tip of the iceberg, and you will find lots of recent research if you search for *ICT4D* or something like *rural ICT* in Google Scholar, and limit your search to the last two years. If you've done interesting research yourself, write a paper or present your research findings through an avenue such as the annual ICT4D conference (*ict4dconference.org*).

The most authoritative publication on ICT and development

World Bank (2016), *World development report 2016; digital dividends*, online. This is a *long* report – even the summary is 38 pages (which is probably why they called it an 'overview' instead of a 'summary'). But the table of contents is hyperlinked so you could take a quick look at the topics and jump to the sections that interest you.

ICT and inclusive innovation

In Table 6.3, about the 'ladder of inclusive innovation', I referred to a brief blog, written by Richard Heeks. If you want to know more about inclusive innovation, you could read a more in-depth paper by the same researcher and a few of his peers: Heeks, R. et al. (2013) "Inclusive innovation: definition, conceptualisation and future research priorities", *Working Paper Series number 53*, Centre for Development Informatics, online.

Or you could watch a one-hour presentation about inclusive innovation by Raghunath Anant Mashelkar (available on YouTube). He gives lots of examples, and in the course of the hour you start to understand why 'doing good' is often good business, and why <u>reverse innovation</u>[26] is both a threat and an important opportunity for ICT companies.

ICT facilitating learning, or not

Many journal websites allow you to search for key words in titles, so it is easy to go to *Information Technology for Development*, for example, and get all the titles that include the word *learning*. Or start with the editorial introduction to a special issue of this journal, on 'ICT and Education': Assar, S., El Amrani, R. and Watson, R.T. (2010) "ICT and education: a critical role in human and social development", *Information Technology for Development*, volume 16, issue 3, pages 151–158, online.

If your optimism needs tempering, read Cristia, J. et al. (2017) "Technology and child development: evidence from the one laptop per child program", *American Economic Journal: Applied Economics*, volume 9, number 3, pages 295–320. This is from the sobering abstract: "This paper presents results from a large-scale randomized evaluation of the One Laptop per Child program. . . . The program [led to] substantial increases in use of computers both at school and at home. No evidence is found of effects on test scores in math and language. There is some evidence, though inconclusive, about positive effects on general cognitive skills." This research includes over 300 schools in rural Peru, and the global programme is much larger still: it has distributed over 2 million computers in

Read Cristia et al (2017)

FIGURE 6.6 The optimist

some 40 countries in the Global South. At $200 per laptop, that is a lot of money for a programme that did not, in Peru at least, increase kids' motivation to learn or to read (even though these laptops are loaded with 200 books), or to dedicate more time to homework, and that did not enhance the quality of school lessons.

And if you are the eternal pessimist, read Mitra, S. and Dangwal, R. (September 2017) "Acquisition of computer literacy skills through self-organizing systems of learning among children in Bhutan and India", *Prospects*, volume 47, issue 3, pages 275–292, online. (There are a few YouTube clips on the Hole in the Wall concept as well.) Or spend some time on the "mobile for development resources" website, which is corporate (set up by GSMA, which represents the interests of mobile operators worldwide) and therefore far from neutral – but interesting nonetheless.

Read Mitra and Dangwell (2017)

FIGURE 6.7   The pessimist

ICT meets special needs

Start with Raja, D.S. (2016) *Bridging the disability divide through digital technology*, World Bank, online. This is a very readable and well-researched background paper of that World Bank 'Digital Dividends' publication mentioned earlier.

Or check out United Nations (undated but I'm guessing 2016) *Toolkit on disability for Africa; information and communication technology (ICT) and disability*, online. Notwithstanding the title, this useful little toolkit is not very Africa-specific at all. It is more like an overview of things you could do and things to keep in mind – pretty much anywhere. On pages 18 and 19, it lists a few other useful resources.

ICT helps farmers

This is a vast field of research and practice. A good starting point could be FAO (2017) *Information and Communication Technology (ICT) in agriculture; a report to the G20 agricultural deputies*, online. Or if you want to see lots of practical examples and the way they are working out, or not, take a look at the December 2018 special issue on 'ICT and agriculture', of *CSI Transactions on ICT*, volume 6, issue 3–4; or FAO and ITU (2017), *E-agriculture in action*, online.

If you have a more specific field of interest, search for recent publications that cover rural ICT in the context of climate adaptation and resilience, extension services, water management, or animal or plant health, or look for knowledge management, e-agriculture, market information, precision farming, or smart farming. Whatever the topic, you're likely to find that more research has been done in India than anywhere else in the world, and that the ICT4D research community is very male-dominated.

ICT diversifies local livelihoods

Research tends to conclude that "ICT users [are] more likely to have diversified income sources as compared to non-users of ICTs." This particular quotation is from Khan, W., Tabassum, S. and Ansari, S.A. (2017) "Can diversification of livelihood sources increase income of farm households? A case study in Uttar Pradesh" *Agricultural Economics Research Review*, volume 30, with the quotation on page 32. Research from other countries uses different methods and comes to similar conclusions. Worthwhile reads are Maniriho, A. and Nilsson, P. (2018) "Determinants of livelihood diversification among Rwandan households: the role of education, ICT and urbanization", *East Africa Research Papers in Economics and Finance*, number 2018–24; and Baird, T.D. and Hartter, J. (2017) "Livelihood diversification, mobile phones and information diversity in Tanzania", *Land Use Policy*, volume 67, pages 460–471. The latter focuses on the Masaai in Tanzania and comes to the conclusion that there is *correlation* between ICT and diversification, but that it is not necessarily a *causal* relationship – an important distinction that research in this field often ignores.

ICT facilitates payments, saving, and lending

Papers often refer to the particularly rapid uptake of mobile banking services in Kenya. This sociotechnical transformation in the financial services sector is described and analysed in, among other papers, Onsongo, E. and Schot, J. (2017) "Inclusive innovation and rapid sociotechnical transitions: the case of mobile money in Kenya", *SPRU Working Paper Series*, 2017–07, online.

Saving and lending systems are lagging behind payment systems. An overview of the reasons for this, and ways to deal with it, is the very readable and only slightly outdated Kumar, K., McKay, C. and Rotman, S. (2010) "Microfinance and mobile banking: the story so far." *Focus Note 62*, Washington DC, CGAP, online.

E-governance and its ability to cut through bureaucracy and reduce corruption

Take a look at recent issues of *EJEG* (which is the 'Electronic Journal of E-governance'), or just do a search with keywords like *e-governance (or e-government)*, *rural development* and then the particular thing you are interested in (e-health, say, or land registry services). For example,

* **About all these internet kiosks and equivalents.** Is e-governance best channelled through mobile phones or public internet access points (PIAPs), such as cybercafés and community centres and suchlike? For a context-specific answer, see Furuholt, B. and Sæbø, Ø. (2017) "The role telecentres play in providing e-governance services in rural areas; a longitudinal study of internet access and e-governance services in Tanzania", *The Electronic Journal of Information Systems in Developing Countries*, volume 84, number 1, 14 pages. Many similar studies find that these PIAPs don't really work, but there are also positive accounts,

such as Hoque, M.R. and Sorwar, G. (2015), "ICT based e-governance services for rural development: a study of union information and service center (UISC) in Bangladesh" *The Electronic Journal of Information Systems in Developing Countries*, volume 71, number 8, pages 1–19. This research also found that, at least within the small number of respondents, the PIAPs *increased* the gender digital divide.

- *About the potential of public–private partnerships in e-governance.* A good read about the use of public-private partnerships in the PIAPs mentioned above is Sharma, R. and Mishra, R. (December 2017) "Investigating the role of intermediaries in adoption of public access outlets for delivery of e-governance services in developing countries: an empirical study", *Government Information Quarterly*, volume 34, issue 4, pages 658–679 (with lots of hyperlinks to related studies in other countries). An older but worthwhile read is Sharma, S. (2007) "Exploring best practice in Public Private Partnership (PPP) in e-government through selected case studies from India", in Ahmed, A. (2007) *World sustainable development outlook 2007: knowledge management and sustainable development in the 21st century*, Routledge. It also has a simple, sensible overview of advantages and key bottlenecks of e-governance, on pages 154–155.

Many research endeavours conclude that initiatives have failed and then try to find the reasons for the failure. But 'failure' is often relative, and much depends on the benchmarks. It is true that very few initiatives deliver all that they promised, but if you compare results with what happened within control groups that did not have access to whatever you're researching, then the picture is often much less bleak.

The drivers of ICT-induced change

For the supply side, take a look at the most recent version of the International Telecommunication Union's *Measuring the information society report*. It is not rural, and it is not focused on the Global South, but if you use the right search words, then this publication will give you state-of-the-art facts, figures and insights.

For the demand side, search for 'diffusion of innovation theory' (about how innovation spreads) and 'uses and gratifications theory' (about the way innovation is adopted and adapted). For a clear and concise description of these theories, in combination with some quality research, read Wei, L. and Zhang, M. (August 2008) "The adoption and use of mobile phone in rural China: a case study of Hubei, China", *Telematics and Informatics*, volume 25, issue 3, pages 169–186, online. A competing paradigm is the 'technology acceptance model' and the closely related 'unified theory of acceptance and use of technology'. These models evolve around 'perceived usefulness' and 'perceived ease of use' and pay little attention to the practical challenges of resource- and ICT-constrained life in the rural Global South.

About the gender digital divide that needs closing for equitable development to stand a chance, see, for example, EQUALS (September 2019) *10 Lessons learned: closing the gender gap in internet access and use; insights from the EQUALS Access Coalition*, online.

If you want to conduct research related to ICT in the context of rural development

Do not start your research before reading at least a few chapters of this challenging but brilliant book: Samoilenko, S.V. and Osei-Bryson, K.M. (2018) *Creating theoretical research frameworks using multiple methods; insights from ICT4D investigations*, Taylor & Francis Group (CRC Press).

The exercise: spot the difference

FIGURE 6.8 Spot the difference

Ritah and Priscilla do not know each other, but their profiles are very similar. They are both literate, rural Ugandan women who trade fish and earn occasional extra money with a range of other activities. They are both HIV positive. They are both single mothers.

Ritah's village has mobile phone coverage, but Priscilla's village does not.

What differences in opportunities do Ritah and Priscilla have?

Notes

1 The school head later told me that she considered these electronic attendance records, rather than better learning results, to be the tablets' most important benefit.
2 See Kaleebu, N. et al. (2013) *SMS story impact assessment report*, VSO, Papua New Guinea, online.
3 Cristia, J. et al. (2017) "Technology and child development: evidence from the one laptop per child program", *American Economic Journal: Applied Economics*, volume 9, issue 3, pages 1–40, with the quotation on page 318.
4 I mention this particular app because my wife uses it, but it is not at all the only one. 'TapTapSee' is another very powerful free app for people with visual impairment, for example.
5 To get a sense of the variety of ways in which a single community uses mobile phones for agricultural purposes, for example, see table 2 on page 25 of the interesting and readable paper of Martin, B.L. and Abbott, E. (Winter 2011) "Mobile phones and rural livelihoods: diffusion, uses and perceived impacts among farmers in rural Uganda", *Information*

Technologies and International Development, volume 7, issue 4, pages 17–34, online. It also has an interesting section about gender differences in phone use.

6   This particular quotation presents a common conclusion. It comes from Dhaka, B.L. and Chayal, K. (September 2010) "Farmers' experience with ICTs on transfer of technology in changing agriculture environment", *Indian Research Journal of Extension Education*, volume 10, issue 3, pages 114–118, with the quotation on page 116. If you want to know more about market information systems that target small farmers, search for any of the systems mentioned on page 129 of Wawire, A.W., Wangia, S.M. and Okello, J.J. (2017) "Determinants of use of information and communication technologies in agriculture: the case of Kenya agricultural commodity exchange in Bungoma County, Kenya", *Journal of Agricultural Science*, volume 9, issue 3, online. The list is not limited to Kenyan initiatives.

7   These and a few other examples are reported on in Duncombe, R. (2016) "Mobile phones for agricultural and rural development", *European Journal of Development Research*, volume 28, pages 213–235; Jensen, R. (August 2007) "The digital provide: information (technology), market performance, and welfare in the South Indian fisheries sector", *The Quarterly Journal of Economics*, volume 122, issue 3, pages 879–924, online, has a fascinating set of graphs that show that the early morning beach price of sardines fluctuated wildly before the introduction of mobile phones, and barely at all after it.

8   Tiny modems that you stick into your USB port to get online.

9   Onsongo, E. and Schot, J. (2017) "Inclusive innovation and rapid sociotechnical transitions: the case of mobile money in Kenya", *SPRU Working Paper Series, 2017–07*, pages 1–28, with the fact mentioned on page 2.

10   Mohseni-Cheraghlou, A. (2013) *Mobile banking: who is in the driver's seat?* World Bank, online.

11   See, for example, Cecchini, S. and Raina, M. (Winter 2004) "Electronic government and the rural poor: the case of Gyandoot", *Information Technologies and International Development*, volume 2, issue 2, pages 65–75. There is an interesting change in tone from the earlier to the more recent papers on e-governance. In 2006, the results of e-governance were still by and large disappointing, as is illustrated in the title of Dada, D. (2006) "The failure of e-governance in developing countries: a literature review", *The Electronic Journal on Information Systems in Developing Countries*, volume 26, issue 7, pages 1–10. The suggestions in the *further reading* section at the end of this chapter are more recent – and tend to be more positive.

12   This is possible because of a large investment in digital IDs for all Indian nationals, resulting in the inclusion of 99% of India's adult population by late 2018 – see Misra, P. (January 2019) "Lessons from Aadhaar: analog aspects of digital governance shouldn't be overlooked", *Background Paper Series Number 19*, Pathways for Prosperity Commission, online, with the fact presented on page 3.

13   In theory, a third reason is that, online, people are more easily able to organize collective action and claim their rights if public money is not used for the stated purpose. The mere risk of being named and shamed on a globally visible platform could serve as an incentive for decision-makers to use the money for its actual purpose. In reality, this collective action potential is not really working yet, outside of urban centres. In fact, even the longest-standing ICT accountability mechanism rarely actually works. This is simply a phone number that people can call in case of problems. The number's existence and use is one of the standard things I check when assessing mobile health clinics, for example. Conversations about this generally start promising and end disappointing: "Yes, absolutely, we have a dedicated phone line for this." "Great! What is the process for handling these complaints, and could I see last month's records please?" My respondents then nearly always admit that the phone line is not currently operational, or at least that phone calls are not logged, and that follow-up is incidental rather than systematic.

14   For a short overview of the various ways in which drones aid agriculture, and why agricultural drones are 'ICT' rather than just 'technology', see Plavevski, O. (June 2017) *11 Cost-effective uses of drones in ICT for agriculture*, ICT Works, online. For a far more

thorough account, see Sylvester, G., editor (2018) *E-agriculture in action: drones for agriculture*, FAO and ITU, online.

15 Wei, L. and Zhang, M. (August 2008) "The adoption and use of mobile phone in rural China: a case study of Hubei, China", *Telematics and Informatics*, volume 25, issue 3, pages 169–186.

16 Onsongo, E. and Schot, J. (2017) "Inclusive innovation and rapid sociotechnical transitions: the case of mobile money in Kenya", *SPRU Working Paper Series*, 2017–07, online, with the fact presented on page 2.

17 International Telecommunication Union (2017) *Measuring the information society report 2017*, volume 1, online, with the quotation from page iv (emphasis added).

18 As of 2016, some half a billion people live in not-yet-connected regions. See World Bank (2016) *World development report 2016: digital dividends*, online, page 4. Living in a connected region does not mean you *are* in fact connected. By the end of 2018, almost half the world's population was not yet using the internet – and they were "particularly women and girls. The statistics show older people also disproportionately remain offline, as do those with disabilities, indigenous populations and some people living in the world's poorest places". This quotation is from UN News (December 2018) *Internet milestone reached, as more than 50 per cent go online: UN telecoms agency*, online.

19 One way forward is obviously to increase a region's connectedness. Another way forward is to work around the connectivity and other infrastructural limitations. For an example of an attempt to design e-learning products that are focused on rural development and that work well in a context of unreliable internet and poor electricity supply, see Chunwijitra, S. et al. (November 2017) *Portable e-learning box for agriculture to support farmer[s] in rural areas: a case study in Thailand*, ECTI-CON 14th international conference, Thailand.

20 There are lots of figures in World Bank (2016) *World development report 2016: digital dividends*, online, and one key observation is that "the internet remains unavailable, inaccessible, and unaffordable to a majority of the world's population" (title of figure O.5, on page 8).

21 The World Bank explores them in detail in World Bank (2016) *World development report: digital dividends*, online.

22 Livia Murray provides a set of plausible reasons for Lebanon's high prices in Murray, L. (April 2015) "Four reasons Lebanon's internet is so slow", *Executive*, online.

23 Partey, S.T. et al. (April 2019) "Scaling up climate information services through public-private partnership business models; an example from northern Ghana", *CGIAR Info Note*, online.

24 For example, in the south Indian Melua, an e-governance project titled "Sustainable Access in Rural India" collapsed in part because of this resistance: "field level staff put up a stiff opposition to accepting applications from the [e-governance] kiosks, as they feared erosion in their authority and opportunities for rent-seeking. . . . However, the field staff did verify the applications for old age pensions in the villages. We suspect this was because the opportunities for corruption are much less in these cases, as the applicants are very old and poor". Kumar, R. and Best, M.L. (2007) "Impact and sustainability of e-governance services in developing countries: lessons learned from Tamil Nadu, India", *The Information Society*, volume 22, issue 1, pages 1–12, with the quotation on page 9.

25 See Box 3.5 of World Bank (2016) *World development report 2016: digital dividends*, online.

26 The development of very low-cost products for poor communities that are then sold elsewhere and become serious competitors of their more expensive equivalents.

7

MIGRATION

Definition of a 'migrant'
  According to the International Organization for Migration, a migrant is any person who is moving or has moved across an international border or within a state away from his or her habitual place of residence, regardless of (1) the person's legal status; (2) whether the movement is voluntary or involuntary; (3) the causes of the movement; or (4) the length of the stay.[1]

Prologue: Adnew's journey

Last year, I met Adnew. He drove me around for a week in Ethiopia. We spent hours talking about his life. His story was impressive.

As a young child, Adnew grew up combining his pastoral duties with basic education. His father's death forced him to drop out of school at the age of 12. By 18, he'd managed to leave his village and move to Addis Ababa. He had hoped to join his older brother or sister there, but neither welcomed or helped him. Adnew ended up as a day labourer, forever unsure of his next day's income.

Adnew did not drink, smoke, or gamble. He did not buy expensive clothes and never partied. After paying for basic food and a bed, he often managed to save a bit of money. He spent this money on motorcycle driving lessons – typically one, sometimes two lessons a month. Eventually, he got his licence. A few years later, he passed his driving test for a 'private vehicle' as well.[2]

Adnew then sold tickets on a microbus during the day. During the night, he was a guard in the garden of a Nigerian diplomat. One day, this man employed Adnew as his driver. In the course of his duties, he learned some English. A few years later, this helped him get a job as a driver for a tourism company.

One of the tourists he drove around headed an international organisation and needed a driver. Adnew applied and got the job, and this is how I met him. I heard this story because he was proud of the journey that had brought him to a point where he had a real contract, was building up a pension, was paid overtime, and was treated with respect. For his siblings, and for the people in the village, Adnew had become a role model.

I am telling this story for two reasons.

First, it serves as a warning. This chapter is about migration flows and their causes and effects on rural economies. We will find that, in many rural communities, migration is common and that global migration flows involve many millions of people, all with their stories and choices, delights and frustrations, fortunes and misfortunes. Too often, politicians, civil servants and journalists forget this – the simple fact that migrants are *people*. This helps explain some of the draconian migration-related policies and hostile media coverage of migrant communities.

Second, I started with Adnew's story because people like him are drivers of migration: they are people who *made it*, inspiring many others to follow, with the same dreams but perhaps with less fortune or discipline. Many don't reach their destination (see Box 7.1) or, if they do, end in abject poverty or detention centres.

BOX 7.1   MIGRANTS DO NOT ALWAYS REACH THEIR DESTINATION

I was once in a bus from Zinder to Agadez, in Niger, West Africa. The man next to me was from Benin and on his way to Libya, where he hoped to find a job. He wore sandals but had nice shoes hanging around his neck.

A few days later, we bumped into each other in Agadez. His plan to hitchhike across the border had not worked. He was now trying to sell his shoes to cover the fare, but I did not buy them. To this day – and it is now nearly 30 years later – I wonder what happened to this man.

What are we talking about?

Migration is of massive economic importance. Some 3.5% of the world's population are international migrants – an estimated 272 million people in total (and a little less than half of them are women and girls).[3] The money these international migrants sent to their low- and middle-income countries of origin amounted to some US$530 billion in 2018. (This is just the officially recorded remittances, and it doesn't include cash informally crossing borders.) This is more than three times the size of the official aid flows in the world and roughly as much as the flow of foreign direct investments to those countries![4] These flows are *so* important, specifically for rural regions, that the UN General Assembly recently made every June 16 the *International day of family remittances*, because "in many developing countries international remittances constitute an important source of income for poor families [and] half will reach rural areas".[5] Another big plus point: remittances are largely resistant to recessions, and there have only been a few brief dips in an otherwise long and steady growth path in the global size of remittances.[6]

Let's take a look at a few major migrant groups.

From the Global South to Europe and North America

Most migrants from the Global South consider Europe and North America to be the most attractive destinations, and people are willing to risk death to get there – *quite literally*. In a survey among 400 people in Dakar, Senegal, half the respondents thought the risk of death of the journey to Europe was 25% or more – yet three-quarters of them were willing to take it.[7]

This is the type of migration that receives the most attention in the media in Europe and North America, and indeed in parts of the Global South. The attention is very often negative, and it intensified because of the Syrian refugee crisis and discussions about the border wall between Mexico and the USA. The tone is harsh and uncompromising: a while ago, I passed by a demonstration of the xenophobic English Defence League, and heard a few men shouting that "all foreigners should go home". They are wrong for many reasons, and one of them is simply that the British economy would crash if 'all foreigners went home'. A French Moroccan woman, frustrated by the anti-immigrant wave that was sweeping through France, suggested on her Facebook page that all immigrants should go on a one-day strike. Just imagine . . . the entire country would grind to a halt.

From the Global South to the Gulf

Relative to its own population, immigration is highest in the Gulf. The United Arab Emirates and Qatar top the list: in 2015, migrants accounted for 88% and 76% of their respective populations.[8] The Gulf's labour market for migrants is highly segmentalised: if you're a woman from Sri Lanka, you will probably be a domestic worker. A taxi driver is probably a man from Bangladesh or Pakistan. An accountant is probably from Egypt.

Within the Global South

There are large migration flows within the Global South. Millions of guest workers in Malaysia and Thailand come from poorer Asian countries such as Cambodia, Laos and Myanmar (and are occasionally rounded up and sent back).[9] Guest workers in South Africa come from many other African countries, and there are several hundred thousand Haitian migrants in the Dominican Republic.

Wherever they migrate to, the work conditions for many of the migrants – and for the illegal ones in particular – are often appalling. If you search the web for the Qatar 2022 World Cup, for example, you'll find pictures of stunning stadiums but also descriptions of the abuse and exploitation of the workers who built them and of the many fatal work accidents.[10] What makes Qatar stand out is not the conditions in which the migrant workers live, but the visibility of their plight: Qatar has the spotlight on it because of the World Cup, and the country's efforts to silence criticism have only increased global interest (somewhat successfully so, as this led to significant changes in Qatar's labour legislation in 2017 and 2019).[11]

Internal migration

Internal migration is even more common than international migration. The 2011 India census found that there were 139 million internal migrants in the country,[12] and a 2014 survey in China concluded that there were 274 million rural-to-urban internal migrants in China.[13]

For the individuals involved, internal migration is not necessarily less dramatic than cross-border migration. The many millions of rural Chinese girls who moved to the city for factory work were likely to face a much larger cultural clash and a more extreme transformation of life than, say, the Egyptian farm workers who moved to farms in Jordan. Imagine the indigenous Amazonians who were driven from the Brazilian rainforest and ended up in São Paulo. What a shock that must have been!

Internal migration consists largely of two types:

- **Rural to urban.** This is massive. It is often one-way migration, from the countryside to the cities.
- **Seasonal migration.** Many people move to wherever agricultural workers are needed, and there are smaller streams to and from tourism hubs, large annual events, and construction centres.

FIGURE 7.1 Moving to the city may be tougher than crossing the border

For each of these types of migration, there's a lot we just do not know. First, the figures are rough. Internal migration is often not registered anywhere,[14] and undocumented international migrants will try to remain unnoticed. Did you notice the vagueness, when I just mentioned that there are "several hundred thousand Haitian migrants in the Dominican Republic"? Three very specific estimates are that there are 311,969; 329,281; and 458,233 of them,[15] but such estimates are examples of false precision.[16] The simple fact is that nobody really knows how many Haitians there are in the Dominican Republic.

Second, models that explain past migration patterns do not predict future patterns well, because they are influenced by many factors and take shape in environments that may change rapidly. The crisis in Syria and the anarchy in Libya have impacted on the migration of Eritreans in ways that nobody could have predicted (essentially, the number of Eritreans attempting to cross the central Mediterranean via Libya went up rapidly and then came down again, for reasons unrelated to the problems in Eritrea, which stayed the same).[17]

What we do know is that migration patterns are complex and that migration often flows both ways. Jordan is an extreme example of this phenomenon. On the one hand, many Jordanians are living abroad, and the remittances they send are of vast economic importance for this small country (and are higher than foreign direct investments or foreign grants).[18] On the other hand, the farmers in Jordan are largely Egyptians, and the domestic workers are largely from Sri Lanka and the Philippines. Jordan's 'economic free zones' are meant to expand Jordan's labour market, but almost all the workers are from China, India, and Bangladesh (with, currently, ambitious plans to add Syrian refugees to the mix).

So what drives all this migration?

Migration drivers

There will not be much migration from a village in which people are happy, healthy, wealthy and safe, with ample opportunities for entertainment and personal growth for adults and the next generation. Conversely, people get pushed out of their village if there's a war or serious oppression, a famine, or drought. These are very raw push factors, and in such cases, people migrate because remaining in place is not an option.

Most rural regions are somewhere in between these two extremes. For such 'in-between' regions, four schools of thought see different decision-making dynamics shaping migration patterns. They see different consequences of migration, too. I will describe these theories briefly.

The first school of thought dates back to 1885 and is called the '**(neo-)classical theory of migration**'. It argues that individuals decide to migrate on the basis of the income differential (and later the *perceived* income differential) between their place of origin and the place they decide to migrate to. This income differential explains both in-country rural-to-urban migration and migration from countries with low salaries to those with higher ones. A second school of thought, which emerged a full century later, is the '**new economics of labour migration**' (or 'NELM'). It saw broadly the same pull factor – the prospect of higher earnings – but recognised that the decision to migrate was often taken by wider families and their communities, rather than by the individual migrants, and that money was often pooled to fund a person's travel. This theory presents migration as a group investment: migrants are meant to make a lot of money and use it to reward those who covered their migration costs.

The resultant money-driven migration pattern is not demographically neutral. In most contexts, young, able-bodied and unmarried men are far more likely to be encouraged to move abroad than women and married men or men from other age groups, or with disabilities that may affect their income-generating capacity. And these young men – and sometimes young women – don't send remittances out of altruism: they are repaying the upfront investment needed for their migration. Later, their remittances serve as insurance, used in the event that they end up returning to their village because of an economic downturn or old age. Older migrants often spend their last years 'back home', partly because of their longing for their motherland but also simply because they have accrued goodwill by sending meaningful sums of money over a period of years, and now they are enjoying the care they have earned.

The migration investment is based on hopes and expectations, which are fuelled by the successes of people like Adnew (see the prologue) and Naeem (see Box 7.2). The stories of those who failed remain hidden, but the people who *made* it in the city or abroad are recounted endlessly and paraded by social media and by companies, like Western Union, which benefit from international migration. Their stories inspire others to follow their footsteps. "Do you know Adnew is a driver now, with a nice car and a high salary?" But others may not have Adnew's stamina or Naeem's luck, and their hopes and expectations are filling the slums of Lagos and the brothels of Europe.

BOX 7.2   THE APPEAL OF SUCCESS

A man recognised my Egyptian friend Karim on the street and thanked him profusely. Seven years earlier, this man had come from his village to England on a tourist visa but with the intention to stay. In a park, he had recognised Karim as a fellow Egyptian and had approached him. After discussing the possibilities, Karim had written two messages on two pieces of paper:

> *My name is Naeem. I am a good cook. I can make Arabic and Western food. I am hardworking and hygienic. Can I show you how I cook?*
>
> *Hello, my name is Naeem. I am a kind man. I treat women with respect. I don't speak English yet, but I will learn quickly. I work as a cook. Will you go out with me?*

The man had laminated both messages and passed by restaurants until somebody asked for a cooking demonstration . . . and hired him. He still works there but nowadays legally and as a UK citizen. The second message appealed to a Polish woman who worked as a waitress in that same restaurant. They dated and then got married. They are still together and have two children.

Just imagine the stories back in the village: "Yes, seriously, all you need to make it in England is two laminated messages saying that you cook well and are good to women!"

FIGURE 7.2   Sometimes, people exaggerate a little

A third school of thought, called the **'migration networks theory'**, dates back to the 1950s and says that the migration dynamics change once the first generation of migrants has established itself somewhere. These initial migrants are strong pull factors for people in their regions of origin. If their host countries permit it, they invite their spouses and children to join them. They also entice their cousins and neighbours with their remittance flows, and help them to make the move as well. These later waves of migrants face lower barriers and risks because they move to an area with an established diaspora community – and after a while, entire streets are inhabited largely by people from a single group of villages. It is easy to see this in Birmingham, the city from which I write this chapter. The Pakistani families in Birmingham are not just 'from Pakistan': they mostly come from a few specific regions *within* Pakistan (such as the Pakistan-controlled part of Kashmir, see Box 7.3), and even within these regions, they are mostly from a few specific areas. Essentially, you are more likely to emigrate if your relatives emigrated as well, and if you do, you are likely to move to the same city – or even street – as these relatives. Migration becomes self-perpetuating: it is normalised, expected and, as long as countries do not add to their immigration obstacles, easier to realise because of ever-stronger migrant networks.

BOX 7.3   THE BLESSINGS AND CURSE OF DIASPORA MONEY

As aid agencies raised funds for the relief response to the deadly Kashmir earthquake of October 2005, the English city of Birmingham proved to be particularly generous. This is where many of the Kashmiri migrants are living.

Birmingham's Kashmiri community was very charitable but may have unwittingly contributed to the death toll. Over the previous decades, the relatively wealthy migrants built villas in the nicest parts of Kashmir. This pushed poorer people to the unstable hills that collapsed when the earthquake hit.

These three schools of thought predict that migration has positive effects on the migrant-sending communities, largely because good things happen when migrants send money back to the households they came from. The key theoretical rival, and the fourth school of thought, is the **'historical-institutional approach'**, which argues that migration is great for the rich *receiving* countries but reinforces poverty in the poorer *sending* ones. This theory argues that migration increases inequality within the rural regions of origin, because the poorest parts of society will not benefit from remittances, as they do not have the resources needed to enable household members to migrate. The historical-institutional approach also emphasises the risks of a brain drain (as highly skilled people are attracted to big cities and foreign lands) and argues that remittances are rarely invested in productive assets that would grow the local economies directly, or spent on locally produced consumables that would cause the local economies to grow indirectly. Instead, the theory postulates that remittances are typically spent on imported luxuries that do not boost the local rural economies and make the growing inequalities within rural communities painfully visible.

Migration discourse

As is often the case with opposing theories, the explanations are either all-negative or all-positive. This is also the case for the discourse among politicians, policy-makers, and the wider public. Until not so long ago, we were in an all-positive era. Remittances were 'the new development mantra'.[19] The transfer of new skills and attitudes back to the sending communities (dubbed 'social remittances'), the economic effects of the circulation of labour and brains, and the developmental force of migrant diasporas were all seen as important benefits of migration.[20] In recent times, however, the tone of the discourse and public mind-set changed and turned overwhelmingly negative. Politics followed and reinforced the tone of discussions, with words such as 'invasion' and with actions such as border walls and mass detention and deportation campaigns.

In the course of only a few years, migrant-focused criticism became so commonplace that policy papers could simply assume, without rationale, that migration was something bad that must be stopped. The 2015 UK aid strategy, for example, pledges that UK's expenditure on 'aid' would "tackle . . . the root causes of mass migration and disease". The strategy provides no explanation as to why halting mass migration is a worthwhile goal to strive for and places 'migration' in a group with 'disease' – both presenting "great global challenges".[21] This change in political framing influences research funding streams as well. A research consortium named 'Migrating out of Poverty' uses UK government funding to explore the benefits of migration within Asia and Africa, but research on potential benefits of migration from either Africa or Asia to Europe is not eligible for funding.

Migration's effects on rural communities

So which theory comes closest to today's real world? That largely depends on the labour and skill gaps the migrants leave behind and on the way remittances are spent – which in turn depends on a complex combination of culture and investment policies. Let's look at some common pros and cons, starting with the cons.

The poorest people do not migrate, or end up as 'modern slaves'

Whatever the drivers, migration requires a level of aspiration and understanding of the possibilities – and it requires money. This is why the economic development of low-income economies initially tends to stimulate, rather than reduce, migration. Even in the largest migrant-sending countries, the very poorest communities are often excluded[22] unless their employer or a middleman pays for their journey. In the 18th and early 19th centuries, this is how people from around Calcutta ended up in the Caribbean; today, it is how Nepali workers end up building the World Cup stadiums in Qatar. The arrangements differ, but the results are broadly the same: you are indebted because you needed support to arrange your permits or to cover travel costs, and you now have to work, sometimes for years, to repay your debts. Often, this is effectively a form of slavery.

Migration may create gaps in the labour market

The labour market effects of migration depend on whether or not there is an over-supply of labour in the regions of origin. If there are more working-age people than jobs, these migrants may leave no labour gaps. Where this is the case, their departure has a positive effect on the people who stay behind, as the same income is now shared among fewer people. Conversely, if labour is in short supply, migration may cause agricultural production to decrease. In the longer term, this is likely to lead to a shift towards less labour-intensive crops. It also leads to changing gender roles: when either men or women are absent,[23] the other sex has to perform duties that were not traditionally theirs. Such changes do not necessarily reduce gender inequality in the wider society. It may well be, for example, that households have less access to credit once the men have left (if indeed it is the men who left), because only land owners – the men – are eligible to sign for a loan.

Not all migrants are farmers, and the impact of migration on the labour market is not limited to manual labour. Sometimes migration causes a 'brain drain' from the village to the city and from low- and middle-income to high-income countries. In many cases, this is not a big problem. A researcher who looked at 33 large labour-exporting countries found that, in two-thirds of them, less than 10% of the best-educated population had migrated.[24] Moreover, the successful migration of highly educated people may inspire people who stayed behind to pursue higher education as well. However, in a few cases, the situation is different, and the effects are particularly negative in the case of health care, where the pull factor is strong. The result is that, for example, there are fewer Malawian doctors in the Malawian countryside, where the vast majority of the Malawians live, than in the country's two big cities. (And if you talk with Malawian health-care professionals, they may tell you there are fewer Malawian doctors in the whole of Malawi than there are in the English city of Manchester, but that is a rumour that does not seem to be true.)[25]

Remittances are a risky source of income, and they may cause the Dutch disease

The expected remittances do not necessarily materialise, and remittances might be too irregular to truly count on. If they *do* materialise and *are* predictable, they may create a type of 'Dutch disease'. Chapter 1 talked about the Dutch disease in the context of underground resources. Here, it is the 'migrant syndrome':[26] migration is *so* attractive that it becomes the norm and negatively affects other economic sectors. First, working in the fields becomes ever-less attractive, both for prospective migrants ('I could earn more if I migrate') and for the people who stay behind ('Now that our children send us money, it no longer seems necessary to work in the fields'). Second, exports become more expensive because the flow of hard currency remittances pushes up the value of the national currency (see Box 1.4 in Chapter 1 for an explanation). The result is that "over time, villages . . . come to specialize in migration (i.e., the exportation of labour), serving as nurseries and nursing homes for their largely migrant workforces".[27]

But it's a massive *source of income, and many millions of households would be far worse off without it*

Remittances increase the overall household incomes – indeed sometimes more than *double* them.[28] These remittances go directly to rural households, and this is getting easier now that mobile banking is reaching increasingly deep into rural regions in the Global South. This increase is spent on refrigerators and televisions, better education for the next generation, better nutrition, and better health (though the results in any one of these areas is also sometimes negative – see the suggestions in the *further reading* section). Moreover, in parts of the Global South, these higher incomes increase productive investments. Even without these investments, increased local consumption is likely to cause a beneficial local 'multiplier effect' (i.e., the effect where a dollar of extra money is spent on local goods and services, which leads to somebody else having a higher income, which may be spent locally again, and so forth).

These remittances reduce poverty in Africa, Asia, and Latin America alike.

- In Latin America and the Caribbean, research that used a 10-country panel data set concluded that "remittances . . . have increased growth and reduced inequality and poverty".[29]
- In Asia and the Pacific, research using panel data for 24 countries concluded that remittances contributed to poverty reduction – especially through their direct effects – *and* benefited overall economic growth.[30]
- Research using data from 34 countries in Africa concluded that remittances significantly reduced poverty – while exports and 'aid' did not (!).[31]

Overall, the positive effects of remittances on the regions of origin are likely to outweigh the negative effects migration may have. These remittances are of such obvious importance to poverty alleviation that one of the Sustainable Development Goal targets for 2030 is to "reduce to less than 3% the transaction costs of migrant remittances and eliminate remittance corridors with costs higher than 5%".[32] (By 2019, this target is still a long way off: "Banks are the costliest channel for sending remittances, with an average cost of 10.3 percent . . . while post offices are lowest at 5.7 percent.")[33]

However, there are large differences across countries, and there are two reasons for this. First, the rest of the local economy: if local markets function well and if a significant portion of what people buy has been produced locally, then the multiplier effect of remittances is significant and the benefits of remittances are not limited to the households that the migrants send money to. Second, government policies matter a great deal – and we will look at them now.

What do governments do?

Some governments recognise the potential benefits of outward labour migration and *want* you to leave, at least temporarily and without major risks to life and limbs. The government of Sri Lanka tries to facilitate the safe migration and subsequent return and re-integration of domestic workers,[34] and training institutes in the Philippines are producing a surplus of nurses in order for them to migrate. Their efforts are paying off, and labour migration is a massive business in such countries – in the Philippines, remittances amounted to some US$34 billion in 2018.[35] In order to ensure the benefits of migration go beyond the migrants' households, some governments – such as the ones of Somalia, Nigeria, Peru, Colombia, and Mexico – have introduced schemes that encourage *collective* remittances. In such cases, diaspora organisations collect money to which home governments add, and the resulting sum is invested in public goods, such as roads, water supply systems, and electrification. Such schemes do not always work particularly well yet. In Mexico, for example, the government quadruples remittances collected by diaspora communities and invests the resulting sum in community projects, but an external assessment found that few projects fulfil the programme's objective of developing infrastructure in Mexico's poorest areas and that, more generally, poorer municipalities are less likely to benefit from the scheme than wealthier municipalities.[36] But that's a matter of design – these systems are in an early stage of development, and their effects will improve over time.

It makes sense for governments to optimise migration and its effects. Doing this requires migration-*specific* policies, as well as the consideration of migration in policies that are, in and by themselves, not migration-specific – such as banking and investment policies. Migrants potentially provide fresh ideas and skills (the 'brain gain'), and if a government creates a somewhat investment-friendly environment, these migrants may invest a sizeable part of their savings productively. They may do this directly, or their banks may do it for them (e.g., Omar sends Amal money, and Amal saves it in a bank that lends it to Fatima, who invests it productively). This is what happened in Malaysia, Korea, and Indonesia, for example, and these investments supported these countries' rapid economic development.

Unfortunately, such enabling environments are not all that common. Often, corruption is rife and governments create a business environment in which everything from land sale to export legislation is difficult. In such cases, a return to the village is unattractive until people retire. The skills learned abroad will not benefit the home community, and remittances might be invested in tomorrow's generation (as money can buy good nutrition and education) but not in today's economic development.

This means that, in such environments, the benefits of remittances are largely confined to the families of the migrants. As these are often not the poorest people in the village, migration may well *increase* local inequalities.

Take Pakistan-controlled Kashmir (referred to in Box 7.3). Many British-based Kashmiri people have built a villa there, but I have come across very few Kashmiri migrants who invested in something that could serve as an economic engine. This seems surprising because many of the British-based people of Kashmiri descent have proven to be very business savvy! But really, it is *not* that surprising at all: corruption in Pakistan is rampant, and the migrants who did invest money in Pakistan's economy found it impossible to make a profit.

Governments may even be actively obstructive. If you are Egyptian and working in television, the government may pose limits on your mobility, out of fear that you will move to one of the satellite channels in the Gulf. Such measures are meant to protect a country's own industry. It's also partly a matter of pride. In Morocco, citizens who choose to migrate can never be civil servants, as they haven't been sufficiently loyal to their country. Frustration plays a role as well: in the 1960s and 1970s, the Moroccan government encouraged its nationals to migrate to Europe, hoping their remittances and newly acquired skills would boost Morocco's economic development. The government now believes that this strategy failed, as so many migrants shipped their families over as soon as they could afford to do so, did not make any investments, and only return to Morocco for vacations.

And some of the obstruction is down to the fear that migrants might come back with ideas and political ideologies that might work against the government. By far the most chilling example of this was Pol Pot, leader of the Khmer Rouge, the Cambodian regime that committed genocide on its own population. The underlying rationale for this genocide had been developed by Cambodian students in France, who had been inspired by French philosophy and the French Communist Party.

Why is all this relevant, and what does it mean for you?

Migrants and their money and influence are too significant to ignore and too useful, potentially, to subject to unnecessary constraints. Directly and indirectly, they affect the lives of hundreds of millions of people in rural regions across the Global South. These flows of people, money and ideas are difficult to monitor and influence, and perhaps this is why governments – in sending, receiving, transit, and hybrid countries – have made life difficult for them, and have often failed to create the environment in which remittances could truly contribute to local economic development. It may also explain why policy-makers so often use negative imagery when reflecting on migration and ignore research that concludes that migration is generally beneficial for the economies of both host and sending communities.

If you are one of the next generation of policy-makers and development professionals, I hope you will not follow the current fashion of fearing and resisting migration. Instead, please help maximise the benefits of remittances and of linkages between diaspora communities and their countries of origin.[37] As you do this, carefully assess the effects of migration and the effects of policies and programmes on migration patterns.[38] In migrant-sending communities, migration may improve or worsen poverty, inequality, investments, land use, and the health and education levels of the next generation. Context is crucial. Migration is not 'good' or 'bad' but a phenomenon that accelerates and amplifies the results of policies and practices that either drive or impede development.

Further reading

Resources that keep you current

Keep an eye on the publications of the *Global Knowledge Partnership on Migration and Development (knomad.org/publications)*. A research consortium named 'Migrating out of Poverty' (migratingoutofpoverty.dfid.gov.uk) also has an ongoing trickle of interesting publications. Key migration-related periodicals are *International Migration* (online) and *International Migration Review* (online, but only few of their publications focus on rural areas in the Global South).

Schools of thought

For an overview, read Haas, H. de (2010) "Migration and development; a theoretical perspective" *International Migration Review*, volume 44, number 1, pages 227–264, online. Two years later, Hein de Haas compared these theories with empirical evidence: see Haas, H. de (2012), "The migration and development pendulum: a critical view on research and policy", *International Migration*, volume 50, number 3, pages 8–25. Mariapia Mendola also provides an inventory of research findings, in Mendola, M. (2012) "Rural out-migration and economic development at origin: a review of the evidence", *Journal of International Development*, volume 24, pages 102–122.

If you want to know more about an individual school of thought, the best reference is the school's own foundational paper. Then click on the Google Scholar's 'citation' button for a list of all publications that ever referred to this paper, and check out a few recent ones to get an impression of key developments since that first paper was published.

About the (neo-)classical theory on migration: It started with Ravenstein, who argued that migration is by and large down to "the desire inherent in most men to 'better' themselves in material respects", in Ravenstein, E.G. (June 1885) "The laws of migration", *Journal of the Royal Statistical Society*, volume XLVIII, part 2, pages 167–227. The theory gained credibility when it moved from *real* income differentials to *expected* income differentials. Michael Todaro made this shift when explaining rural-to-urban migration in the Global South, in Todaro, M.P. (1969) "A model of labor migration and urban unemployment in less developed countries", *The American Economic Review*, volume 59, number 1, pages 138–148, online.

About the New Economics of Labour Migration (NELM): Stark, O. and Bloom, D.E. (1985) "The new economics of labour migration", *The American Economic Review*, volume 75, number 2, pages 173–178, online. Cited over 2,000 times, this six-page paper synthesized the research done in previous years and gave the emerging new approach its name.

About the historical-institutional approach: It probably started in the 1960s, with Andre Gunder Frank's synthesis of the 'dependency theory', which argued that development in the industrial world and the persistent lack of development (*under*-development, he called it) elsewhere are two sides of the same coin. Frank did not cover migration explicitly, but his followers do and the line of argument is that migration from the 'periphery' to the 'core' makes rich countries richer and keeps poor countries poor. Read Frank, A.G. (1966) "The development of under-development", *Monthly Review*, volume 18, September 1966 (reprint in 1989).

About the migration networks theory: This started in the 1950s, with Gunnar Myrdal's 'circular and cumulative causation of migration', which is well-explained and elaborated on in Massey, D.S. (September 1988) "Economic development and international migration in comparative perspective", *Population and Development Review*, volume 14, number 3, pages 383–413.

Empirical research

For insights into the impact of migration on rural development, you could take a look at FAO (2018) *The state of food and agriculture; migration, agriculture and rural development*, online. Or read Vargas-Lundius, R. et al. (2008) *International migration, remittances and rural development*, IFAD, online. It is over a decade old but not yet dated.

For empirical research on a more specific issue, use Google Scholar to find a recent paper on that issue. In its references, this paper will generally list other pieces of empirical research on the same topic. Or you could take one or more of the following papers as a starting point.

Why do so many people **not** migrate out of their village?

See Brauw, A. de, Mueller, V. and Lee, H. L. (2014) "The role of rural-urban migration in the structural transformation of Sub-Saharan Africa", *World Development*, volume 63, pages 33–42. This paper is one of only a few attempts to explain why so many rural people in Africa do *not* migrate. The somewhat disappointing conclusion is that the data needed to reach firm conclusions do not yet exist.

What are remittances spent on?

This has been the focus of a lot of research, conducted with variable methodological rigour. A large-scale piece of research is reported on in Démurger, S. and Wang, X. (2016) "Remittances and expenditure patterns of the left behinds in rural China",

China Economic Review, volume 37, pages 177–190, online. As is often the case, the paper concludes that increases in consumption are much larger than increases in productive investments (but keep in mind the multiplier effect: increased consumption may benefit the wider community). Disturbingly, the paper also identified a strong negative impact on education expenditure! Which makes you wonder,

What does migration do for the next generation?

This all depends on the context, as is illustrated by the diametrically opposed conclusions of these two publications:

- Hu, F. (2012) "Migration, remittances and children's high school attendance: the case of rural China", *International Journal of Educational Development*, volume 32, pages 401–411. The conclusion: remittances only partly compensate for the negative effects of the absence of adults, and the effects of this absence of adults are particularly negative for girls. Other publications come to similar conclusions – but not this one:
- Yang, D. (2008) "International migration, remittances and household investment: evidence from Philippine migrants' exchange rate shocks", *The Economic Journal*, volume 118, number 528, pages 591–630, online.

For a comparison of 20 studies that assess the effects of remittances on nutritional status (ten of which were focused on child nutrition in particular), see Thow, A.M., Fanzo, J. and Negin, J. (2016) "A systematic review of the effect of remittances on diet and nutrition", *Food and Nutrition Bulletin*, volume 37, number 1, pages 42–64, online. Key conclusions are that (1) research is often insufficiently robust; (2) effects vary significantly across countries and are positive, negative, or mixed; and (3) children with the highest risk of under-nutrition live in the poorest households, and these households will not receive any remittances because they do not have the resources to fund migration.

What does migration do for the poorest segments of society?

- Abdelmonein, Y. and Litchfield, J. (2015) "Does migration improve living standards of migrant-sending households? Evidence from rural Ethiopia", *Working Paper 41*, Migrating out of Poverty Research Consortium, online. This is one of very few studies that attempt to create a counter-factual: 'what would have happened with these households *without* the migration of one or more of the household members?' The key conclusion: yes, migration leads to a 7% average increase in household consumption, . . . but migration caused the *poorest* households to be worse off.
- A paper that has a different research question and uses different methods but comes to an equally disheartening conclusion is Fuente, A. de la (2010)

"Remittances and vulnerability to poverty in rural Mexico", *World Development*, volume 38, number 6, pages 828–839. The paper's conclusion is that people with a high likelihood of future poverty have a low likelihood of receiving remittances.

What do remittances mean for work done in the villages of origin?

You will find a well-written and concise overview of past research in the introductory section of Démurger, S. and Li, S. (2012) "Migration, remittances and rural employment patterns; evidence from China" *Gate Working Paper 1230*, online. The rest of the paper is also worth reading. And check out the methods used in Gray, C.L. and Bilsborrow, R.E. (2014) "Consequences of out-migration for land use in rural Ecuador", *Land Use Policy*, volume 36, pages 181–191, online. The authors first use econometric analysis to find the impact of migration on land use in rural Ecuador. Then they use remote-sensing methods to verify the 'greenness' of the lands. Could it be that outward migration leads to a reduction in agricultural activity? If so, does this lead to a regrowth of native vegetation? Does migration therefore help biodiversity conservation? If the findings interest you, you may want to compare them with Urama, N.E. et al. (2017), "International migrant remittances and labour supply in Nigeria", *International Migration*, volume 55, number 1, pages 37–50, online; and Abdelali-Martini, M. and Hamza, R. (2016) "How do migration remittances affect rural livelihoods in drylands", *Journal of International Development*, volume 26, pages 454–470 (it focuses on Syria).

To what extent do remittances cause the 'Dutch disease'?

In 2018, Farid Makhlouf published a meta-analysis (this is essentially an assessment of 'what all the research combined has found') that comes to the conclusion that together, the research findings "support the view that in spite of their utility for the recipient households, remittances pose a challenge to the developing country on the macroeconomic level." See Makhlouf, F. (2013) "Remittances and Dutch disease: a meta-analysis", *CATT-UPPA Working Paper*, number 8, online.

How do governments facilitate or hinder migration and its contribution to (rural) development?

There are plenty of country studies, so a quick search on your country of interest should get you what you need. Three publications mentioned in the endnotes are

- ILO (November 2015) *Sri Lankan migrant domestic workers; the impact of Sri Lankan policies on workers' right to freely access employment*, online.
- OECD (2017) *Interrelations between public policies, migration and development in the Dominican Republic*, online.

- Aparicio, F.J. and Meseguer, C. (2012) "Collective remittances and the state: the 3x1 program in Mexican municipalities", *World Development*, volume 40, number 1, pages 206–222, online.

Exercise

The assignment

See the following texts about Maharena and Kamal. Please assess Maharena's situation first and Kamal's second. Then discuss the following questions for each of them:

1 What are the risks associated with each of their options? What option would you have chosen, if you were them, and why?
   From the perspectives of rural development and migration,
2 What could the governments in the sending and receiving countries usefully do?
3 What could non-governmental organisations active in each of the sending countries usefully do?

Maharena

Maharena lives in a rural area close to Lalibela, the site of Ethiopia's famous medieval churches and an important place for pilgrimage and devotion. It is a *very* poor part of the country, and her village has no electricity or running water. Maharena never quite understood *why* the village was so poor, as there is a river close by (but no irrigation system) and a beautiful national park only an hour's walk away. And why do all the tourists go to Lalibela but never to the medieval church right next to her village? But poor it is – the only real asset is a good school, from which Maharena has recently graduated.

Notwithstanding the poverty, Maharena loves the land on which she is living and is proud to be from the Lalibela region. That makes her sad to leave, but leave she must.

Maharena will probably follow in her sisters' footsteps. Both sisters had moved to Lebanon and had been among the 250 young women from the Lalibela region who worked in Beirut. These women saw each other regularly and often worked together to help their relatives to come to Lebanon too. They almost invariably work as domestic workers and are always a little afraid to get in trouble with the families they work for, as they have few rights and several Ethiopian women ended up in a Lebanese prison because their employers had accused them of stealing.

For five long years, Maharena's sisters had saved almost their entire salary. They then returned to Ethiopia and settled in its capital, Addis Ababa. They invested their savings wisely, and their business was doing reasonably well. Perhaps that was another possibility. Maybe Maharena should not go to Lebanon at all but to her sisters in Addis Ababa.

Maharena is nervous, uncertain of the life ahead of her and sad to leave her motherland.

Kamal

Kamal is from Nepal and has been in India for almost ten years now. He is a construction worker and, notwithstanding the rampant discrimination against Nepali workers, has been earning relatively good money.

Kamal has almost saved enough to 'start his life', as he calls it, back in the village. And then the earthquake hit Nepal. More than anything in the world, he had wanted to go home, after the earthquake, to be with his parents, brothers, and sisters. They were still alive, but their houses – all in the same village – had collapsed. He, and so many of his Nepali colleagues (many from the same group of villages), wanted to help. They knew about construction but were afraid to leave India and lose their jobs. There wouldn't be much they could do either, as everything was scarce, and it was obvious that the organisations that worked there had overlooked his village.

Kamal is no longer sure he wants to return. First, the country is a mess, with a huge trauma and little hope of a speedy recovery. Second, government officials are bound to give him a hard time with whatever he would want to do. Some officials see migrants as wealthy and disloyal to Nepal, and they make these people pay bribes for the simplest of things.

Last year, one of Kamal's friends was smuggled into Malaysia, and he wrote to Kamal to tell him that all had gone well and that he should come too. Perhaps that was a good idea.

Notes

1 IOM (2016) *IOM definition of "Migrant"*, online.
2 As opposed to a taxi licence, which is harder and more expensive to get and which allows you to drive commercial vehicles.
3 For a brief overview of international migration figures, see UN (17 September 2019) *The number of international migrants reaches 272 million, continuing an upward trend in all world regions, says UN*, online. For the database itself, see bit.ly/Migration2019.
4 World Bank (2019) *Leveraging economic migration for development: a briefing for the World Bank Board*, online, page 14 and Figure 2.6 on page 15. For this sort of stats, the regular and online *World Bank Migration and Development Brief* is also a useful source.
5 United Nations General Assembly (18 June 2018) *Resolution A/RES/72/281*, online.
6 World Bank (2019) *Leveraging economic migration for development: a briefing for the World Bank Board*, online, Figure 2.6 on page 15. The brief 2015–16 dip in remittances was the first one in 30 years and caused short-lived worries – see World Bank (April 2017) *Remittances to developing countries decline for second consecutive year*, online.
7 Mbaye, L.M. (2014) "'Barcelona or die': understanding illegal migration from Senegal", *IZA Journal of Development and Migration*, volume 3, pages 1–19, online.
8 IOM (2018) *World migration report 2018*, page 56.

9　The Malaysian government recently committed to finding, arresting and repatriating over two million illegal immigrants. This is tough for the migrants, of course, but also quite a challenge for the government. What do you do if the home governments do not acknowledge that these people are their citizens, for example?

10　In 2014, the International Trade Union Confederation looked at accident figures in previous years and extrapolated them on the basis of the number of additional workers entering Qatar for construction work. It concluded that at least 4,000 workers would lose their lives in the construction process. See International Trade Union Confederation Special Report (March 2014) *The case against Qatar: host of the FIFA 2022 world cup*, page 14, online.

11　The implementation of the 2017 legislation is slow and problematic – see Amnesty International (2019) *Reality check; the state of migrant workers' rights with four years to go until the Qatar 2022 world cup*, online. The October 2019 legislation is far more ambitious and will probably be easier to implement – see ILO (October 2019) *Landmark labour reforms signal end of kafala system in Qatar*, online.

12　Sharma, K. (2017) *India has 139 million internal migrants: they must not be forgotten*, World Economic Forum, online.

13　According to the 2014 "Rural – urban migration monitoring survey" of the National Bureau of Statistics in China. See Démurger, S. and Wang, X. (2016) "Remittances and expenditure patterns of the left behinds in rural China", *China Economic Review*, volume 37, pages 177–190, figure on page 178.

14　With a sense of frustration, De Brauw, Mueller, and Lee explain that household surveys often lack a migration component, and panel surveys often only track the migratory behaviour of the household heads. See Brauw, A. de, Mueller, V. and Lee, H.L. (2014) "The role of rural-urban migration in the structural transformation of Sub-Saharan Africa", *World Development*, volume 63, pages 33–42.

15　All three estimates are presented in OECD (2017) *Interrelations between public policies, migration and development in the Dominican Republic*, online, Table 2.4 on page 45.

16　False precision occurs when very specific figures are presented while, in reality, they are very rough estimates. False precision is bad because it creates unjustified confidence in the quality of the figures.

17　For insight into the unlivable situation in Eritrea, see the *Wall Street Journal* (2016) *Thousands flee isolated Eritrea to escape life of conscription and poverty*, online. For an explanation of the changing Eritrean human smuggling patterns, see the *Economist* (2017) *Migration from Eritrea slows*, online.

18　Jordan Strategy Forum (2018) *The economics of Jordanian remittances; some issues we should be happy about & enhance*, online, with the facts mentioned on page 10.

19　See Kapur, D. (April 2004) "Remittances: the new development mantra?" *G-24 Discussion Paper Series Nr 29*, UNCTAD, online.

20　See Castles, S. (December 2009) "Development and migration – migration and development: what comes first?" *Theoria – a Journal of Social and Political Theory*, volume 56, issue 121, page 19, online.

21　HM Treasury and DFID (2015) *AK aid: tackling global challenges in the national interest*, online, with the quotation from the foreword on page 3.

22　For an empirical study of this 'poverty trap', see, for example, Golgher, A.B. (2012) "The selectivity of migration and poverty traps in rural Brazil", *Population Review*, volume 51, issue 1, pages 9–27.

23　Generally, men dominate the first-phase migration flows (i.e. before the process of family reunification starts), but there are exceptions. The most notable exception is Sri Lanka, where, in the 1990s, three-quarters of the migrants were women (a phenomenon sometimes referred to as the 'feminisation of migration'), and where men have only recently caught up (it's now 50–50).

24　Adams, R.H. (2003) "International migration, remittances and the brain drain", *World Bank Policy Research Working Papers*, online.

25 I first saw this Manchester point mentioned in the Joint Learning Initiative (2004) *Human resources for health: overcoming the crisis,* pages 18 and 19, online, but understood that the rumour had existed at least since the 1980s. The statement was discredited in a BBC follow-up investigation: see Health and Development (January 2012) *More Malawian doctors in Manchester than Malawi?* online. About the brain drain in Malawi's health care system in general, and about possible ways forward, see The African Capacity Building Foundation (2018) "Brain drain in Africa: the case of tackling capacity issues in Malawi's medical migration", *Occasional Paper Number 31,* online.

26 The term 'migrant syndrome' was coined in Reichert, J.S. (1981) "The migrant syndrome: seasonal U.S. wage labor and rural development in central Mexico", *Human Organisation,* volume 40, issue 1, pages 56–66. In essence, "Instead of providing a source of capital with which residents could strengthen the local economy, high annual income earned in the United States has merely encouraged more people to migrate, thereby making the town and its inhabitants increasingly dependent on U.S. wage labor as a source of livelihood. This dependency is not merely reflected in economic trends. It has also become part of the local value system."

27 Taylor, J.E. (1999) "The new economics of labour migration and the role of remittances in the migration process", *International Migration,* volume 37, issue 1, online, with the quotation on page 64.

28 For example, on Tonga, remittances amounted to more than 50% of the overall village income in three of the four Tongan villages examined. Faeamani, S.U. (1995) "The impact of remittances on rural development in Tongan villages", *Asian and Pacific Migration Journal,* volume 4, issue 1, pages 139–155, online.

29 Acosta, P. et al. (2008) "What is the impact of international remittances on poverty and inequality in Latin America?" *World Development,* volume 36, issue 1, with the quotation on page 89. 'Panel data' are data that are gathered at multiple points in time, from the same people or companies, with the aim of identifying trends.

30 Imai, K.S. et al. (2014) "Remittances, growth and poverty: new evidence from Asian countries", *Journal of Policy Modeling,* volume 36, pages 524–538. (In case you can't find this paper: 'Modeling' really is written with one 'l'.)

31 Ellyne, M. and Mahlalela, N. (17–19 May 2017) *The impact of remittances on poverty in Africa: a cross-country empirical analysis,* paper presented at the 14th African Finance Journal Conference, online.

32 Sustainable Development Goals, Target 10.c.1.

33 Ratha, D. et al. (October 2019) "Data release: remittances to low- and middle-income countries on track to reach $551 billion in 2019 and $597 by 2021", *World Bank Blogs,* online.

34 There is some controversy, as "rising opposition against women migrating as domestic workers based on reports of negative impacts on the children and families of women domestic workers has led to a number of policies and practices to stem the migration of women to the domestic work sector". This led, in 2013–14, to two government 'Circulars' that required a 'Family Background Report' for female domestic workers, meant to ensure the care and protection of their children. There is no such requirement for male migrants. See ILO (November 2015) *Sri Lankan migrant domestic workers: the impact of Sri Lankan policies on workers' right to freely access employment,* online, with the quotation from the abstract.

35 See World Bank (April 2019) *Record high remittances sent globally in 2018,* online.

36 Aparicio, F.J. and Meseguer, C. (2012) "Collective remittances and the state: the 3x1 program in Mexican municipalities", *World Development,* volume 40, issue 1, pages 206–222, online.

37 These long-term ties are easier to maintain as a result of new communication technologies, and they are the focus of the 'transnational theory of migration' – yet another school of thought.

38 Such assessments are really difficult, so you may want to use specialist evaluators.

8

SOCIAL ASSISTANCE

Note on terminology: 'social assistance', 'social safety nets', and 'social welfare' are equiv-alents. They provide <u>non-contributory</u>[1] transfers in cash or in kind, which are targeted at poor and vulnerable people. Social assistance is a sub-group of 'social protection'. Social protection is not necessarily focused exclusively on poor and vulnerable people and includes, for example, labour and child protection policies. If this is not entirely clear, read on, and things will come into focus.

Prologue: the fisherman's metaphor and the elephant in the ~~room~~ fishpond

Few sectors are as male-dominated as the world of fishermen, so I don't want to stereotype but my metaphor is more about John than Mary.

As a student in international development or suchlike, you will have grasped that you should not 'give John a fish' but 'teach John to fish' (indeed there is even an organisation with that name – *teachamantofish.org.uk*). Much of what you learn builds on this metaphor. You learn, for example, that the world is full of training programmes, but that training does not automatically lead to skill gains (and may be subject to perverse incentives – see Box 8.1). You learn that it's not just about skills and that John won't be in the position to fish unless he has access to fishing grounds and to the capital required to get fishing gear.

You learn that fishing grounds must be managed, or else John and his peers will quickly overfish and deplete stocks. You learn that climate change might dry up the lake or that the lake might get polluted and that diseases and oxygen-poor waters might kill off the fish.

You learn that there needs to be a functioning, not-too-corrupt market where John's fish fetch a fair price. You learn that this requires salespeople (this is where Mary typically enters the story), roads, and transport options that connect the

BOX 8.1   BEWARE OF PERVERSE INCENTIVES

Where organisations train poorer members of a community, they typically provide financial compensation for the assumed income loss. This provides a perverse incentive: some people look around for training opportunities to gain dollars rather than skills. Once, I interviewed a woman who explained how a micro-enterprise training course had *almost* changed her life and how the *only* thing she now needed before establishing a small company was a few more training days. When I mentioned that I was actually interviewing her because of a different training course, on local conflict mediation, she needed a few seconds to make the mental switch and then explained, with equal enthusiasm, how *that* training had *almost* enabled her to mediate local conflicts and how the *only* thing now required was a few more training days to hone her skills.

village to the market, as well as parallel industries that sell ice to keep the fish fresh and snacks to get Mary through the long, hot day.

Much of a degree in international development is about understanding that 'development', 'livelihoods', and 'empowerment' are complex concepts and that progress often requires addressing a range of different bottlenecks.

But here's what has long been the elephant in the room: what if John, for whatever reason, can't fish? What if, temporarily or permanently, John and other members of his household are incapable of undertaking activities that allow the household to earn an income or even grow subsistence crops?

Then life looks very grim indeed. Then the household will need support to make ends meet, to get food, to keep the children in school. They might only need it for a while – perhaps until the harvest season or until a key income earner recovers from an illness. Or they might need it permanently – perhaps as a consequence of old age, or a chronic illness, or an incapacitating disability.

If such support is somewhat regular and predictable, it is called 'social assistance'. Social assistance is non-contributory and targets various types of poor and vulnerable people. Until recently, social assistance didn't receive much attention in the development sector. Country governments and development practitioners did not like the concept. They feared that social assistance was prone to corruption and would be a disincentive to work. More fundamentally, the prevailing ideal was that people should be empowered to take care of themselves and be (or grow into) productive members of society.

In recent times, this has changed. Perhaps it's because many of the world's informal family- and community-based safety nets are eroding. Maybe it has become clear that, even in conditions of overall economic growth, there are groups that are left behind. Or perhaps leaders came to realise that large groups

FIGURE 8.1 Sometimes, skills are not enough

of very poor and vulnerable people may destabilise government. I do not know. What I do know is that some of the Latin American countries showed the way by upscaling their social assistance programmes in the 1990s. Their success gained visibility during the 'triple F crisis' of 2007–08, when a global financial crisis was preceded by sharp rises in food and fuel prices (see Chapter 5). Around the world, the poorest segments of society suffered more than other groups – but in a few Latin American countries, social assistance systems shielded the poorest households from the worst effects. Within the international donor community, a view emerged that low-income countries in Africa and Asia could also develop such systems, and key donors such as the World Bank and DFID invested heavily in supporting the capacity of many governments to do so. Now, only a little over a decade later, social assistance systems are much more common and sizeable than they were at the time of that triple F crisis. Their importance is highlighted in the Sustainable Development Goals (see Box 8.2), and they have considerable ownership among a range of governments throughout the Global South. As they grow, they are creating a 'neighbourhood effect' (see Chapter 1): if the countries around you have social assistance programmes in place, you do not want to be the only country in the region that does not seem to care about the plight of its most vulnerable citizens.

BOX 8.2 TARGET 1.3 OF THE SUSTAINABLE DEVELOPMENT GOALS

"Implement nationally appropriate social protection systems and measures for all, including floors,[2] and by 2030 achieve substantial coverage of the poor and the vulnerable."

Source: SDGs, *Goal 1 targets*, online.

What are we talking about?

Nowadays, developing countries spend an average of 1.5% of their GDP on social assistance.[3] This spending takes different forms, and the most important ones are as follows (with the 'winner' – cash transfers – appearing last):

1 of 4: public work programmes

These are social assistance programmes that pay poor people money or sometimes give them food – but only if they work on a road, irrigation canal, dike, or anything else that does not require advanced skills and that is meant to benefit a community.

The idea is that these programmes target the poorest people through self-selection: you really do not want to be part of it unless you *desperately* need the money. The programmes are not meant to compete with other money-earning opportunities, and their wages are meant to be a little below the lowest paid for any of the local jobs. They are also often time-bound: they are meant to avoid hunger and distress sales in the months before the harvest or to provide a minimum income after a natural disaster.

Public work programmes often have two significant drawbacks.

1   These programmes are often not much more than a relatively expensive way to give people cash (or food). Because the infrastructure is not their primary purpose, it is often of poor quality and not very useful. More than once, I have driven *next to* rather than *on* a road that had recently been constructed by a public work programme, because the road had deteriorated beyond use. In the case of a road, this is bad. In the case of a construction that is meant to prevent disasters, such as a dike or drainage system, it is worse: it looks like a duck, it quacks like a duck, but when the floods come, it does not actually float.

2   Work requirements come with the risk of excluding the people who need the money most. You need to be able to do work and live relatively close to a work site, so people with severe disabilities, elderly people, people who live remotely, and women with child-care responsibilities are unlikely to benefit from a public work programme, unless the programme is deliberately and carefully inclusive. Sometimes they are. At the time of writing, the government of Rwanda is piloting a programme that targets young mothers who cannot travel far from home and have little time to spare. They get part-time and local assignments and a fixed monthly sum. It seems to work.

The reason that public work programmes get a sizeable proportion of social assistance funding in Sub-Saharan Africa, South Asia and the Middle East is largely political. Governments do not like the idea of hand-outs and do not want to be seen to be providing them. 'You'll have to work for your money – even if that work is a matter of digging holes and filling them in again.'[4]

2 of 4: in-kind support in general and food support in particular

People receive school uniforms, housing, seeds, solar-powered lights, and – far more important than all these things combined – food. Some of this food support is ready-made and meant for immediate consumption in nutrition clinics or schools. (School meals, in fact, are such an important part of in-kind support that statistics often show them as a separate type of social assistance.) Other support takes the form of raw ingredients or nutritional bars and the like, which is meant to be taken home. Sometimes the targeting is very restrictive, such as nutritional support to households with malnourished children. More commonly, all people who belong to an easily identifiable group qualify, such as all children in a group of schools or all pregnant and lactating women in a certain region.

In-kind support can be useful but is often unnecessarily restrictive (you wouldn't like your income to be paid in fish either) and more expensive than it would be to give poor households the money needed to buy whatever you're distributing.

One of the reasons such support still exists is the 'awe factor' that sometimes comes with the distribution of *things*, and I recall having succumbed to its appeal in a few of my earlier evaluations. The first time I visited a school with a school-feeding programme, my host's argument for the programme was that 'it takes a meal out of the family's tight daily budget'. At the time, I was merely impressed by the small blackened kitchen, in which a single cook prepared the same simple meal every day without electricity or any of the other conveniences that I was used to seeing in a school kitchen. It was only later that I realised the host's explanation was deeply unsatisfactory, for two reasons. First, these programmes are meant to provide *supplementary* meals, not *substitute* meals. Second, school meals are an expensive way of taking the pressure off a family's budget, as providing school meals often costs more than the monetary worth of the equivalent ingredients in cash. The direct programme costs are high, especially if the food is imported, as is often the case. Before the food is eaten, it needs to be bought, transported, possibly sent through customs, stored, distributed over regions and then over schools, and *then* cooked and given to children. That's a lot of steps. Moreover, some of the organisations involved are bureaucracies with enormous overhead costs.[5] Donated food does not necessarily reduce costs: "The flexibility of the [Food for Education] program design . . . is often limited by the in-kind donations to WFP, which result in higher costs and therefore lower the overall cost-efficiency of the program."[6]

A better reason for school feeding programmes is that they lead, very directly, to schoolchildren eating food that typically has a relatively high nutritional value. This is a good thing, even if this meal is partly *substitute* food instead of *additional* food (as in, even if it results in the children getting less food at home). Moreover, the food may help children to concentrate whilst in school. School meals even increase school enrolment and attendance, especially in combination with a few other measures, such as making sure there are functioning latrines and that they are segregated for girls and boys, so that girls don't have to go home halfway through the school day. This, then, gives you a clue about appropriate targeting: school feeding programmes make the most sense in areas and grades where there is a lot of non-enrolment and dropping out. A well-targeted school meal programme could, for example, be one that only provides meals to children in grades 5 and 6, if these are the 'drop out years', or one that gives extra take-home food to girls, if girls are particularly likely to discontinue their education.

3 of 4: discounts and fee waivers

They exist for education, health care, and other services, and they count as social assistance, provided they are targeted at particularly poor households. *General* subsidies for food, fuel, and electricity are also common (and in fact cost more than all social assistance types together, in some countries) but do not qualify as social assistance. This is because such subsidies are not targeting poor people in particular. And they don't necessarily reach them either, as only the wealthier groups have access to electricity and use petrol-consuming equipment.

4 of 4: cash transfers

People receive a periodic sum of money. Sometimes, it comes with one or more conditions: you get it if your children get vaccinated or stay in school, or only if you attend information sessions about nutrition. Generally, cash transfers should not discourage you from earning money: they are meant to *add to* rather than *substitute* other sources of income.

When I implemented my first-ever cash transfer programme (for the UNHCR in Jordan, focused on Iraqi refugees, in the mid-1990s), I was worried that the money would be spent on booze and cigarettes. At the time, their impact on consumer behaviour was simply unknown, but there has since been a lot of research on spending patterns. As it turns out, people tend to spend cash transfers wisely. Recently, an evaluation of a large cash transfer programme in Kenya even concluded that recipients "spend significantly more of their overall income (*not just the cash transfers*) on food, health and clothing, and significantly less on alcohol and tobacco".[7] The reason might be a reduction in negative coping behaviour: if your problems seem less insurmountable, you may be less inclined to 'drink-to-forget'.

There has been much debate about the pros and cons of each of these options, but the verdict is in, and, in most cases, cash transfers are the better option. There are three reasons for cash transfers outperforming other types of social assistance:

- Cash transfers are empowering, as you leave the spending decisions to the recipients instead of assuming that you know their needs better than they do. Compared to cash transfers, all other forms of social assistance are restrictive.
- Cash transfers are cheaper than other forms of social assistance. Unless there *is* no local food market, the distribution of food is often a costly option, for example. The cost advantage is even bigger now that technological innovation is making cash transfers ever-easier and ever-cheaper. Nowadays, you rarely have to queue to receive actual coins and bills. Instead, it is transferred to your debit card or SIM card – even in countries such as, say, Zimbabwe.
- Cash transfers are easy to monitor. If people are on the beneficiary list and should get a thousand rupees every month, you can ask them how much they received. If it's a thousand rupees every month, there is no 'leakage'. (But be careful how you ask your questions! Quick surveys and hasty interviewers will often miss important information. In this particular case, hastiness would risk missing hidden costs, such as the bribe you pay to get on the eligibility list or the money you pay somebody to 'help you use the ATM machine'.)

Countries are increasingly recognising the superiority of cash. In most countries, cash transfers are now amounting to more than 50% of social assistance[8] and most other countries will probably follow soon. Therefore, much of the rest of this chapter zooms in on cash transfers.

What does social assistance aim to achieve?

Some programmes focus simply on 'poor people'. Others focus on the elderly, pregnant and lactating women, young mothers, or people with disabilities. Depending in part on the target groups, different programmes aim to achieve different things. Here are some key objectives.

1 – Increase and smooth people's consumption. The basics are simply this: if you are very poor, and you regularly receive a bit of money, then you regularly have a bit of extra money. If you receive food, clothes or free health services, you have extra food, clothes, or better access to health services. If the support is regular, you adapt your consumption behaviour.

For as long as you receive this regular support, and provided that the in-kind support is actually useful, you are a little less poor and vulnerable than you would otherwise have been. This has immediate effects. It may be the difference between being hungry a lot or not, or between being sick and in pain or not. It may also have hard-to-measure but important effects on your sense of self-worth and dignity (see Box 8.3).

BOX 8.3   DRESSED FOR THE OCCASION

In the south of Bangladesh, I was interviewing women who were recipients of a cash transfer programme. Most of them talked about meals-per-day, no doubt because the organisation behind the programme had asked them to do so, as this was how they measured success. In addition, some respondents mentioned better access to health services or showed me the improvements in their dwellings.

And then there were a few women who linked the cash transfers to their dignity and self-esteem. One described the rags she used to wear and the difference the cash had made in this regard: "because I now look like others, I was invited to a wedding in the village. It was the first party ever that I attended as a guest, not as a beggar".

---

2 – Empower women and girls, in part by reducing inequalities within the household. If you are a woman and the social assistance is channelled through you (as is often the case), you may find that the support changes the household dynamics to your advantage. You may also find that the periodic support enhances the chances of your daughter's safe transition from adolescence to adulthood by reducing risky behaviour like having unprotected sex, as this is often <u>transactional</u>[9] and driven by poverty-induced desperation and lack of alternatives.

3 – Strengthen resilience and help 'graduate' people out of poverty. Beyond the effect of immediate poverty alleviation, social assistance often aims to have longer-term effects. First, a bit of support during particularly harsh times may keep you from making distress sales (which, as you will recall, are asset sales at low prices to meet today's urgent needs at the cost of future prospects). Second, you might manage to build some savings that would help you cope with the hard times that may be coming or invest part of the support you receive. In principle, such investments could gradually grow your assets. You start with a few chickens, say, and sell chicks or eggs until you have money to buy goats, which may help you save for cattle – at which point, you 'have graduated out of poverty'. Some lenders accept future social assistance payments as an informal form of collateral, so you could even use your regular extra income to get a loan, to speed up your asset acquisition.

4 – Help achieve a brighter future for the next generation. Social assistance may benefit the prospects of your children and therefore *their* children (and so on), thereby breaking the inter-generation transfer of poverty. If you receive a school uniform or a meal every day you are in school, or your mother receives a monthly sum of money, you are more likely to attend classes. If the support is targeting girls in particular, it may have equalising effects as well.

The idea is that your school attendance causes you to learn useful things, which leads to later-age benefits that range from better income-earning opportunities to better parenting. Similarly, the expectation is that you eat more nutritious meals (because you receive supplementary food or cash to buy it) and that this leads to better growth, health, and cognitive development, all of which improve your prospects as a 'grown-up'.

5 – Have positive effects on the local economy. This could happen in three ways, or so the theory goes. First, if your social assistance takes the shape of public work programmes, a beneficial side-product could be useful infrastructure, which may reduce the effects of natural hazards (dikes prevent flooding) or support the local economy (roads facilitate trade).

Second, the mere fact that the poorest members of a community get a bit of support may benefit the wider community's economy, through the 'multiplier effect'. In essence, recipients will spend that extra money in the local shop or use it to pay for somebody to repair their bicycle or vaccinate their goat or plough their plot of land. This money does not disappear; it goes into the pockets of members of the community who also buy things locally, and so on.

Third, the existence of a social safety net may change people's approach to risk-taking. Essentially, a social safety net could give you the comfort of knowing that you will not fall into desperate destitution if your livelihood plans fail, and this may encourage you to strive to *maximise* your income (which requires a risk-taking attitude) instead of *stabilising* it. If lots of people aim to maximise their income, there will be individual losers, but overall, the community's income will probably grow.

FIGURE 8.2   The multiplier effect

So that's the theory, and these are the claims that often make programme proposals look attractive (see Box 8.4). Next, how is all this panning out in practice?

BOX 8.4   BEWARE OF UNREALISTIC AIMS

People who develop proposals make the plans sound as attractive as possible to attract funding. This makes sense, as they are generally competing with other proposals that also exaggerate their likely achievements. Therefore, you should generally take proposals with a grain of salt, as they are unlikely to achieve all they promise. Some of the DFID business cases,[10] for example, envision that programmes are going to empower the recipient households' women; increase the households' savings and productive assets; strengthen their resilience to climate change; and improve the health, nutritional status, and education of the households' children. Evidence suggests that each of these outcomes is possible, but that a single programme is unlikely to achieve all of them.

What does social assistance achieve in practice?

Cash transfers are generally better than their alternatives but do *not* generally achieve all the hyped-up impact claims listed in the previous section, because households are held back by more than money alone (see the Chapter 5 prologue). In reality, it is like this:[11]

If you give Mary money, she can buy things. Receiving money will generally lead to *spending* money, unless a household faces a crippling debt that urgently needs paying off. Therefore, as you would expect, cash transfers almost always increase a household's total expenditure as well as the specific expenditure on food. All other links are less direct, and their effects are weaker and less consistent (or not yet thoroughly assessed – see Box 8.5).

BOX 8.5   MIGHT SOCIAL ASSISTANCE HELP CONSOLIDATE PEACE?

When countries emerge from a conflict, they generally face a devastated economy and have groups that are deeply distrustful towards one another. To keep the peace, these groups need to feel that they are not forgotten and that life is better now than it was during the conflict. In the longer term, this requires equitable economic development, among many other things that foster social cohesion. More immediately after the conflict, a broad provision of social assistance could help prevent a further deterioration of living standards (potentially

---

caused by the disappearance of a war economy that includes armies' food transports to loyal regions and the like). This is why the social assistance budgets in many post-conflict countries are higher than in most other countries. Nobody in Rwanda's government will mention it, but I suspect that the government's strong and genuine drive towards a country-wide social assistance system is in part inspired by the notion that very poor rural Hutu groups could potentially be a serious threat to the country's stability.

It makes sense, and literature often *assumes* this peace consolidation effect, but there is very little research that actually *assesses* the contribution of social assistance to peacebuilding efforts. Indeed, there is some evidence of adverse impacts if targeting is on the basis of ethnic and other group identities rather than needs.[12]

Transferring cash to Mary rather than her husband or brother will probably strengthen Mary's decision-making power within the household and may reduce the risk of abuse. This increased decision-making power is easy to understand: Mary now has money, and with money comes power. The abuse is more complex. On the one hand, an improved overall position of a household's women may reduce abuse, as these women can 'bargain themselves out of abuse'. The reduction in poverty-related stress will also play a role, as abuse is often triggered by stress and frustration. On the other hand, in a few cases, cash transfers have actually *increased* domestic abuse. Perhaps some men feel the need to reassert their dominance by abusing the women in the household or because the abuse is meant to ensure that the spending decisions are in line with the man's preferences? Nobody really fully understands the dynamics yet, and the evidence is relatively flimsy, but the risk of abuse seems to be highest if there is a large age difference between the man and the woman, and if the man is uneducated.[13]

And her daughters may be less likely to resort to risky sexual behaviour. In many households, the cash also enables girls and women to make choices in relation to fertility and sexual activity (i.e., out of free will and when ready, rather than under pressure or out of economic necessity). It is a little different for boys: cash transfers do not seem to reduce *their* risky sexual activity and may even increase it.

Mary may save or invest some of the money she receives. Studies often − but not always − find positive links between cash transfers and savings, livestock ownership, and spending on agricultural inputs. This is understandable: once you have met your most basic needs, it is smart to think of the future or save a bit of cash in case of adversity. But the effect is neither very impressive nor guaranteed, and most people need more than a bit of extra cash to 'graduate out of poverty'.

And her kids may go to school (but this might be a waste of time). Cash transfers often improve school attendance − even without the cash being conditional upon it. But, sadly, this school attendance does not lead to a clear pattern of improved learning outcomes. In other words, cash transfers may lead to kids spending their days being bored in schools in which they do not actually *learn* things. This shows the multidimensionality of the learning challenge: attending school is necessary, but for attendance to be *useful*, you need *quality* education, which is not something all schools offer.

To avoid stunting, kids need more than a bit of extra money. Once people receive cash transfers, their use of health services and dietary diversity increase, and there are some <u>anthropometric results</u>.[14] However, to reduce the risk of child stunting, people need more than cash transfers alone, as undernourishment is as much a matter of the *absorption* of nutrients as it is of nutritional *intake* (see endnote 8 in Chapter 1).

And there is some evidence that these cash transfers make a minor contribution to local economies, but that this does not have much effect on the poorest members of the communities. There is not enough evidence to confirm that people act more entrepreneurially if there is social assistance to fall back on in case of failure. The opposite could also be true: people might behave more entrepreneurially in contexts without social assistance "for the simple reason that without social safety nets, many [people] must hustle or starve".[15] We just don't know yet. We do know that cash transfers have a multiplier effect, caused by John spending the dollar he got in Mary's shop, who makes 20 cents in profit, which she spends on locally grown tomatoes, which means a ten-cent profit for the farmer, and so on. Research suggests that this multiplier ranges from $1.08 (in Nyanza, Kenya) to $1.81 (in Hintalo, Ethiopia).[16] However, the poorest members of communities do not benefit much from this multiplier effect. Because they are poor, they have few productive assets, so they are not the people you go to when you want to buy things.

Is this not a little disappointing?

Well, yes, for people who had unrealistic hopes. Cash transfers are no magic bullet. But keep in mind three things. First, cash transfers are great in achieving what they are primarily meant to achieve: alleviating crippling poverty and improving people's quality of life, even if only for the duration of the cash transfers. That in and by itself is well worth a considerable investment.

Second, for many governments this is new, and they are on a learning curve (see Table 8.1 for weaknesses that are still common). Over time, the targeting and the size and regularity of the payments will improve, and this will increase their impact – including some of the more ambitious, less direct, longer-term types of impact.

Third, social assistance can't do all the heavy lifting by itself, but in combination with other types of support, great things are possible. Make cash transfers conditional on school enrolment, for example, and you get children in school. Combine this with a concerted effort on the supply side (so better teachers, who receive reasonable salaries and teach a useful curriculum on the basis of methods that encourage learning in schools with adequate facilities), and children will read, write, and more. Provide poor people with locally produced food, and combine this with

TABLE 8.1 Common cash transfer flaws

1: Targeting

Three types of targeting errors

- Eligibility errors: the eligible group is not particularly poor. Rwanda uses a set of home-grown *Ubedehe* criteria, which are related to people's embeddedness in local communities. These criteria are only loosely correlated with poverty.
- Inclusion errors: you receive transfers, but you are not actually part of the eligible group. In a maternal programme in Nigeria, fake urine samples initially led to the inclusion of women who were not in fact pregnant. Rumour goes that they used the urine of pregnant donkeys.[17]
- Exclusion errors: cash transfers that require people to do public work often exclude people who need the money most – such as people who live in remote locations and women whose hands are tied by child-care responsibilities.

Implication

You spend more money than needed, and do not reach all those you aim to reach.

2: Transfer size

The determinants

Often, the transfer size is based on the cost of a food item or basket, or a percentage of the national poverty line. Both benchmarks are artificial: not all money is spent on food, and the national poverty line does not accommodate price differences across regions. Public work programmes often pay an amount that is loosely based on local labour costs, rather than anything related to poverty indicators.

When setting the transfer size, affordability plays a role as well. This is because there is a trade-off between transfer size and coverage: you can afford to make payments to more people if you pay each person less.

Implication

If the transfer size is too low, it will not make a meaningful difference in the lives of the recipients. Equally, if the transfer size is higher than necessary to achieve an objective, you reach fewer people than you could.[18] Some governments also worry that anything more than *really* low transfer sums might discourage economic activity – but I have not come across examples in the Global South where this was an actual issue.[19]

3: Timeliness

The situation

If a cash transfer programme has accepted you as an eligible recipient, you are typically entitled to a monthly or quarterly sum of money.

Often, you do not receive all the money you are officially entitled to, you receive it later than promised, or the cumulative monthly payments are paid only a few times per year. When assessing ten large cash transfer programmes in Africa and Asia, I found that only three of the programmes made most of their payments broadly on time (give or take ten days or so).[20]

Implication

Cash transfers aim to change behaviour. Better food intake, school enrolment, use of health services, asset acquisition – you know the list by now. But for people to change their behaviour, they need to feel confident that the money will actually arrive, in full and at the scheduled time. Without this, cash transfers never give a sense of predictability and remain some sort of manna from heaven: welcome, for sure, but not something you base your spending decisions on.

Overall lesson: beware of hidden agendas. Improving cash transfer programmes is not just a matter of learning about good practice principles. There are vested interests to keep in mind. In some countries, the government is running dozens of small and inefficient cash transfer programmes. They often leak, too. Technically, it is fairly easy to merge programmes and to reduce these leaks. However, attempts to do so typically encounter strong resistance from people who see 'their' funds as a source of prestige or as a way to gain and reward supporters and, perhaps, as an opportunity to siphon off a portion of the budget.

technical support to farmers (who now have an assured buyer of their produce), and you might create a positive spiral of rural economic development.[21]

An impressive example of a multi-faceted approach is BRAC's 'poverty graduation' programme. It started in Bangladesh in 2002, and was inspired by BRAC's observation that its work did not manage to be truly useful to the poorest people.

In every community, this BRAC programme starts with a very careful participatory process that identifies the community's poorest and most vulnerable members. Once BRAC knows whom to target, it combines relatively small cash transfers with support such as asset grants (often some sort of livestock), animal vaccinations, food supplements, entrepreneurial and other training, and hygiene awareness raising. The results are impressive. Because of the weekly cash transfers, beneficiaries do not need to sell their assets as soon as adversity hits them, and a large majority of beneficiaries achieves substantial improvements in their socio-economic status. In most cases, the results continue after households have exited the programme, even in the face of climate shocks. The model is not replicable everywhere, because it requires a diversified rural economy and a high population density. It may also perform less well in times of economic downturn and is costlier than standard cash transfers. But still, the results are impressive, and BRAC and a number of other organisations are currently trying to replicate the programme's success in other countries.

Why is all this relevant, and what does it mean for you?

Cash transfers are a very efficient and immediate way to get money into the hands of poor people, and they are changing the face of rural poverty. In regions where cash transfer programmes are well targeted, timely, and sizeable enough to amount to a meaningful addition to a household's income, they reduce poor people's levels of deprivation. If people face temporary hardship, cash transfers alleviate it. If poor people are permanently unable to earn an income – because of old age, say – cash transfers make them less poor than they would otherwise have been.

Cash transfer programmes are here to stay. Many different modalities and target groups exist, and many programmes have moved well beyond their pilot phases. Over time, they will increase their geographical coverage – which is currently often limited – until they are truly country-wide. They will continue to innovate, and this will reduce overhead costs and improve targeting and reliability. Transfer amounts will increase, and this is important because the amounts currently paid are often so small that the transfers are empty gestures.[22] Paradoxically (if not unexpectedly), low-income countries need these programmes most, but their governments are least able to afford and manage them. In the foreseeable future, these countries will continue to rely on the international donor community for technical support and some of the finances.

If you work for a government in the Global South, please steer your country towards more cash transfer programming and less towards its alternatives (with the possible exception of food distribution as part of the promising Institutional Demand approach – see endnote 21). Steer your country away from public work programmes, as these tend to be expensive and often exclude groups that need social assistance but are unable to do work in locations at significant distances from their homes. Do not push for *conditional* cash transfer programming if the imposed conditions do not actually improve things: school enrolment is only useful if children actually *learn* things, and nutritional classes are only useful if they lead to behavioural change. This explains why conditional cash transfers "throughout Latin America, the Caribbean and some other countries have reported improved health outcomes, while programmes in Africa have achieved mixed success".[23] Then make sure to measure results – and be realistic about what cash transfers can and cannot achieve. Realise that the problem of, say, poor maternal health or education is most often on the supply side.

If you are a technical advisor, please help improve the design and implementation of cash transfer programmes, as they achieve the most when they are well-targeted and when the payments are meaningful, predictable and timely. Realise that most of today's cash transfer programmes exclude some of the poorest groups in society, such as homeless people and illegal migrants. Build government capacity to expand coverage, but also realise that not all problems have technical solutions: some are caused by hidden interests and agendas, and may require political influencing. Lastly, realise that some forms of social assistance will always be needed (such as pensions), but other forms are established in response to a failed harvest, an economic downturn, war, or civil unrest. They should be phased out when they are no longer needed. This is tough (see Box 8.6).

BOX 8.6 'THATCHER, THATCHER, MILK SNATCHER'

Do you suffer from hyperinflation, a big recession, or civil unrest? Increase the food subsidies, or give people money. During the Arab Spring, the knee-jerk response of the Libyan and Saudi governments was to do exactly that. Such measures have great short-term popularity, but there is a flipside: these subsidies are hard to remove, so you are left with an additional burden on the government long after the demonstrations have ceased.

A famous example of this 'status quo bias' is related to British school milk: Margaret Thatcher was called "Thatcher, Thatcher, milk snatcher" long after reducing UK's school milk programme in the early 1970s – even though many kids did not particularly like the milk and classrooms often had a sour smell because of hidden milk cartons and milk-filled plant pots.

Further reading

Ever since the turn of the century, there has been a lot of funding for research in the field of social assistance. Some donors fund research because they want to promote it and find out what works best. Others feel they are taking risks by supporting such programmes (some UK papers tend to write about social assistance in very derogatory terms, for example) and therefore need to make sure their support is very, *very* much rooted in evidence.

So there is plenty of research on the issue. However, the nature and design of social assistance programmes are changing so rapidly that a Google Scholar search is probably more useful than reading the publications that seem so cutting edge at the time of writing. Search for 'cash transfers', 'social assistance' and 'social protection', with or without the addition of the word 'rural'. Use the 'advanced search' to limit your search to material that was published recently. Or consider the following:

Social assistance in general

The World Bank has a flagship series on the subject. At the time of writing, the third and latest issue is World Bank (2018) *The state of social safety nets*, online. It is a massive book, but the summary is just a few pages. Every version of this publication has a few 'special issue' chapters, and if you want to understand how rural and urban social assistance differ, you may want to look at the 2015 version (section 5).

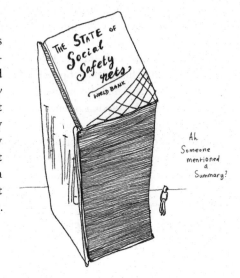

FIGURE 8.3   Somebody mentioned a summary?

Social protection (including social assistance) and agriculture

Tirivayi, N., Knowles, M. and Davis, B. (September 2016), "The interaction between social protection and agriculture: a review of evidence", *Global Food Security*, volume 10, pages 52–62.

Volume 16 of the quarterly *Global Food Security* (March 2018) included a special issue on social protection and agriculture. It starts with a wonderful four-page overview that synthesises all other papers into a single paragraph each: Croppenstedt, A., Knowles, M. and Lowder, S.K. (March 2018) "Social protection and agriculture: the introduction to this special issue", *Global Food Security*, volume 16, pages 65–68.

Cash transfers

In 2016–17, I assessed DFID's cash transfer work (the resulting report is available on *icai.independent.gov.uk*). As part of this assessment, I asked many DFID staff and implementers for their intellectual sources of inspiration. By far the most common answer was this book: Hulme, D., Hanlong, J., and Barrientos, A. (2010). *Just give money to the poor. The development revolution from the Global South*, Kumarian Press.

For a meta-study (i.e., a study that looks at the available evidence, gathered by lots of other studies), see Bastagli, F. et al. (2016) *Cash transfers: what does the evidence say?* ODI, online.

Public work programmes

For a meta-evaluation report, see Subbarao, K. et al. (2013) *Public works as a safety net: design, evidence, and implementation*, World Bank, online. It's a massive publication, but has a one-page overview of 'key messages' in the executive summary.

Food aid

School feeding interventions are common, and you'll probably find one or more recent assessments for whichever country you might be interested in. For a report that presents the findings of 14 country studies and synthesises a few key lessons, see Drake, L. et al., editors (2016) *Global school feeding sourcebook; lessons from 14 countries*, The Partnership for Child Development and Imperial College Press, online.

As is the case in so many fields, be aware of the organisation behind the publication you're reading. The World Food Programme (WFP), for example, has a vested interest in school feeding programmes. This doesn't mean that the findings it reports are untrue – but the selection of findings are likely to be biased towards the positive. For a good example, see the 24 Wonderful Findings reported in WFP (January 2019) *The impact of school feeding programmes*, online. (It includes a hyperlink to a far more detailed report on page 1.) In such cases, read the publication, feel uplifted, and learn about important achievements. Then check some of the references and snowball from there for nuance and more critical findings.

In general, more detailed and niche-focused WFP publications are less biased. For a strikingly honest evaluation of a relatively new type of food distribution programmes that links investments in local agricultural production with food aid to the poorest community members, see WFP (2015) "P4P impact assessments; synthesis of preliminary findings", *PWP Global Learning Series*, online. (P4P means 'Purchase for Progress'.)

Exercise on social assistance

You are a technical advisor, and you need to suggest ways to reduce costs and increase coverage of a social assistance programme.

Because of the recession in Stabilistan, your budget is under pressure. At the same time, the proportion and number of very poor households is on the rise. You need to reduce the costs of your social assistance programme, while increasing coverage.

At the moment, eligible households are entitled to

- A monthly sum of money that depends on the size of the family (900 Qs for one person, going up to a maximum of 3,000 Qs for large families). For households with children, the transfers are conditional on their school enrolment and attendance.
- A biannual voucher to buy clothes at *SuperCheap*, a countrywide chain of textile shops (900 Qs per person).
- Free medical care in a countrywide chain of Stabilicare clinics. These private clinics are small but good and have a reference system for specialist care.
- Per year, a minimum of 30 days of employment at a public work programme, which is meant to build rural infrastructure and teach marketable skills. This work takes place in the agricultural off-season.

Your task is to reduce the costs of this programme significantly while increasing the coverage modestly. To make this happen, the discussion will focus on three things:

1   Which parts of the programme are likely to provide the best value for money from the point of view of the eligible households, and why?
2   Which parts of the programme are most likely to present opportunities for corruption, and why?
3   Which parts are therefore best reduced, cancelled, or replaced by something else, on the basis of which arguments?

Now that you're going to change this programme at any rate, you also wonder,

4   Does that education-related conditionality to the cash transfers make sense, or should it be eliminated? If you do not feel you are in the position to make a decision, what information do you need?

Notes

1   'Non-contributory' means that it is not based on you paying to buy an entitlement. Most types of insurance, for example, are not part of social assistance, as they are 'contributory': you essentially buy protection to guard against possible adversity.
2   The International Labour Organization is the inventor of the concept of 'social protection floors' as the minimum amount of support needed to ensure all fundamental needs are met. Or the more convoluted official definition: these floors are "nationally defined sets of basic social security guarantees that should ensure, as a minimum that, over the life cycle, all in need have access to essential health care and to basic income security which together secure effective access to goods and services defined as necessary at the national level." See ILO (undated) *Social protection floor*, online, accessed on 12 October 2019.
3   World Bank (2018) *The state of social safety nets 2018*, foreword, online, page 16. This average hides major differences across countries.
4   This was the title of a public works study of ODI, some time ago. McCord, A. and Farrington, J. (2008) "Digging holes and filling them in again? How far do public works enhance livelihoods?" *Natural Resource Perspectives*, issue 120, ODI, online.

5 For good research on school meal costs, see Gelli, A. et al. (2011) "New benchmarks for costs and cost-efficiency of school-based feeding programs and food-insecure areas", *Nutrition Bulleting,* volume 32, issue 4, pages 324–332; or Kristjansson, E.A. et al. (2016) "Costs, and cost-outcome of school feeding programmes and feeding programmes for young children. Evidence and recommendations", *International Journal of Educational Development*, volume 48, pages 79–83. These studies do not consider the significant indirect cost of keeping organisations such as WFP going.

6 See Gelli, A., Al-Shaiba, N. and Espejo, F. (2009) "The costs and cost-efficiency of providing food through schools in areas of high food insecurity", *Food and Nutrition Bulletin*, volume 30, issue 1, United Nations University. (This paper also makes a case for fortified biscuits, which the research found to be both cheaper and more nutritious than the alternatives.)

7 ICAI (January 2017) *The effects of DFID's cash transfer programmes on poverty and vulnerability: an impact review*, online, with the quotation from paragraph 4.10 on page 14.

8 For raw data, go to the World Bank ASPIRE database. For a country-by-country overview of a sample of 112 countries for which data is available, see Appendix D of World Bank (2018) *The state of social safety nets 2018*, online. For regional overviews, see Figure 2.14 on page 30 of that same publication, but note that it does not include health-related fee waivers because of the many data inconsistencies across countries. The 'more than 50%' statement is about the sum total of three types of cash transfers: conditional cash transfers, unconditional cash transfers, and social pensions.

9 Transactional sex refers to sexual encounters or relationships in which the one-way giving of money or other presents is an important factor.

10 Admirably, DFID business cases are all available through DFID's 'development tracker' (*devtracker.dfid.gov.uk*).

11 This overview of the achievements and limitations of cash transfers is largely based on Bastagli, F. et al. (2016) *Cash transfers: what does the evidence say? A rigorous review of programme impact and of the role of design and implementation features*, ODI, online. The review team considered over 38,000 studies against pre-defined quality criteria. The review findings are based on the 200 studies that passed that quality test.

12 See Carpenter, S., Slater, R. and Mallett, R. (October 2012) "Social protection and basic services in fragile and conflict-affected situations", *Working paper 8*, Secure Livelihoods Research Consortium, online, section 5.5; and Idris, I. (2017) *Conflict-sensitive cash transfers: social cohesion*, K4D, online.

13 Francesca Bastagli and her team discuss possible explanations in section 11.3 of Bastagli, F. et al. (2016) *Cash transfers: what does the evidence say? A rigorous review of programme impact and of the role of design and implementation features*, ODI, online.

14 Anthropometry is the measurement of the size and proportions of the human body. Common anthropometric measurements are height-for-age, weight-for-age, weight-for-height, and head circumference (for under-2s, when the brain and head are meant to grow rapidly).

15 This quotation is from The *Economist* (30 June 2016) *Opportunities galore*, online.

16 See Thome, K. et al. (2016) *The local economy impacts of social cash transfers: a comparative analysis of seven Sub-Saharan countries*, FAO, online. I am not aware of similar comparative analyses conducted on other continents.

17 I used this example because the creativity of these women made me smile. A much more common problem is that the targeting is just not very carefully done and that people flex the truth a little when answering eligibility questions.

18 It depends on the objective. For example, $5 per month may be enough for a girl to attend school, but it will not make life much easier for a household of people too old to work.

19 A DFID literature overview comes to the conclusion that "there is no evidence that cash transfers reduce labour market participation overall. Indeed, in some contexts cash transfers can increase the labour market participation of poor households, promote

employment, help to lessen the burden of childcare responsibilities, cover the costs of job-seeking, and also reduce days of work lost due to ill health". See DFID (2011) *Cash transfers*, online, page 38.

20 Reported in ICAI (January 2017) *The effects of DFID's cash transfer programmes on poverty and vulnerability: an impact review*, online, table 3 on page 25.

21 'Institutional Demand' programmes support the professionalisation of smallholders and buy part of their produce for distribution to poor and vulnerable households. They are complex, because they link expertise in smallholder support, purchasing *and* social assistance, and *everything* needs to work well for the programmes to be successful. Nonetheless, a massive worldwide growth of this sort of programming seems likely, in the coming few decades. For a review of a few such programmes, see WFP (2015) "P4P impact assessments: synthesis of preliminary findings", *PWP Global Learning Series*, online. (P4P means 'Purchase for Progress'.)

22 In low-income countries, these transfers only amount to 13% of the incomes of eligible people. See World Bank (2018) *The state of social safety nets 2018*, online, figure 3.20 on page 54.

23 See Marshall, C. and Hill, P.S. (July 2015) "Ten best resources on conditional cash transfers", *Health Policy and Planning*, volume 30, issue 6, pages 742–746, online. And if you are into good arguments wrapped in theatrics, you may want to look at Freeland, N. (2007) "Superfluous, pernicious, atrocious and abominable? The case against conditional cash transfers", *IDS Bulletin*, volume 38, issue 3, pages 75–78.

9

CLIMATE CHANGE

Climate change aggravates many of the problems and threats that rural communities are facing. It adds importance and urgency to what would also be good practice without climate change.

In earlier chapters, we discussed a range of good practice principles. This final chapter refers to them but does not revisit them. To understand this chapter, you therefore need to have read the others.

Prologue

Once there were lots of dinosaurs. Then, one day, some 66 million years ago, an enormous asteroid crashed into the earth.

The impact immediately killed all life in the vicinity. Wildfires and an enormous tsunami killed life further away. Elsewhere, it continued for a while, but dust darkened the skies and evaporated sulphur chilled the planet. This killed most of the plants. Their death caused starvation further up the food chain, until most life on the planet had died.[1]

We are the 21st-century dinosaurs. We have spotted the asteroid, and we named her Climate Change.

What are we talking about?

This book's first chapter is largely a positive one. It says that we're doing really well in many different ways. It points at progress in addressing infant mortality, gender gaps, illiteracy, inequality and extreme poverty, among other things. But it also says that climate change is presenting us with unprecedented challenges.

This is not fear-mongering. Climate change is a well-evidenced phenomenon, and climate change deniers are wrong. We know that

- The world's average temperature is increasing. The Intergovernmental Panel on Climate Change (IPCC, the international body responsible for reviewing the science of climate change) estimates that human action has caused the average temperature in the world to be between 0.8 and 1.2°C higher in 2017 than it was prior to the Industrial Revolution.[2] Temperature fluctuations have become more pronounced, and there are more frequent, longer-lasting heat waves.
- These higher temperatures are causing land ice to melt, and the melt water is causing sea levels to rise.
- There are more extreme weather events than before. In some regions, there are more droughts, as rainfall is sparser and water evaporates more quickly than it used to. Rainfall is also less predictable and sometimes heavier when it finally comes; this causes flash floods[3] on dried-out soil. In other regions, there is more frequent and heavier flooding, caused by *rises* in rainfall, higher sea levels, and storms and cyclones that are increasing in frequency and severity as a consequence of warming seawater.

These three phenomena will get progressively worse in all scenarios considered by IPCC[4] – though the *speed* and *severity* with which this will happen depends on our collective action in the years to come.

Climate change is not new (you'll recall the occurrence of ice ages), but today's *rapid* change is caused by us. The best-known cause is the burning of fossil fuel, which releases carbon dioxide into the air. Like all other economic sectors, agriculture burns fossil fuel as well, but this is only a small part of its contribution to greenhouse gas emissions. When we cut forests to create farmland, for example, and when we till the soil, we reduce the trees' and soil's carbon storage, which means that more of the world's carbon ends up in the atmosphere. Livestock produces methane gas – another greenhouse gas that, like carbon, traps the heat in the atmosphere and warms the world.

The effects of climate change on life are diverse. Cold climates get a little warmer and greener. Warm climates get hotter and less green. Sea fish move from warmer waters, and lake fish might die or adapt. Coral reefs bleach, die, and lose their role as breeding grounds for fish and other sea creatures.

In many cases, climate change reinforces and deepens phenomena and trends that exist already. Cyclones are not new, but climate change causes their frequency and intensity to increase. Overfishing has affected fish stocks – and the warmer water and its lower levels of oxygen add to the pressure on the remaining fish.

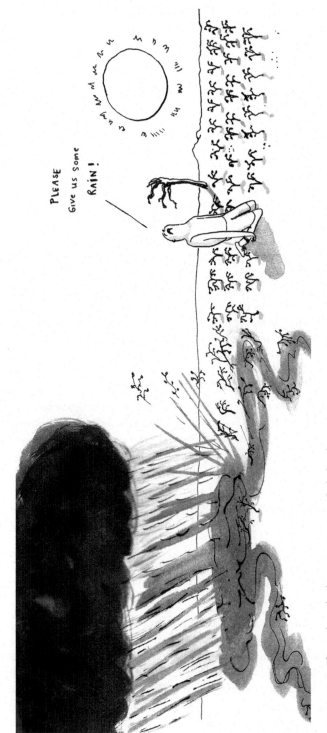

FIGURE 9.1 After a drought, heavy rain causes flash floods

For rural populations in particular, climate change makes problems worse and threats graver

So far, climate change has affected rural areas more than urban ones. This is because agriculture, fishing, pastoralism and foraging all use natural resources (soil, water and forests), and are all heavily affected by the weather (wind, rain, sunshine and temperature).

For some farmers in colder climates, the heating effect of climate change is wonderful news, at least for now. But for most rural communities in the Global South, climate change takes problems and makes them worse; and takes threats and adds to their likelihood and probable impact. For a few illustrations of climate change as a 'problem and threat multiplier', take a look at some of the problems and risks we covered in previous chapters (see Table 9.1).

Climate change aggravates problems. In turn, some of these problems accelerate climate change. The forest fires that burn more fiercely because of the dryness of the wood add to deforestation and thus further reduce the global forests' carbon storage capacity. Wind erosion aggravated by climate change releases large volumes of soil-kept carbon as well. In a vicious circle, this release of forest- and soil-held carbon accelerates the planet's warming process. This causes frozen lands to thaw a little faster, which releases yet more soil carbon into the atmosphere, and so on.

So what does this mean for rural folks?

Climate change accelerates change and heightens risks

In regions where climate change is already noticeable, it will be aggravating two problems: it will be accelerating the changes rural folks are facing, and will be heightening the risks they are exposed to. To cope with this, rural communities and other stakeholders need to plan and act with the effects and threats of climate change in mind.

Often, this is largely a matter of following the good practice principles discussed in this book. Climate change adds weight and urgency to these principles, but doesn't fundamentally change them. Let's consider a few examples. I'll talk mostly about farmers, but the challenges for fishing and pastoralist communities are broadly comparable.

Problem 1: climate change accelerates the changes that farmers are facing

Climate change affects the rhythm and amount of rainfall; the start and duration of growing seasons; the average, volatility and predictability of temperature; and the soil's moisture, salt levels and nutrients. Without modifications in farming practice, such changes often reduce agricultural income. As the world's climate continues to evolve, farming requires an ongoing process of adaptation, rather than just a one-off change of practice.

Helpful modifications include the adoption of farming types that are new to the world or a region, such as floating farms,[9] insect farming, riverbed farming,[10]

TABLE 9.1 How climate change adds to problems and threats

What the chapter says	How climate change is making it worse
Chapter 1 covers a few key obstacles that have stood in the way of development over the last 50 years. It argues that development is nearly impossible in countries that are heavily affected by conflict or fragility.	The ever-continuing conflicts and instability of South Sudan are not caused by climate change. They have to do with violent leaders, cultivated ethnic tensions, unnatural borders and grinding poverty, in combination with oil reserves (among other things). But climate change *has* made South Sudan hotter and drier than it was before. For farmers and pastoralists, this makes life even more difficult and adds to friction and violence within and between these groups.
Chapter 2, on agricultural production practice, says that many poor farmers face challenges because farming practices caused, and are still causing, soil erosion, declining water reserves, and pests' resistance to pesticides and medication.	Climate change adds to erosion because stronger winds blow topsoil nutrients away, and longer droughts aggravate the wind's eroding effects by dehydrating the soil. Higher temperatures expose plants and livestock to new diseases, heat stress and, in 2020, locust swarms the size of cities. Climate change accelerates the decline in water levels, because it causes higher levels of evaporation and, in some parts of the world, declining rainfall. Rains are also less predictable, and this has implications for the start and duration of growing seasons. Rain is not declining everywhere – and *that* can be problematic as well. Bangladesh is facing frequent flood and water logging, and climate change is making it worse: since 1980, the volume of its annual rainfall has been on the rise.[5]
Chapter 3, on common goods, discusses the pressure on the world's remaining forests. A key driver of deforestation is the expansion of agricultural land, for which stretches of forests are burned down.	The Brazilian wildfires of 2019 were not caused by climate change. Instead, these man-made fires were the consequence of a complex interplay between farmers' thirst for new agricultural land, protests (and specifically a 'day of fire' that was meant to draw attention to a region's unemployment), and a gradual decline in the rights of indigenous people and in forest policing budgets. But drought and heat *added* to the problems, as they made it harder to terminate the fires and caused accidental fires to ignite more easily.

(Continued)

TABLE 9.1 (Continued)

What the chapter says	*How climate change is making it worse*
Chapter 4, on trade, says that the price volatility of agricultural products means that farming income is unpredictable. Crop prices are affected by oil prices, harvest volumes and shifting consumer preferences, among many other things.	Do you remember that one of the components of the 2007–08 'triple F crisis' was a spike in food prices? This hike was caused by a combination of factors, and the effects of climate change were one of them. The 'Big Dry' in Australia's Murray-Darling Basin and a particularly hot season in much of India, for example, reduced wheat harvests, and this pushed prices yet more upwards.
Chapter 5, on microfinance, says that poor people often take loans from different sources, in part to service older debts. By doing so they incur ever-higher fees and fines, until they are trapped by an unrepayable volume of loans. This causes great harm, up to and including forced labour and debt-related suicides.	Such debt traps often start with a shock that requires quick money – such as a failed harvest, a blown-away boat, or destructive floods. Poor people are unlikely to have the reserves required to cope with such shocks, so they borrow money instead. The chances of such disasters happening increase as climate change causes longer, hotter, drier periods and a higher frequency and severity of tropical storms and flash floods.
Chapter 6, on ICT, talks about the gulf between those who easily access modern ICT and those who do not. The people on the wrong side of this 'digital divide' are typically among the poorest and most marginalised people already. ICT increases the gap between them and the others, as the others benefit from ICT while they do not.	Many of the people who are on the wrong side of the digital divide are *also* likely to be disproportionately affected by the effects of climate change. There are two reasons for this: First, the remote rural areas that do not have phone and internet coverage are also often areas that are vulnerable to hazards that are aggravated by climate change, such as wind erosion, drought and heat. Second, the groups with least access to ICT – such as remote rural women, older people and illiterate people – often don't have easy access to other channels of information and advice either. They are therefore less likely to gain the knowledge needed to shield their plots from erosion, catch (or 'harvest') scarce rainwater, or minimise evaporation. This reduces their income-earning potential and increases their exposure to shocks. Both climate change and the digital divide consolidate and deepen the inequalities between particularly poor and marginalised people and their less remote, more literate, wealthier and ICT-connected peers.

What the chapter says	How climate change is making it worse
Chapter 7, on migration, says that there are many reasons that compel or force people to migrate. Opportunities, violence, migratory traditions, friends or relatives abroad or in the city: it is often a combination of factors that causes people to stay or move.	In this multitude of reasons to stay or go, climate change may tip the balance towards migration. People have moved to the US for lots of reasons, for example, and for rural (but not for urban) Mexicans, one of these reasons was rising temperatures.[6]
	For fishing communities in particular, climate change is likely to play a role in migration decisions. For coastal communities, rising sea levels, declining fish stocks, the intrusion of salt water into fresh water systems and the additional flooding risks of extreme weather events may all add reasons to migrate. For lake-based fishing communities, retreating lakes and the effects of rising water temperatures and drops in oxygen levels on the lake's fish have the same effect.
	Often, only one or two of a household's members leave the village, with the aim of sending remittances to supplement their household's income. But in some regions, entire communities move out. This may happen if the loss of farm or fishing income is causing the wider local economy to collapse or if the risk of extreme weather grows too high. Parts of the south of Bangladesh are extreme examples of this phenomenon, and the migration of millions of people seems inevitable.[7] In a few countries, climate-driven migration is actively pushed by governments: the governments of Fiji, Papua New Guinea, and Vanuatu have relocated entire communities to reduce their exposure to storms and high water.[8]
Chapter 8, on social assistance, discusses the importance of cash transfers for people who face hardship. It mentions that many cash transfer programmes are still largely funded by international donors and that country-wide roll-outs of such programmes remain beyond the capacity of governments in many low-income countries.	The rural income variability and drops that climate change effects are causing add to the importance of cash transfer programmes – but also to their costs and management challenges.
	In cases of prolonged drought, for example, government-led social assistance programmes are often unable to meet the needs of their drought-affected citizens. In such cases, international donors are

(Continued)

TABLE 9.1 (Continued)

What the chapter says	*How climate change is making it worse*
	tempted to bypass government structures and work through non-governmental organisations instead.
	Where this happens, the effects of climate change effectively undermine the long-term transfer of financial and organisational responsibility from international donors and organisations to national governments.

Most people live in societies where women and men have distinctly different roles and rights, and climate change therefore has different effects on women and men. Men return to the shore without shrimp, and women then lose their shrimp-peeling income. Women walk for longer to fetch water for the household, and men walk for longer to feed and water their cattle. Often, when climate change causes farm income to decline, the first school dropouts are girls, the first people to migrate are young men, and the last to farm in deteriorating conditions and under a hotter sun are women. Women have, on average, less access to assets to draw on in times of hardship; shocks will therefore hit them harder.

FIGURE 9.2 Climate change amplifies threats

or <u>strip cropping</u>[11] (there are many other examples). Alternatively, farmers may make incremental improvements to, say, their irrigation or rainwater harvesting techniques or their use of pesticides. It may also be useful to move to new types of livestock (from cows to camels, say) or crops (from rice to the less thirsty potato, or from summer to less water-consuming winter crops) or to different varieties of the same crops, such as quicker-growing or less water-consuming varieties of rice.

Change is never easy, and such modifications require careful, aligned planning and action on many fronts. We have discussed this in previous chapters. For farmers to swap to more climate-resilient crop varieties, for example, localised research needs to identify or develop varieties that are suitable for the specific conditions of that particular region's climate and soil. Farmers need to be actively engaged in this research, and there need to be effective incentives for them to try out new varieties (see Chapter 2). The seeds, seedlings, or saplings of these varieties must be readily available and affordable, and so must other inputs, such as fertiliser, extra labour, and whatever equipment is needed to make it all work (Chapters 2, 4, and 5). These new crops and practices may require irrigation to control watering or terraced farming or greenhouses to reduce overall water requirements (terraces avoid downward streams; greenhouses reduce evaporation). For farmers to invest in such changes, they need to be confident of their long-term access to the land they farm (Chapter 2). Public works could help, by digging irrigation networks and flattening agricultural lands (Chapter 8, but note the quality concerns of public works' infrastructure), so could programmes that add government funding to collective remittances, for the purpose of financing infrastructure investments (Chapter 7).

For farmers to embrace and benefit from these changes, they may need new skills (as cows and camels have their own specific requirements, for example). For this, face-to-face engagement is important − and this is often the role of extension workers (Chapter 2). These extension workers are increasingly supported by virtual 'climate information services'. Such ICT applications initially just provided virtual weather forecasts, but nowadays they also give real-time advice on the action needed to ensure the best possible harvest − such as a crop's water needs, which depend on each particular day's sunlight and temperature. In this context, we discussed a Ghanaian climate information app (Chapter 6), but it doesn't all need to be cutting edge, and good old radio broadcasts are also still being used.[12] Where none of this action prevents a reduction in farm income, households may increase their income and reduce the pressure on the lands by sending some of their members to the city or abroad. Governments could facilitate this process and help ensure that migration risks are effectively mitigated and that benefits for the home village are significant (Chapter 7). Throughout the change process, products and services reach and affect men and women differently. Without a deliberate and monitored effort to ensure equitable access to these products and services, they will often reach and benefit more men than women. You will recall that only 21% of the subscribers to that Ghanaian app were women, for example, and this app's benefits will mostly accrue to landowners, who are generally male.

Problem 2: climate change heightens the risks that farmers are exposed to

It doesn't just *reduce* agriculture income; it also *increases its volatility*. In one year, all might go really well – and then the next year, the monsoon starts weirdly late or the soil gets *so* dry that it's no longer able to absorb the water when it finally starts raining, or the wind is *so* strong that it's impossible to go fishing. For many people, it's this *unpredictability*, more than the average income *size*, that makes life particularly tough.

In previous chapters, we discussed the good practice principles that reduce or mitigate the effects of volatility in weather and income. Again, climate change adds to the importance of these principles and the urgency of their application, but it doesn't really change them. The following examples illustrate the point:

The volatility amplified by climate change adds to the attraction of the multi-product nature of integrated farming (Chapter 2). Microfinance also supports income diversification, by enabling investments into new lines of business (Chapter 5). Well-functioning markets (Chapter 4) and ICT products (Chapter 6) facilitate this diversification effort by increasing the efficiency of the rural gig economy. All these income diversification methods help reduce a household's overall income volatility. Some of these multiple activities require healthy commons, as people resort to foraging and subsistence fishing in times of particular hardship (Chapter 3). In really bad years, micro-insurance helps farmers, pastoralists and fisherfolk cope with income shocks by making pay-outs on the basis of climatic and other indicators (Chapter 5). Where disaster risks are too high even after risk reduction efforts (see Box 9.1), governments could facilitate orderly and safe migration to regions with more potential. This requires attention to people who don't have the means or social networks to move without support (Chapter 7). If all else fails, cash transfers and other forms of social assistance could provide a safety net (Chapter 8).

BOX 9.1 DISASTER RISK REDUCTION

Climate change contributes to natural hazards. Depending on your level of preparedness, such hazards may or may not turn into disasters.

Not all countries are equally prepared. Consider the Dominican Republic and Cuba, for example – two countries that face the same cyclones. Cuba has carefully developed plans that are regularly rehearsed. They start at the top and end at street level. When the government announces the threat of a cyclone, Benita knows that there's a woman with three young children on the third floor of her building and a man in a wheelchair on the ground floor – and that it is her task to get them to the shelter. The Dominican Republic does not have such detailed, well-rehearsed plans. Consequently, when Hurricane Georges hit both countries, there were 380 casualties in the Dominican Republic and only six in Cuba.[13]

In countries that learn from experience, there are also large differences over time. Look at the casualties of three otherwise comparable cyclones in Bangladesh:

- 1970: 300–500,000 casualties
- 1991: 138,000 casualties
- 2007: 4,000 casualties[14]

The 2007 cyclone was a terrible disaster, but it was incomparable to the gravity of what happened in 1970 and 1991.

Countries that are well-prepared for natural hazards share a few key features:

1 A government that recognises the importance of being prepared and the need to engage a wide range of stakeholders.
2 Real-time data about what hazards are likely to happen when and where.
3 Well-maintained forms of protection that cushion the blows, such as dikes and healthy mangrove forests.
4 Well-maintained structures that protect people and their livestock from such blows, such as flood-resistant buildings (they stand on legs) and shelters.
5 Actionable plans to respond to upcoming hazards, rooted in local knowledge and with a clear allocation of tasks and responsibilities.
6 A population that is aware of risks and response plans, and that's supported by well-rehearsed evacuation plans, stockpiles, and real-time communication about threats. People with disabilities are not overlooked in communication (so that the blind have a siren to hear, the deaf a flag to see, and so on) and during the response (so that people with mobility impediments can get to the shelter too).
7 Actionable plans for a speedy post-disaster recovery, which cover wide-ranging issues such as tracking systems to reunite displaced children and their parents, reconstruction efforts, and material and psychological support for those who need it.

Efforts to reduce the effects of disasters are guided by the Sendai Framework for Disaster Risk Reduction 2015–2030.

It is in the direct interest of individual farmers and other rural folks to modify their practice to address the problems of accelerated change and heightened risks. This is not the case for a third problem: the fact that agricultural practice *contributes* to climate change.

Agriculture accelerates climate change

As mentioned at the start of this chapter, livestock produces greenhouse gases, and the mere act of tilling soil reduces its carbon storage. In addition, farmers often burn their harvest residues, and some farm operations burn fossil fuels. It all adds up, and, collectively, the global agricultural sector contributes some 11.5% of the world's total greenhouse gas emissions.[15] It's more if you add the effects of forests that are burned down to expand agricultural land, or the greenhouse gas emissions caused by the transport of agricultural inputs and outputs.

Again, a few of the good practice principles and tools we discussed in previous chapters could help reduce agriculture's contribution to climate change. Integrated farming reduces transport emissions and agricultural residuals (Chapter 2), for example. Sound management of common forests reduces deforestation (Chapter 3), and ICT tools collect data that could inform mitigating action (Chapter 6). And so forth.

A key obstacle to better practice is that the effects of farmers' individual contributions to greenhouse gas emissions are both negligible and irrelevant to their direct interests.[16] For example, economic growth has increased the demand for meat in China, and meat producers in Argentina and Brazil have jumped at the export opportunities this provides (which got even more profitable after swine fever killed over 100 million pigs in China, in 2018–19). The forest-burning to create space for this extra meat production, the meat production itself, and the long-distance transport all contribute to greenhouse gas emissions – but the stakeholders involved won't feel any direct pain as a consequence of these particular emissions.

People are unlikely to take voluntary steps toward more sustainable land use or move to more water-efficient crops or stop expanding into forests (or, even better, contribute to *re*forestation) unless this is in their own and fairly short-term interest. So how could you incentivise good behaviour?

Pay for it.

Governments, often with the support of the international donor community, *pay* for action that is in the long-term national and global interest. There is a term for this: "Payment for Ecosystem Services", or PES. PES systems give people and community organisations money to conserve, restore, or improve soil, forests, coastal systems, and aquifers. Some of the community-based natural resource management systems that we discussed in Chapter 3 are examples of such systems, but PES systems also extend to privately owned forests and other natural resources. These systems are often criticised for paying insignificant amounts, for prioritising conservation over people, and for being of most benefit to people who verifiably own land (thereby possibly increasing inequality within communities). Still, in a few Latin American countries in particular, some PES systems have successfully reversed deforestation (see Box 9.2).

BOX 9.2 FOREST PROTECTION AND REFORESTATION IN COSTA RICA

In 1950, 70% of Costa Rica was covered by forest. By 1996, it was down to 48%. The main cause of this deforestation was the conversion of forests to agricultural and cattle grazing land.

Legislation in 1996 banned further forest conversion, and the government initiated a PES scheme to encourage the protection of what was left, as well as large-scale reforestation. The scheme was not equally effective across the country, but the overall result has been that the country's percentage of forested area increased, after a long period of decline, to almost 55% in 2016. The transfer of hundreds of millions of dollars to individuals, legal entities, indigenous groups, and cooperatives was key to the process. For many recipients, the transfers form a stable source of income, and in remote rural areas, the PES funding is one of the principle sources of cash.

Sources: Porras, I. et al. (2013) *Learning from 20 years of Payments for Ecosystem Services in Costa Rica*, International Institute for Environment and Development, online; and the indicator titled 'Forest area (percentage of land area)' of *data.worldbank.org/indicator*.

Why is all this relevant, and what does it mean for you?

This chapter covered three problems:

1 Climate change makes problems worse.
2 Climate change makes threats graver.
3 Agriculture accelerates climate change.

The first two problems mostly just add importance and urgency to the good practice principles discussed throughout this book and to the suggestions made towards the end of each of the previous chapters. In essence, climate change necessitates modifications in rural practice, and many things need to go well for this to happen. It does not matter that the seeds of a new drought-resistant maize variety are available and that the world is full of eager maize buyers – if farmers are unaware of the opportunity, feel no enthusiasm for it, or cannot afford to grow it. So search for the weakest links in a rural region's adaptive capacity (often extension services and engagement with farmers), and strengthen them. Identify the barriers to the adoption of good practice, and work to overcome them. In doing so, keep in mind that your actions will have different effects on women and men and that, if you don't pay particularly careful attention, the least visible, vocal, educated, and empowered people are the least likely ones to benefit from your efforts. Addressing these first two problems is really tough and requires a massive concerted effort (*and you need to think of effective disaster risk reduction* – see Box 9.1), but it might all *just* be doable.

The third problem is even tougher to address. The fragile 2015 Paris Agreement and initiatives such as the Extinction Rebellion movement show widespread support for reducing greenhouse gas emissions. But we have not yet solved the 'free rider' problem that underpins climate change: it is caused by individuals and companies who are not individually incentivised to change their behaviour, as their individual changes would require sacrifice but would not have a meaningful effect on their individual prospects or global trends.

Millions of individual farmers and other rural folks won't change their practice unless they have clear and strong incentives to do so. The PES systems that pay people and communities for the conservation and restoration of natural resources are a starting point. In countries with strong monitoring systems and little corruption, subsidies for certain crops and sustainable farming practices might also help – even if the agricultural subsidies of the last few decades have been costly and largely ineffective. In some contexts, carbon taxing could be helpful. But none of this will truly do the trick, and I hope the next generation of policymakers will develop new and more effective incentives to move agriculture towards emissions-reducing and forest-conserving practices.

The last five decades gave us good reason to be optimistic, and policymakers in a number of Asian countries in particular have much to be proud of. Lots of things improved, and often rapidly so. But in this process of rapid rural and broader development, we have accelerated climate change, even long after the evidence of its impact was strong and unambiguous. So there we are: the older generation of policymakers is handing over a range of achievements, lots of good practice to build on, some challenges to deal with, and one absolutely massive problem for the next generation to resolve.

Further reading

On climate change

Collectively, we are not yet taking the action needed to reduce the speed of climate change and to adapt to evolving realities, but this is not because climate change isn't sufficiently well-documented or discussed.

The most powerful start of your reading would be a five-page article that was signed by over 11,000 scientists worldwide: Ripple, W.J. et al. (November 2019) "World scientists' warning of a climate emergency", *Bioscience*, online. After that, keep up to date with reports from the Intergovernmental Panel on Climate Change via *ipcc.ch*. Some of the technical reports are tough, but they have readable 'summaries for policy-makers'. Or sign up for regular newsletters at *climatechangenews.com*, which cover climate change effects, international climate change negotiations, and projects and innovations related to mitigation and adaptation. If you find all the bad news and doom scenarios demoralising, go to the website of the *Poverty-Environment Initiative* to find practical examples of ways in which poverty reduction could go hand in hand with environmental protection and restoration.

For insights on the linkages between climate change and poverty, start with World Bank (2016) *Shock waves: managing the impacts of climate change on poverty*, online. It covers areas such as food security, disaster mitigation, health, safety nets, climate-informed development, and pro-poor climate policies. Or if you are interested in a particular theme – health, education, refugees or small islands, say – then take a look at the website of whichever UN organisation takes the lead on that particular theme, and you'll probably find a fact sheet on climate change with hyperlinks to relevant publications. Many of the large annual flagship reports from UN organisations and suchlike include a section on climate change as well, and many such reports have recently had a 'climate change'-themed issue.

On agriculture and climate change

For a two-minute rundown of the various ways in which agriculture contributes to climate change, read Russel, S. (May 2014) *Everything you need to know about agricultural emissions*, World Resource Institute, online. For more specific data on agriculture's contributions to climate change, go to the *Agriculture* link under the *Sectors* tab in *climatewatchdata.org*. Then, for much more data and many more reports, click on *Resources for Action*, or read parts of FAO (2016) *The state of food and agriculture; climate change, agriculture and food security*, online (which is one of many examples of a 'climate change'-themed issue of a UN flagship report, mentioned in the previous paragraph).

For insights, examples, and suggestions in relation to climate-smart agriculture,[17] check the table of contents of the 570-page FAO (2014) *Climate-smart agriculture sourcebook*, online. If this massive publication feels daunting, read this 17-page literature review (excluding extensive references) instead: Loboguerrero, A.M. et al. (March 2019) "Food and earth systems: priorities for climate change adaptation and mitigation for agriculture and food systems", *Sustainability*, volume 11, issue 5, online. It focuses on family-based farms in developing countries. Or, for a steady trickle of reports on all things related to the interplay between agriculture, food security, and climate change, see the *themes* tab of *cdkn.org*, the website of the Climate & Development Knowledge Network, or check new issues of *Climate Risk Management*, an open-source journal.

Because climate change makes problems worse and threats graver, it is covered in many of the references suggested in this book's earlier chapters. For themes that did not get their own chapter, a quick Google Scholar search should help. Take the first big problem covered in Chapter 1 as an example: a Google Scholar search with the terms *conflict* and *climate change* would bring you to publications such as

- Price, R. (January 2019) "Climate change as a driver of conflict in Afghanistan and other fragile and conflict affected states", *K4D Helpdesk Report*, Institute of Development Studies, online. This is a 14-page overview of literature about the links between climate change and conflict, and it's a good read. The title suggests that it's mostly about Afghanistan, but this is not in fact the case, simply because Roz Price found very little Afghanistan-specific research to report on, so she expanded her review to include other regions as well.

- Huntjens, P. and Nachbar, K. (2015) "Climate change as a threat multiplier for human disaster and conflict policy and governance", *Working Paper 9*, The Hague Institute for Global Justice, online.

Exercise

This text describes an entirely useless visit from a UN official to a village. Could you find as many shortcomings as possible and suggest a more appropriate approach?

The roads are good in the dry season, so they reach the village early. John, a UN engagement officer on his first international posting, is pleased with the preparations done by the Waqf Welfare Institute, his local counterpart. There is a small podium on the village square, and there are a few banners and at least 60 men. John even sees a few people who look different – possibly refugees from nearby Fragilistan.

John gets introduced in the local language and takes the floor. He has three messages and feels he conveys them well, because he talks slowly and doesn't use long words:

1   Climate change is a massive global problem. Stabilistan must help solve this problem and has agreed to a PES system, with funding from the Green Climate Fund. It is part of the government's REDD+ strategy. In essence, slash and burn agriculture is no longer allowed, and satellite imagery will monitor compliance. But this is actually really good news for farmers, because each of them will receive a sum of money every month, proportional to the size of their current farmlands.

2   He is aware that climate change is leading to local problems and that the crops have failed a few times, in recent years. He is therefore excited to announce that CGIAR and its partners developed a new, even more drought-resistant type of maize, and seeds are now available in Stabilistan as well. The men should go to the local extension centre to get trained on how to best grow this maize. He has a leaflet about it (he raises it in the air so that people can read its large-printed title: 'How to grow maize in 2020'). There's also an app that gives information about this type of maize. John then asks who has a smartphone. There is no real response, initially, but when the Waqf man quickly says something, a few hands go up, confirming that the investment in the app was probably a good one.

3   This type of maize needs irrigation, so the government will be digging a main canal nearby, in the next few months. There will be a public works programme

to dig branch canals and distributaries. The farmers will then have to dig their own field channels, for the water to reach their fields.

Unusually, there's still a bit of time left when John has finished his presentation, so he asks if there are any questions. There is one, from a man in the front of the group:

السلام عليكم يا خواجة. احنا مفهمناش قوي انت كنت بتقول ايه عشان احنا مبتكلمش إنجليزي. لكن انت سألت عن تليفوناتنا. لو تقصد الكهربا، بعد الانتخابات الكهربا اتقطعت ومن ساعتها مرجعتش تاني. لو سمحتوا ترجعوهالنا.[18]

John looks at the Waqf guy. He says that the man raised a different issue and that he'll deal with it and then says, to the man and the group:

لا، هو بيتكلم عن الغابة. الخواجة بيقول إنكم لازم تسيبوا الغابة في حالها ولو عملتم كده، الحكومة حتديكم فلوس. حقول لكم الحكاية بعدين. دلوقتي بس صقفوا له عشان يمشي وإلا حيفضل قاعد لنا هنا بقية النهار.[19]

The people look content, and there's a bit of a 'thank-you' applause, so the Waqf man's response must have been good. John feels the event has been successful. He signs the attendance sheet so that the attendants get a small stipend for their travel to the village square, waves goodbye, and leaves for the next village. If all visits go as smoothly as this one, he'll be home before dinner.

Notes

1 Recent research in the crater showed that 130 metres of debris filled it the day after the impact, illustrating just how massive the hit had been. The debris contained no sulphur – it had all evaporated. See Gulick, S.P.S. et al. (9 September 2019) "The first day of the Cenozoic", *PNAS*.

2 IPCC (2018) *Global warming of 1.5°C: summary for policymakers*, Intergovernmental Panel on Climate Change, online, fact from paragraph A.1. The "1.5°C" in the title is a prediction, not a realised rise in temperature.

3 Flash floods are sudden floods. They are typically caused by heavy rain. They form particularly quickly on soil that is hard and dry, as such soil that doesn't absorb water well.

4 See Pachauri, R.K. and Meyer, L.A., editors (2014) *Climate change 2014: synthesis report. contribution of Working Groups I, II and III to the Fifth Assessment Report of the Intergovernmental Panel on Climate Change*, Intergovernmental Panel on Climate Change, online. The IPCC's next synthesis report will be published in 2022.

5 In addition, *within* years, Bangladesh faces a trend of declining rain in the winter months and increasing rain in the wet season. For more on these trends, see Mondol, M.A.H. et al. (November 2018) "Precipitation concentration in Bangladesh over different temporal periods", *Advances in Meteorology*, volume 2018, online.

6 Nawrotzki, R.J. et al. (November 2015) "Climate change as a migration driver from rural and urban Mexico", *Environmental Research Letters*, volume 10, online.

7 Kniveton, D., Rowhani, P. and Martin, M. (April 2013) "Future migration in the context of climate change", *Climate-Related Migration in Bangladesh Briefing Paper*, issue 3, online.

8 International Organization for Migration (2019) *Climate change and migration in vulnerable countries: a snapshot of least developed countries, landlocked developing countries and small island developing states*, IOM, online, page 25.

9 In Bangladesh, floating farms are often built onto frames of plastic containers, bamboo, and water hyacinths. They drift but do not move, as they are anchored. They help

Bangladeshi farmers cope with floods. These farms produce vegetables, fish, and ducks. They are a good example of climate change adaptation, and it will not be long before floating farms are common in other countries' coastal communities as well.

10 Riverbeds that run dry after the rainy season are potential plots for quick-growing single-season crops. Riverbeds often remain unused, and sometimes their utilisation requires the introduction of crops that are new to the region.

11 Strip cropping is the technique of growing rows of crops that don't have great or indeed any market value but prevent erosion next to rows of crops that are valuable but don't prevent erosion.

12 At the time of writing for example, a Filipino radio campaign aiming to raise awareness about sustainable agricultural techniques among small-scale farmers was being broadcast, in different dialects, by some 200 radio stations. See Navarro, R.L. et al. (2019) "Harnessing rural radio for climate change mitigation and adaptation in the Philippines", *CCAFS Working Paper Number 275*, CCAFS, online.

13 Figures are from Guiney, J.L. (January 1999) *Preliminary report Hurricane Georges: 15 September – 1 October 1998*, National Hurricane Centre, online, table 5.

14 For insight into the way Bangladesh managed to dramatically reduce the loss of lives over the past decades, and an analysis of its evolving 'whole-country' response, see Tatham, P., Spens, K. and Oloruntoba, R. (2009) *Cyclones in Bangladesh – a case study of a whole country response to rapid onset disasters*, POMS 20th annual conference, online, with the figures mentioned on page 17. In this publication, the stated number of 2007 casualties is 4,234, but this is an example of the 'false precision' that we discussed before; in other publications, the estimated number of casualties ranges from 3,447 to 15,000.

15 See the *Drivers of Emissions* tab under *Agriculture*, under *Sector*, in *climatewatchdata.org*, accessed on 3 November 2019. The 11.47% (which I rounded to 11.5% in the text) is an estimate of the situation as it was in 2014. Over the last decades, the proportional contribution of countries in the Global South has increased, with particularly significant contributions from China and Brazil.

16 The same applies to most readers of this book: the world would be better off if we all took fewer flights, as flights burn lots of fossil fuel . . . but the specific flights *you* take won't make a difference; similarly, the world would be better off if we all ate less meat, but your personal decision not to eat meat won't reduce the speed of climate change.

17 'Climate-smart agriculture' refers to agricultural practice that deals with the problems of accelerated change and heightened risks *and* reduces agriculture's contribution to climate change as well as its other harmful effects, such as its negative effect on biodiversity.

18 "Peace be upon you stranger. We don't really understand what you were saying because we don't speak English, but you asked about our phones so if this is about electricity: after the elections the electricity stopped and we'd like it back please."

19 "No, this is about the forest. The foreigner says that you should leave it in peace and if you do this the government will give you money. I'll tell you the details later. Now applaud the foreigner or he'll be here all afternoon."

CONCLUSIONS

In many ways, the world's population is doing really well. Globally, the infant mortality rate is lower, life expectancy is higher, and people are more literate than ever before. Gender gaps are slowly narrowing, and extreme poverty has been on an uninterrupted decline for decades.

Progress in some Asian countries – like China, India, Indonesia, Malaysia, and Thailand – has been particularly fast. These countries avoided unserviceable debt burdens. They cut excessive bureaucracy, resolved conflicts (or at least kept them local), and changed policies that killed entrepreneurialism. They also invested heavily in their rural regions, allowing a 'Green Revolution' to unfold. In these and other parts of the Global South where the Green Revolution was successful, efficiency gains in farming methods and improvements in plant and animal varieties drove a rapid expansion in agricultural production. This kick-started strong positive spirals of economic diversification and development.

Further agricultural growth is needed if the decades-long positive trends in human development are to continue. It is possible to achieve such growth without depleting water reserves and soil – two key resources on which rural economies are based. But for this to happen, farmers need to feel certain of having long-term control over the land they are farming, and they need to be able and committed to using the right inputs at the right time in the right manner. This, in turn, requires further crop, water, and soil research, as well as investments in farmers' abilities and in incentives for them to follow good practice. It also needs an environment in which property is safe, effective support services are available, and negotiated access to water reserves is based on their replenishable capacity.

Further growth should not deplete the world's remaining common forests, grazing lands and fisheries. The livelihoods of millions of people depend on them. They are the custodians of biodiversity, and some offer protection against wind, waves and erosion.

The privatisation or nationalisation of such common resources does not usually conserve them and often harms the communities that depend on them. Instead, conserving commons requires community engagement. Such engagement is key in two types of management systems for common resources. The first type, 'customary systems', is rooted in deep knowledge of the local commons but is often unashamedly sexist and exclusionary, and sometimes incites violence. Many such systems are also losing their authority and, with that, their effectiveness. The second type is a group of more recent 'community-based natural resource management systems'. Such systems are sometimes reasonably successful, but often they are not. Failures are almost inevitable where they are donor-driven, short-term, designed with only the fleeting participation of unrepresentative community segments, and implemented under the watchful eyes of government authorities reluctant to relinquish power.

Effective common resource management systems follow the 'design principles' the late Elinor Ostrom first presented in 1990. These principles are about the active participation of a wide range of stakeholders and the perceived legitimacy of the commons' management system. They are also about the clarity of boundaries, rules, entitlements, monitoring arrangements, sanctions, and conflict management. Adherence to these principles is a precondition for, but not a guarantee of, success. Research in the years to come will further refine our insight into what else is needed for common resources not to be overfished, over-foraged and over-farmed.

Very few people fish, forage or farm solely for their own consumption. Almost universally, at least part of it is done to earn money through trade. Unfortunately, poverty affects the quality and volume of production, and remoteness raises the costs of transport to all but the most local buyers. The things poor and remote people offer for sale are therefore often relatively unappealing, and the prices they fetch are low. They are also unattractive buyers, as they are hard to reach and don't have much to spend. This affects the availability, affordability and quality of virtually all products, except those produced locally.

The only option for many rural people is to sell their products close to where they live, because of the ease of market access, transport and storage. This keeps earnings modest, as local demand is limited and undiversified, and (again) prices are low. Cooperatives give access to larger markets and better prices. They often enjoy sustained success but also often fail because of disappointing trade volumes, inefficiencies, and corruption.

These local markets and cooperatives may be the starting points of complex global value chains. Where rural economies depend on such chains, the preferences and priorities of international companies shape people's livelihood choices. So do the tariffs, non-tariff barriers, and subsidies of international trade arrangements. Their effects differ widely across countries and regions. They may strengthen rural economies but may also reinforce grinding poverty for people without alternatives or negotiation leverage. In response to the latter effects, 'fair trade' and 'making markets work for poor' programmes seek to improve the levels, stability and predictability of the income of poor farmers and rural workers. Results vary. There are successes, but problems – including very serious issues like forced labour – are still common.

People who draw the short straw in trade are often trapped in poverty – especially if they are also landless, illiterate and malnourished. Their poverty traps deepen because of 'intersectionality': power structures and perceptions about people's identities that compound the challenges they face. "She can't have a market stall here because she is. . . [fill in gender, age, race, ethnicity, religion and whatever else decision-makers feel are her 'weaknesses']."

These poverty traps are multifaceted, and for most people, a bit of money won't be enough to escape them. This helps explain why the achievements of fair trade to date have been modest. This simple truth applies to microfinance as well: even if people have access to microfinance products (and more remoteness generally means less access), benefits are not normally transformational. Moreover, microloans sometimes cause unmanageable debts or disempower women by providing money they don't control but must repay.

Nonetheless, the prospects of microfinance are bright. Microfinance institutions are innovating rapidly. They are penetrating more distant rural areas and offer credit, saving schemes, insurance, leasing and pension products that are increasingly appropriate for and appealing to rural folks. In all likelihood, microfinance products will increasingly improve income, inspire healthy risk-taking, reduce short-term hardship by smoothing consumption, cushion shocks, avoid distress sales, and empower women and girls – provided that two conditions are met. First, there must be a level of stability and a functioning cash-based economy. Second, the various non-financial problems that keep people poor – such as illiteracy, malnutrition and discrimination – must be addressed as well, as only a multifaceted package of improvements may improve a poor household's livelihood and strengthen its sustainability.

Paradoxically, better livelihoods will increase, not reduce, rural outward migration. This is because migration requires a level of aspiration and understanding of the possibilities, and it requires money. The decision to spend this money is often made by households and wider social networks, rather than individuals, and is largely based on the expectation of remittances. This is why economic migrants are often single, young, able-bodied men and women: they have the highest earning potential.

If their savings are modest, rural migrants move to cities or follow seasonal opportunities within their own countries. If they have a bit more, or if they can borrow money, they may go to neighbouring countries. Or they could try make the yet more expensive, cumbersome and uncertain move to the Gulf, Europe and North America, or to high-income countries in other regions. Wherever they go and eventually end up, many migrants face risks, hardship and discrimination, and migration-averse media and politicians often aggravate these problems. If migrants are successful nonetheless, their remittances will increase the income of their close relatives back in the village. For their larger communities of origin, the picture is more complex. For them, migration is not 'good' or 'bad' but a phenomenon that accelerates and amplifies the results of government policies and practices that either facilitate or impede local economic activity and other forms of development.

Such government policies and practices evolve, and so do government priorities and financial allocations. Governments are influenced by public pressure, through voting or otherwise, and by changes in the governments around them, multilateral organisations, and worldwide trends. In recent years, these various pressures led many governments to increase their investments in social safety nets. A few Latin American countries provided inspiration, when their social assistance programmes limited the harm poor people suffered because of the 2007–08 'triple F crisis' (which, you will recall, was caused by price hikes in food and fuel and a near-collapse of the global financial sector and led to long-term adversity for the world's poorest people in particular).

Governments around the Global South ramped up their investments in social safety nets. They provided public work, fee waivers, food support and cash transfers. Whilst these are all potentially useful forms of social assistance, they are not all equal. Most research concludes that, where functioning markets exist, cash transfers are superior to other types of social assistance. They increase consumption and empower recipients, as they support people without making assumptions about their needs. They reduce negative coping behaviours and intra-household inequalities. Overhead costs are relatively low, and cash transfers are easy to monitor and therefore difficult to corrupt.

But cash transfers are not a solution for all problems and have been overhyped a bit. Recent research found that objectives related to health, nutrition, resilience, and children's learning are not generally being met. This may change with better targeting, better timeliness of payments, and more appropriate (and generally larger) transfer sizes. Even if the design and operationalisation of cash transfer programmes improve, they won't, in isolation, enable people to escape poverty. Instead, cash transfers are like microfinance products: they are a potentially useful *part* of multi-faceted poverty reduction approaches.

Cash transfers, microfinance products, and almost everything else covered in this book have become more efficient and effective because of ICT. You wouldn't immediately say so if you walk through the average village, but the effects of ICT have been profound, and they are growing. Many ICT applications support agricultural production processes, trade and the efficient use of rural people's time and assets. ICT also facilitates transactions, savings and insurance. It supports people with disabilities, increases government accessibility, and potentially reduces bureaucracy and corruption.

ICT innovation is fast and varied, and some ICT hardware (radios, smartphones) and applications (weather forecasts, online banking) have spread quickly and reached deep into remote rural lands. However, access is unequal, and a 50-year-old illiterate rural woman in the Global South could benefit massively from ICT opportunities but is on the wrong side of several 'digital divides'. These divides could increase inequalities, if the least-connected people (who are often the poorest people) lose their market share to better-connected competitors – as the latter are more quickly and fully informed about market needs and opportunities and thus better able to respond to them. Healthy competition among providers of ICT products and networks reduces this divide by lowering ICT prices. This must be combined with investments in rural ICT infrastructure. In some parts of the world, public-private partnerships and conditionalised contracting ('you can connect region X but only if you connect region Y as well') have worked well.

ICT is solving problems. Climate change is causing them. It accelerates erosion and declines in water reserves. It causes heat stress and disease threats to fish, livestock, and plants. It also adds volatility to harvest volumes and prices and increases the frequency and intensity of extreme weather events. Women are often hit harder than men, because they have fewer assets to cushion shocks and fewer options for adapting their livelihood strategies to evolving realities.

The effects of climate change add weight and urgency to many of the good practice principles discussed in this book. However, these principles won't help reduce agriculture's considerable contribution to greenhouse gas emissions. For emission reductions, individual actors need to be appropriately incentivised. So far, money appears to be the most persuasive incentive, and there have been some successes with "Payment for Ecosystem Services". These give people and community organisations money in return for the conservation, restoration and improvement of soil, forests and coastal systems. They help but won't suffice. The world needs new and better ideas, and I hope this book has provided a few ingredients for you to develop some.

INDEX